OLD ENGLISH WORD STUDIES:
A PRELIMINARY AUTHOR AND WORD INDEX

old english word studies: a preliminary author and word index

ANGUS CAMERON
ALLISON KINGSMILL
ASHLEY CRANDELL AMOS

published in association with
The Centre for Medieval Studies, University of Toronto
by University of Toronto Press
Toronto Buffalo London

© University of Toronto Press 1983
Toronto Buffalo London
Printed in Canada

ISBN 0-8020-5526-5

Canadian Cataloguing in Publication Data

Cameron, Angus, 1941-
  Old English word studies : a preliminary word and
author index

(Toronto Old English series ; 8)
ISBN 0-8020-5526-5

1. Anglo-Saxon language — Bibliography. 2. Anglo-
Saxon language — Glossaries, vocabularies, etc.
I. Kingsmill, Allison, 1923-   II. Amos, Ashley
Crandell.   III. University of Toronto. Centre for
Medieval Studies.   IV. Title.   V. Series.

Z 2015.A1C35   016.429   C 82-095277-X

This book has been published with the help of a grant from
the Publications Fund of University of Toronto Press.

contents

toronto old english series

general editor's preface

The Toronto Old English Series, an offshoot of the Dictionary of Old English project, has three reasons for existence. The first is to publish Old English texts not yet in print, in order to provide citations for the Dictionary. The second is to replace editions whose treatment of the text is unsatisfactory for dictionary use. The third is to provide bibliographies, semantic studies, and other tools useful for the Dictionary.

The present volume fits into the last category. The authors have drawn up this list of word studies for their own use in writing dictionary entries, but hope that their work will inform and delight anyone interested in exploring the sometimes unsmooth course of Old English lexicographical scholarship.

The General Editor wishes to thank the Editorial Board of the series for its continuing support, Anna Burko for her expert and meticulous copy-editing, and Elaine Quanz for skillfully and cheerfully typing the camera-ready copy. The publication of this volume marks the end of the preliminary, information-gathering stage of the Dictionary project. It is a tribute to the remarkable vision and leadership of Angus Cameron that all the preparatory tasks he set for his team twelve years ago have now been completed.

R.F.
September 1982

abbreviations

diss.	dissertation
ed(s).	edited by, edition, editor(s)
impr.	impression
intro.	introducer, introduction
MS(S)	manuscript(s)
N.F.	Neue Folge
no(s).	numbers(s)
n.s.	new series
OE	Old English
o.s.	original series
pt.	part
repr.	reprint, reprinted
rev.	revised
ser.	series
s.s.	supplementary series
trans.	translated by, translation, translator
vol(s).	volume(s)

For abbreviations of journal titles and short titles of collections see the Introduction, pp. x-xii and xiii-xiv. Other abbreviations are those used in Stanley B. Greenfield and Fred C. Robinson, *A Bibliography of Publications on Old English Literature* (Toronto 1980), and in the *MLA International Bibliography*.

introduction

From the earliest days of the Dictionary of Old English project, we realized the importance of collecting and consulting the works of scholars past and present on matters of vocabulary. This collection of word studies was begun to help us in writing entries. The task has turned out to be both larger and longer than we expected. Although we now present a first version of our materials, we realize that our work is far from ended.

We have mixed feelings about publishing our indexes at this stage. The field of search is not tidy; this list of word studies has a clear focus in the semantic studies of individual Old English words and groups of words, but its circumference is much less clearly defined. As the collection accumulated, the difficulties of separating vocabulary from the other levels of language soon became apparent. Studies which were primarily etymological, phonological, morphological, or syntactic in intent were often focussed on specific words and contained materials invaluable for the study of meaning. In addition to the work of linguists and philologists we have noted relevant discussions in the works of literary critics, textual critics, historians, students of place and personal names, archaeologists, and numismatists. We have collected books, chapters in books, articles, and theses, but have had to exclude book reviews, although they, too, sometimes contain helpful information on vocabulary. In the few cases where reviews are included, they are entered under the reviewer's name rather than under the work reviewed.

We have to admit that our goals of completeness and consistency have not yet been attained. Still, we have found the lists in the word index invaluable in writing our dictionary entries and we expect that others will find them helpful as they take up studies of individual words or sections of the vocabulary. The reader can take delight in being able to follow up some fine academic quarrels. Scholars from the turn of the century such as Schlutter and Holthausen let fly at one another with astonishing skill and vehemence, while contemporary scholars such as Greenfield and Hill show that the art has not been totally lost.

The other reasons for publishing our indexes now are practical and financial. The likelihood that research and publication funds will diminish over the next few years raises the possibility that we might not be able to publish at all if we wait until the most obvious time, after the appearance of the Dictionary. The decision to publish now has made us aim for and, we hope, achieve more rigorous standards of accuracy in collecting, indexing, and citing the word studies than we would have done if we had been gathering the material strictly for our own use. Most of all we anticipate that publication now will prompt our readers, whether in reviews, articles, or private communications, to bring new items, omissions, and inaccuracies to our attention. We hope to be able to publish a revised second edition of the indexes, with entries keyed to the headwords used in the Dictionary, after the Dictionary has appeared.

A description of how we went about forming our collection of materials may be useful here. We began by checking the standard bibliographies and consulted the following:

Anglo-Saxon England 1- (Cambridge 1972-)

Annual Bibliography of English Language and Literature (Cambridge 1921-)

Bibliographie linguistique: Linguistic Bibliography (Utrecht 1939-)

Dissertation Abstracts International, earlier called *Microfilm Abstracts* and *Dissertation Abstracts* (Ann Arbor 1938-)

English and American Studies in German (Tübingen 1969-)

Gipper, H. and Schwarz, H., *Bibliographisches Handbuch zur Sprachinhalts-forschung* (Cologne 1962-)

Greenfield, S.B. and Robinson, F.C., *A Bibliography of Publications on Old English Literature to the End of 1972* (Toronto 1980)

Index to American Doctoral Dissertations, earlier called *Doctoral Dissertations accepted by American Universities* (New York and Ann Arbor 1932-)

Index to Theses Accepted for Higher Degrees in the Universities of Great Britain and Ireland (London 1954-)

Kennedy, A.G., *A Bibliography of Writings on the English Language* (Cambridge, Mass. 1927)

Letopis' zhurnal'nykh statei (Moscow 1926-) vols. for 1952-75

MLA International Bibliography of Books and Articles on the Modern Languages and Literatures (New York 1922-)

Old English Newsletter 1- (New York, Columbus, Binghamton 1967-)

Sawyer, P., *An International Medieval Bibliography* (Leeds 1967-)

Stein, G., *English Word-Formation over two Centuries: In Honour of Hans Marchand on the Occasion of his Sixty-Fifth Birthday, 1 October 1972,* Tübinger Beiträge zur Linguistik 34 (Tübingen 1973)

Terasawa, Y., *Chūsei Eigo Eibungaku Kenkyū Gyōseki List* [A bibliography on medieval English language and literature] , Chūsei Igirisu Kenkyū Shiryō Centre, Tokyo Daigaku Kyōyōgakubu (Tokyo 1979)

Watson, G., *The New Cambridge Bibliography of English Literature:* Vol. 1, *600-1600* (Cambridge 1974)

As individual articles and books came to our attention, we checked their bibliographies and footnotes and gained many additional references. In addition, we checked the following journals and series as fully as possible and added a number of items which had been missed in the bibliographies:

Academy *The Academy: A Weekly Review of Literature, Science, and Art* [partial]

Anglia

AION-SG *Annali: Istituto Universitario Orientale (Naples), Sezione Germanica*

AJP	*American Journal of Philology*
An Med	*Annuale Mediaevali* (Duquesne)
Archiv	*Archiv für das Studium der neueren Sprachen und Literaturen*
ArL	*Archivum Linguisticum*, old and new series
Athenaeum	*The Athenaeum: A Journal of English and Foreign Literature, Science, the Fine Arts, Music, and the Drama* [partial]
BBzA	Bonner Beiträge zur Anglistik [partial]
Beibl	*Anglia Beiblatt*
Beiträge zur Kunde der indogermanischen Sprachen [partial]	
BGdSL	*Beiträge zur Geschichte der deutschen Sprache und Literatur*
EA	*Etudes anglaises*
EG	*Etudes germaniques*
EGS (EPS)	*English and Germanic Studies*, later *English Philological Studies*
EHR	*English Historical Review* [partial]
ELN	*English Language Notes*
E&S	*Essays and Studies by Members of the English Association*, old and new series
ES	*English Studies*
EStn	*Englische Studien*
Expl	*Explicator*
Germania	
GRM	*Germanisch-romanische Monatschrift* [partial]
IF	*Indogermanische Forschungen*
Jahrbuch des Vereins für niederdeutsches Sprachforschung [partial]	
JEGP (JGP)	*Journal of English and Germanic Philology*, formerly *Journal of Germanic Philology*
Language	*Language: Journal of the Linguistic Society of America*
Language Dissertations, supplement to *Language*	
LM	Language Monographs, published by the Linguistic Society of America
Leeds Studies	*Leeds Studies in English and Kindred Languages*, old and new series
MÆ	*Medium Ævum*
MLN	*Modern Language Notes*
The MLQ	*The Modern Language Quarterly*, 1897-1904
MLQ	*Modern Language Quarterly*, 1940-present
MLR	*Modern Language Review*
MP	*Modern Philology*
MS	*Mediaeval Studies*
MSzS	*Münchener Studien zur Sprachwissenschaft*
Neophil	*Neophilologus*

NM	*Neuphilologische Mitteilungen*
NQ	*Notes and Queries* [partial]
NSpr	*Die neueren Sprachen* (Marburg)
OEN	*Old English Newsletter*
PLL	*Papers on Language and Literature*
PMLA	*Publications of the Modern Language Association*
PQ	*Philological Quarterly*
RES	*Review of English Studies,* old and new series
SEP	Studien zur englischen Philologie
SGG	*Studia Germanica Gandensia*
SN	*Studia neophilologica*
SP	*Studies in Philology*
Speculum	
Sprache	*Die Sprache: Zeitschrift für Sprachwissenschaft* (Vienna)
TNTL	*Tijdschrift voor Nederlandse taal- en Letterkunde* [partial]
TPS	*Transactions of the Philological Society* (London)
Traditio	*Traditio: Studies in Ancient and Medieval History, Thought, and Religion*
TSLL (UTSE)	*Texas Studies in Language and Literature,* 1959-present; formerly *University of Texas Studies in English* [partial]
WBEP	Wiener Beiträge zur englischen Philologie
Wörter und Sachen	
YES	*Yearbook of English Studies*
ZAA	*Zeitschrift für Anglistik und Amerikanistik* (East Berlin)
ZDW	*Zeitschrift für deutsche Wortforschung*
Zeitschrift für Dialektologie und Linguistik, formerly *Zeitschrift für Mundartforschung*	
ZfdA and Anzeiger	*Zeitschrift für deutsches Altertum und deutsche Literatur*
ZfdPh	*Zeitschrift für deutsche Philologie*
ZfM	*Zeitschrift für Mundartforschung*
ZvS	*Zeitschrift für vergleichende Sprachforschung*

The abbreviations used here and elsewhere are those in the *MLA International Bibliography* supplemented by those in Stanley B. Greenfield and Fred C. Robinson, *A Bibliography of Publications in Old English Literature from the Beginnings through 1972* (Toronto 1980). We have tried to make our journal listings complete through 1980, although with some periodicals we have had to be satisfied with the most recent issue to reach the shelves of our library.

This version of *Old English Word Studies* consists of two main indexes, the first for books and authors, and the second for words discussed. We present the author index in book form, while the much larger word index is in microfiche.

The author index comes in three parts. The first is a list of sixteenth- and seventeenth-century manuscript glossaries and dictionaries. In making this list we have benefitted greatly from the work of M.S. Hetherington, *Old English Lexicography, 1550-1659* (U. of Texas, Austin diss. 1973). The second part is a list of Old English dictionaries, concordances, and glossaries to specific texts. These are arranged alphabetically by editor or compiler. The third and largest part of the author index is the list of vocabulary studies arranged alphabetically by author's name and date of publication. Authors known only by their initials appear at the beginning of each letter of the alphabet, and un-signed pieces appear under Anonymous. When, as frequently happens, an author has published more than one item in a year, these are distinguished by successive letters of the alphabet immediately following the date. The sequence of items within one year is as follows: books are listed before articles, and articles in books are listed before articles in journals or series. Within the same year, journals are listed alphabetically.

Items with more than one author come after items which the first author has written by himself, so that the articles written by A.S.C. Ross with his various collaborators appear after the articles written by Ross himself. We have left titles as they appear on title pages and in journal headings, except that we standardize capitalization, punctuation, and references to words and their meanings (the words are italicized, the meanings enclosed in quotations). A small number of *Festschriften* and collections of essays which we cite frequently are referred to by the following short titles:

Atwood and Hill *Studies* Atwood E.B. and Hill, A.A., eds. *Studies in Language, Literature, and Culture of the Middle Ages and Later* (Austin 1969)

Brodeur Festschrift Greenfield, S.B., ed. *Studies in Old English Literature in Honor of Arthur G. Brodeur* (Eugene 1963)

Chadwick Memorial Volume Fox, Sir C. and Dickins, B., eds. *The Early Cultures of North-West Europe,* H.M. Chadwick Memorial Studies (Cambridge 1950)

Creed *Essays* Creed, R.P., ed. *Old English Poetry: Fifteen Essays* (Providence 1967)

Klaeber Festschrift Malone, K. and Ruud, M.B., eds. *Studies in English Philology: A Miscellany in Honor of Frederick Klaeber* (Minneapolis 1929)

Koziol Festschrift Bauer, G., Stanzel, F.K., and Zaic, F., eds. *Festschrift Prof. Dr. Herbert Koziol zum siebzigsten Geburtstag,* WBEP 75 (Stuttgart and Vienna 1973)

McGalliard Festschrift Nicholson, L.E. and Frese, D.W., eds. *Anglo-Saxon Poetry: Essays in Appreciation for John C. McGalliard* (Notre Dame and London 1975)

Magoun Festschrift Bessinger, J.B. and Creed, R.P., eds. *Franciplegius: Medieval and Linguistic Studies in Honor of Francis Peabody Magoun, Jr.* (New York 1965)

Meritt Festschrift Rosier, J.L., ed. *Philological Essays: Studies in Old and Middle English Language and Literature in Honor of Herbert Dean Meritt* (The Hague and Paris 1970)

Mertner Festschrift Fabian, B. and Suerbaum, U., eds. *Festschrift für Edgar Mertner* (Munich 1969)

Pope Festschrift Burlin, R.B. and Irving, E.B., Jr., eds. *Old English Studies in Honour of John C. Pope* (Toronto and Buffalo 1974)

Stenton Collected Papers Stenton, D.M., ed. *Preparatory to Anglo-Saxon England: Being the Collected Papers of Frank Merry Stenton* (Oxford 1970)

Whitelock Festschrift Clemoes, P. and Hughes, K., eds. *England Before the Conquest: Studies in Primary Sources presented to Dorothy Whitelock* (Cambridge 1971)

The third part of the author index has itself been indexed, with two exceptions, according to the words discussed; this word index appears in microfiche only. The two exceptions are items marked with an asterisk (*), which for one reason or another do not lend themselves to indexing although they do include discussions of vocabulary, and items marked with a dash (−), which we have not seen but included because they appear to be relevant either from their titles or from the references we have to them. Many of these unseen items are by Russian or Japanese authors, and we would appreciate more information on them.

The word index has been prepared for microfiche using a computer-editing system. While this has had many advantages for us it has also had a few disadvantages, one of which is that diacritics appearing in authors' names have had to be omitted. Words are usually listed in the form that the author uses, although we have represented both ð and þ by þ and have occasionally normalized forms by dropping final double consonants.

We have tried to index only substantial discussions of lexical items and not mere citations of Old English forms for comparative purposes. It has sometimes been difficult to know where to draw the line, and we have probably over-indexed more often than we have under-indexed.

While the simplest way of treating the orthographical variants would be to tie them to a standardized list of Old English headwords, this headword list will not be ready until the Dictionary itself is complete. In the meantime we have referred to the headword lists in the existing dictionaries, particularly that in H.D. Meritt's edition of J.R. Clark Hall's *A Concise Anglo-Saxon Dictionary* and have begun to sort out the welter of forms by giving a system of cross-references through which users are guided from one spelling to other likely spellings. Although we have tried to make these cross-references as complete as possible, there are, inevitably, gaps and the user should be forewarned. We have also done our best to disambiguate homographs and to sort out most of the true homonyms in the word list. Wherever forms have close semantic relationships, as in the case of related nouns and adjectives, we have left them unsorted.

Ordinarily we have cross-referenced inflected forms of nouns and verbs; positive, comparative, and superlative forms of adjectives and adverbs; discussions of a single, difficult word, usually a gloss, even if indexed under widely varying emended forms; and different spellings of the 'same' word. We have not cross-referenced *ge-* and unprefixed forms of a word; weak and strong forms of a verb; inflected forms of pronouns and articles; compounds to their constituent elements; phrases to any of their elements; or forms of words with prefixes, suffixes, or infixes to their simple forms. Homonyms are disambiguated either by grammatical label (n., v., pron., adj., etc.), by cross-referencing to an appropriate group of associated spellings, or by a very rough gloss intended only as a label.

Although this work appears under our names and we are responsible for its shortcomings, it represents work done by all the members of the Dictionary of Old English staff. We would particularly like to thank Antonette diPaolo Healey, who read and indexed hundreds of articles in our collection; Sharon Butler, who proofread the word index; Anna Burko and Elaine Quanz, who typed and edited various recensions of the work; and Joan Holland. Sophie Skoric, one of the many helpful librarians on the staff of the University of Toronto Library, gathered and checked the Russian references, while our Japanese titles were transliterated and translated by Yasko Nishimura. Among our student research assistants we wish to thank Bella Schauman, who began the work; Martha Emelity, Gregory Waite, and Peggy Seiden. Of the many scholars who have sent us copies of their own work and helped us to gather our collections, we wish to acknowledge Helmut Gneuss and his colleagues in the Institut für englische Philologie at the University of Munich, especially Karl Toth; Manfred Görlach of the University of Heidelberg, René Derolez of the University of Ghent, and Bruce Mitchell of St. Edmund Hall, Oxford. When we circulated a first version of the author index, Eric Stanley of Pembroke College, Oxford, T.F. Hoad of St. Peter's College, Oxford, Fred C. Robinson of Yale University, and Carl Berkhout of the University of Arizona gave us particularly helpful comments.

The research and gathering of materials for this work have been generously supported by the Canada Council and its successor, the Social Sciences and Humanities Research Council of Canada, through their Grants in Aid of Research and Major Editorial Grants programmes. Finally we wish to thank

Professor Roberta Frank, who has encouraged us at every stage and has allowed the work to stand (microfiche and all) in the Toronto Old English Series.

A.C., A.K., A.C.A.
September 1982

OLD ENGLISH WORD STUDIES:
A PRELIMINARY AUTHOR AND WORD INDEX

reference works 1

SIXTEENTH- AND SEVENTEENTH-CENTURY MANUSCRIPT DICTIONARIES
OF OLD ENGLISH

Anonymous
[Old English - Latin Glossary] Bodleian Library MS. James 42

D'Ewes, Simonds
'Dictionarium citeriorum, saeculorum Anglo-Saxonicum-Latinum' British
   Library MSS. Harley 8 and 9

Dugdale, William
'Dictionarium Saxonicum' Bodleian Library MS. Dugdale 29

James, Richard
'Glossarium Saxonico, Anglicum' Bodleian Library MS. James 41
'Collectio vocum Saxonicarum' Bodleian Library MS. Selden Supra 62

Joscelyn, John
'Dictionarium Saxonico-Latinum' British Library MSS. Cotton Titus A.XV
   and A.XVI, Lambeth Palace MS. 692

Junius, Francis
'Dictionarium Saxonicum' Bodleian Library MSS. Junius 2 and 3
'Etymologicon linguae Anglicanae' Bodleian Library MSS. Junius 4, 5, and 77
'Anglosaxonicum glossarium Cottonianum' Bodleian Library MSS. Junius
   84 and 112
'Dictionarium ... Anglo-Saxonicum ...' [and other Junius MSS] Bodleian
   Library MSS. Fell 8-18, British Library MS. 4720

Nowell, Laurence
'Vocabularium Saxonicum' Bodleian Library MS. Selden Supra 63, Lambeth
   Palace MS. 692, Bodleian Library MS. Junius 26. See **Marckwardt**, 1952.

Parker, John
'Dictionariolum' Bodleian Library MS. Bodley 33

Twyne, Brian
'Collectio vocum Saxonicarum' Bodleian Library MS. Add. C.250 (30278)

Wheelocke, Abraham
'Lexicon Saxonicum Latinum' British Library MS. Harley 761, Cambridge
   University Library MS. Gg.2.2

DICTIONARIES, ENCYCLOPAEDIAS, CONCORDANCES, GLOSSARIES,
SELECTED GLOSSARIES IN EDITIONS AND FACSIMILES

Arngart, O.S.
1956 *The Durham Proverbs: An Eleventh Century Collection of Anglo-Saxon Proverbs edited from Durham Cathedral MS. B.III. 32,* Lund Universitets Årsskrift, *N.F.* Avd. 1, Bd. 52, Nr. 2 (Lund)

Assmann, B.
1889 *Angelsächsische Homilien und Heiligenleben,* BaP 3 (Kassel; repr. with intro. by P. Clemoes, Darmstadt 1964)

Bately, J.
1980 *The Old English Orosius,* EETS s.s. 6 (London)

Benson, T.
1701 *Vocabularium Anglo-Saxonicum* (Oxford)

Bessinger, J.B., Jr.
1960 *A Short Dictionary of Anglo-Saxon Poetry* (Toronto)

Bessinger, J.B., Jr. and Smith, P.H., Jr.
1969 *A Concordance to Beowulf* (Ithaca)
1978 *A Concordance to the Anglo-Saxon Poetic Records* (Ithaca and London)

Blackburn, F.A.
1907 *Exodus and Daniel: Two Old English Poems,* Belles Lettres Series (Boston)

Blake, N.F.
1964 *The Phoenix,* Old and Middle English Texts (Manchester)

Bosworth, J.
1838 *A Dictionary of the Anglo-Saxon Language* (London)
1848 *A Compendious Anglo-Saxon and English Dictionary* (London)

Bosworth, J. and Toller, T.N.
1898 *An Anglo-Saxon Dictionary,* ed. Toller (London)

Braasch, T.
1933 *Vollständiges Wörterbuch zur sog. Caedmonschen Genesis*, AF 76 (Heidelberg; repr. Amsterdam 1967)

Brooks, K.R.
1961 *Andreas and The Fates of the Apostles* (Oxford)

Brown, T.J.
1969 *The Durham Ritual: A Southern English Collectar of the Tenth Century ...*, with a contribution by F. Wormald, A.S.C. Ross, and E.G. Stanley, EEMF 16 (Copenhagen)

Campbell, A.
1938 *The Battle of Brunanburh* (London; reissued Oxford 1974)
1972 *An Anglo-Saxon Dictionary: Enlarged Addenda and Corrigenda* (Oxford)

Carlson, I.
1978 *The Pastoral Care edited from British Library MS. Cotton Otho B.ii,* completed by Lars-G. Hallander together with Mattias Löfvenberg and Alarik Rynell, Stockholm Studies in English 48 (Stockholm)

Carnicelli, T.A.
1969 *King Alfred's Version of St. Augustine's Soliloquies* (Cambridge, Mass.)

Chapman, H.W.
1905 *An Index to the Old English Glosses of the Durham Hymnarium*, YSE 24 (New York; repr. in F.C. Robinson, *Word-Indices to Old English Non-Poetic Texts* [Hamden 1974])

Clark Hall, J.R.
1894 *A Concise Anglo-Saxon Dictionary* (Cambridge; 2nd ed. 1916; 3rd ed. 1931)

Clark Hall, J.R. and Meritt, H.D.
1960 *A Concise Anglo-Saxon Dictionary,* 4th ed. with supplement by Meritt (Cambridge)

Classen, E. and Harmer, F.E.
1926 *An Anglo-Saxon Chronicle,* Modern Language Texts, English Series (Manchester)

Clubb, M.D.
1925 *Christ and Satan: An Old English Poem*, YSE 70 (New Haven)

Cockayne, T.O.
1864-6 *Leechdoms, Wortcunning, and Starcraft of Early England*, Rolls Series 35, 3 vols. (London; repr. with intro. by C. Singer, 1961; New York 1965)

Cook, A.S.
1894 *A Glossary of the Old Northumbrian Gospels* (Halle; repr. New York 1969)
1900 *The Christ of Cynewulf: A Poem in Three Parts* (Boston; repr. with preface by J.C. Pope, Hamden 1964)
1911 *A Concordance to Beowulf* (Halle; repr. New York 1968)
1921 *The Old English Physiologus*, YSE 63 (New Haven)

Dickins, B. and Ross, A.S.C.
1934 *The Dream of the Rood*, Methuen's Old English Library (London; 4th ed. 1954)

Doane, A.N.
1978 *Genesis A: A New Edition* (Madison)

Dobyns, M.F.
1973 *Wulfstan's Vocabulary: A Glossary of the Homilies with Commentary* (Illinois diss.; *DAI* 34:7701A)

Dodd, L.H.
1908 *A Glossary of Wulfstan's Homilies*, YSE 35 (New York; repr. Hildesheim 1968; also repr. in F.C. Robinson, *Word-Indices to Old English Non-Poetic Texts* [Hamden 1974])

Dunning, T.P. and Bliss, A.J.
1969 *The Wanderer*, Methuen's Old English Library (London)

Ettmüller, E.M.L.
1851 *Vorda Vealhstôd Engla and Seaxna: Lexicon Anglosaxonicum ... cum synopsi grammatica* (Quedlinburg and Leipzig; repr. Amsterdam 1967)

Farrell, R.T.
1974 *Daniel and Azarias*, Methuen's Old English Library (London)

Finnegan, R.E.
1977 *Christ and Satan: A Critical Edition* (Waterloo)

Förster, M.
1944 'Vom Fortleben antiker Sammellunare im Englischen und in anderen Volksprachen' *Anglia* 67-8: 1-171

Fowler, R.
1972 *Wulfstan's Canons of Edgar*, EETS 266 (London)

Fry, D.
1974 *The Finnsburh Fragment and Episode*, Methuen's Old English Library (London)

Garmonsway, G.N.
1939 *Ælfric's Colloquy*, Methuen's Old English Library (London; 2nd ed. 1947; repr. 1965)

Geisel, I.
1915 *Sprache und Wortschatz der altenglischen Guthlacübersetzung* (Basel diss.)

Gelling, M.
1976 'The Old English Charter Boundaries of Berkshire' in *The Place-Names of Berkshire*, Part III.1, English Place-Name Society 51 (Cambridge): 615-792

Gneuss, H.
1963 'Ergänzungen zu den altenglischen Wörterbüchern' *Archiv* 199: 17-24

Goolden, P.
1958 *The Old English Apollonius of Tyre* (London)

Gordon, E.V.
1937 *The Battle of Maldon*, Methuen's Old English Library (London; 2nd ed. 1957)

Gordon, I.L.
1960 *The Seafarer*, Methuen's Old English Library (London)

Gosser, L.G.
1926 *Some Studies in the Vocabulary of Old English* (Chicago diss.)

Gradon, P.O.E.
1958 *Cynewulf's Elene*, Methuen's Old English Library (London)

Grein, C.W.M.
1861-4 *Sprachschatz der angelsächsischen Dichter*, Bibliothek der angelsächsischen Poesie 3-4 (Kassel)

Grein, C.W.M., Holthausen, F., and Köhler, J.J.
1912-14 *Sprachschatz der angelsächsischen Dichter*, ed. Köhler (Heidelberg)

Grimm, C.
1906 *Glossar zum Vespasian Psalter und den Hymnen*, AF 18 (Heidelberg; repr. Amsterdam 1967)

Groschopp, F.
1883 *Kleines angelsächsischen Wörterbuch von Christian W.M. Grein* (Kassel)

Grünberg, M.
1967 *The West-Saxon Gospels* (Amsterdam)

Harris, M.A.
1899 *A Glossary of the West Saxon Gospels*, YSE 6 (Boston; repr. in F.C. Robinson, *Word-Indices to Old English Non-Poetic Texts* [Hamden 1974])

Harrison, J.A. and Baskervill, W.M.
1885 *A Handy Anglo-Saxon Dictionary: Based on Groschopp's Grein* (New York)

Healey, A. diPaolo
1978 *The Old English Vision of St. Paul*, Speculum Anniversary Monographs 2 (Cambridge, Mass.)

Hill, L.L.
1947 *A Glossary of the Marginal Homilies of MS. 41, Corpus Christi College, Cambridge* (U. of Texas, Austin diss.)

Holthausen, F.
1934 *Altenglisches etymologisches Wörterbuch*, Germanische Bibliothek, IV. Reihe, Wörterbuch 7 (Heidelberg; 2nd ed. with rev. bibliography by H.C. Matthes, 1963)

Hoops, J.
1911-19 *Reallexikon der germanischen Altertumskunde* (Strassburg; 2nd ed. ed. H. Beck et al., Berlin and New York 1968-)

Irving, E.B., Jr.
1953 *The Old English Exodus*, YSE 122 (New Haven)

Jember, J.K. et al.
1975 *A Modern English-Old English Dictionary* (Denver)

Kemble, J.M.
1845 *Codex diplomaticus aevi Saxonici* III (London; repr. Vaduz 1964): xvi-xlii

Kendrick, T.D. et al.
1956-60 *Evangeliorum quattuor codex Lindisfarnensis,* glossary by A.S.C. Ross and E.G. Stanley, 2 vols. (Olten-Lausanne)

Klaeber, F.
1922 *Beowulf and The Fight at Finnsburg* (Boston; 3rd ed. with 1st and 2nd supplements, 1950)

Köbler, G.
1974 *Verzeichnis der Übersetzungsgleichungen der älteren altenglischen Glossare*, Arbeiten zur Rechts- und Sprachwissenschaft 2 (Göttingen)

Kuhn, S.M.
1965 *The Vespasian Psalter* (Ann Arbor)

Leo, H.
1872-7 *Angelsächsisches Glossar* (Halle)

Leslie, R.F.
1961 *Three Old English Elegies*, Old and Middle English Texts (Manchester; repr. 1966)
1966 *The Wanderer*, Old and Middle English Texts (Manchester)

Liebermann, F.
1903-16 *Die Gesetze der Angelsachsen* (Halle; repr. Aalen 1960)

Liles, B.L.
1967 *The Canterbury Psalter: An Edition with Notes and Glossary* (Stanford diss.; *DA* 28: 1053A)

Lindelöf, U.
1897 *Glossar zur altnorthumbrischen Evangelienübersetzung in der Rushworth-Handschrift (die sogenannte Glosse Rushworth²)*, Acta societatis scientiarum Fennicae 22, no.5 (Helsingfors)
1901 *Wörterbuch zur Interlinearglosse des Rituale ecclesiae Dunelmensis*, BBzA 9 (Bonn)
1909-14 *Der Lambeth-Psalter*, Acta societatis scientiarum Fennicae 35.i and 43.iii (Helsinki)

Lucas, P.J.
1977 *Exodus*, Methuen's Old English Library (London)

Lye, E.
1743 *Francisci Junii Francisci filii etymologicum Anglicanum* (Oxford)

Lye, E. and Manning, O.
1772 *Dictionarium Saxonico- et Gothico-Latinum*, ed. Manning (London)

Malone, K.
1933 *Deor*, Methuen's Old English Library (London; 4th ed. 1966)
1962 *Widsith* (Copenhagen)

Marckwardt, A.H.
1952 *Laurence Nowell's Vocabularium Saxonicum*, University of Michigan Publications, Language and Literature 25, ed. Marckwardt (Ann Arbor and London; repr. New York 1971)

Menner, R.J.
1941 *The Poetical Dialogues of Solomon and Saturn*, MLA Monograph Series 13 (New York, repr. 1973)

Mertens-Fonck, P.
1960 *A Glossary of the Vespasian Psalter and Hymns: Part I: The Verb*, Bibliothèque de la Faculté de philosophie et lettres de l'Université de Liège, Fasc. 154 (Paris)

Molloy, M.A.
1907 *The Vocabulary of the Old English Bede* (Cornell diss.)

Montagnani, F.
1979 *Il glossario botanico nella biblioteca della cattedrale di Durham* (Florence)

Morris, R.
1874-80 *The Blickling Homilies*, EETS 58, 63, 73 (London; repr. 1967)

Needham, G.I.
1966 *Ælfric: Lives of Three English Saints*, Methuen's Old English Library (London)

Norman, F.
1933 *Waldere*, Methuen's Old English Library (London; 2nd ed. 1949)

Plummer, C.
1892-9 *Two of the Saxon Chronicles Parallel*, 2 vols. (Oxford; reissued by D. Whitelock, 1952)

Pope, J.C.
1967-8 *Homilies of Ælfric: A Supplementary Collection*, EETS 259, 260 (London)

Raith, J.
1933 *Die altenglische Version des Halitgar'schen Bussbuches*, BaP 13 (Hamburg; repr. Darmstadt 1964)

Reichenbächer, E.
1934 *Glossar zum ae. Regius-Psalter* (Jena diss.; Kahla)

Rhodes, E.W.
1889 *Defensor's Liber scintillarum*, EETS 93 (London; repr. New York 1973)

Roberts, J.
1979 *The Guthlac Poems of the Exeter Book* (Oxford)

Rypins, S.
1924 *Three Old English Prose Texts in MS. Cotton Vitellius A xv*, EETS 161 (London)

Schaubert, E. von
1963 *Heyne-Schückings Beowulf*, 18th ed. (Paderborn)

Schröer, A.
1885-8 *Die angelsächsischen Prosabearbeitungen der Benediktinerregel*, BaP
2 (Kassel; repr. with appendix by H. Gneuss, Darmstadt 1964)
1888 *Die Winteney-Version der Regula S. Benedicti* (Halle)

Schulte, E.
1904 *Glossar zu Farmans Anteil an der Rushworth-Glosse (Rushworth[1])*
(Bonn)

Schwab, U.
1967 *Waldere: Testo e Commento* (Messina)

Sedgefield, W.J.
1899 *King Alfred's Old English Version of Boethius' De consolatione philosophiae* (Oxford; repr. Darmstadt 1968)

Seebold, E.
1970 *Vergleichendes und etymologisches Wörterbuch der germanischen
starken Verben*, Janua linguarum, series practica 85 (The Hague and Paris)

Simons, R.
1899 *Cynewulfs Wortschatz: oder, Vollständiges Wörterbuch zu den Schriften Cynewulfs*, BBzA 3 (Bonn)

Skeat, W.W.
1879 *An English-Anglo-Saxon Vocabulary* (Cambridge; repr. with intro. by
J.D. Pickles, Binghamton 1978)

Smith, A.H.
1933 *Three Northumbrian Poems*, Methuen's Old English Library (London;
2nd ed. 1968)
1956 *English Place-Name Elements*, English Place-Name Society 25, 26
(Cambridge and New York; repr. Cambridge 1970)

Somner, W.
1650 'De lingua Anglica vetere ...' in M. Casaubon, *De quatuor linguis
commentationis pars prior* (London): 1-72
1659 *Dictionarium Saxonico-Latino-Anglicum* (Oxford; repr. Menston
1970)

Spindler, R.
1934 *Das altenglische Bussbuch* (Leipzig)

Stilwell, R.
1947 *A Glossary for the Vercelli Prose Homilies* (U. of Texas, Austin diss.)

Stracke, J.R.
1974 *The Laud Herbal Glossary* (Amsterdam)

Swanton, M.
1970 *The Dream of the Rood*, Old and Middle English Texts (Manchester)

Sweet, H.
1885 *The Oldest English Texts,* EETS 83 (London)
1896 *The Student's Dictionary of Anglo-Saxon* (Oxford)

Thomas, P.G. and Wyld, H.C.
1904 'A Glossary of the Mercian Hymns' *Otia Merseiana* 4: 84-130

Timmer, B.J.
1952 *Judith*, Methuen's Old English Library (London; 2nd ed. 1961)
1954 *The Later Genesis* (Oxford; rev. ed.)

Toller, T.N.
1921 *An Anglo-Saxon Dictionary: Supplement* (London)
1922-4 'Additions to the *Supplement* of the Bosworth-Toller *Anglo-Saxon Dictionary*' *MLR* 17 (1922): 165-6 / 19 (1924): 200-4

Tupper, F.
1910 *The Riddles of the Exeter Book* (Boston; repr. Darmstadt 1968)

Twysden, R.
1652 *Historiae Anglicanae scriptores X ... Ex vetustis manuscriptis ... glossario ...* (London)

Ure, J.M.
1957 *The Benedictine Office*, Edinburgh University Publications in Language and Literature 11 (Edinburgh)

Vleeskruyer, R.
1953 *The Life of St. Chad* (Amsterdam)

Wheloc, A.
1644 *Archaionomia, sive De priscis Anglorum legibus libri, sermone Anglico, vetustate antiquissimo ... Gulielmo Lambardo interprete ...* (Cambridge)

Whitelock, D.
1939 *Sermo Lupi ad Anglos*, Methuen's Old English Library (London; 3rd ed. 1963)
1967 *Sweet's Anglo-Saxon Reader*, 15th ed. (Oxford)

Williamson, C.
1977 *The Old English Riddles of the Exeter Book* (Chapel Hill)

Woolf, R.E.
1955 *Juliana*, Methuen's Old English Library (London; 2nd ed. 1966)

Wyatt, A.J. and Johnson, H.H.
1891 *A Glossary to Ælfric's Homilies* (London)

Zettersten, A.
1979 *Waldere*, Old and Middle English Texts (Manchester)

Zeuner, R.
1891-1910 *Wortschatz des sogenannten Kentischen Psalters*, 2 vols. (Gera)

Ziegler, W.
1978 *Die unveröffentlichten lateinisch-altenglischen Glossare in der HS. Bodleian, Bodley 730 (2709): Ausgabe und Kommentar* (Vienna diss.)

a

Abbott, W.C.
1904 'Hrothulf' *MLN* 19: 122-5

Adams, A.
1907 *The Syntax of the Temporal Clause in Old English Prose*, YSE 32 (New York)

Adams, E.
1858 'On the Names of Ants, Earwigs, and Beetles' *TPS* (1858): 93-107
1859 'On the Names of Spiders' *TPS* (1859): 216-27
1860-61a 'On the Names of the Wood-Louse' *TPS* (1860-61): 8-19
1860-61b 'On the Names of Caterpillers, Snails, and Slugs' *TPS* (1860-61): 89-112

Adams, J.F.
1958 *'Wulf and Eadwacer:* An Interpretation' *MLN* 73: 1-5

Adams, R.W.
1974-5 *'Christ II:* Cynewulfian *Heilsgeschichte' ELN* 12: 73-9

Addy, S.O.
1899 'The Dings in York' *N&Q* ser. 9, 4: 270-71
1927 'The *stapol* in *Beowulf:* Hall and Chamber' *N&Q* 152: 363-5

Adolf, H.
1947 'OHG *wuntarôn* and the Verbs of Fear and Wonder (A Study in Onomasiology)' *JEGP* 46: 395-406

Adzhiashvili, Sh. D
1973 'Remeslennaia terminologiia v drevneangliiskom iazyke (Terminologiia priadeniia i tkachestva)' Moscow, Universitet, *Vestnik,* ser. 10, *Filologiia* [28] 5: 63-75 [The artisan terminology in OE (terms of spinning and weaving)]
1974 'Leksika kuznechnogo remesla v drevneangliiskom iazyke' Moscow, Universitet, *Vestnik,* ser. 10, *Filologiia* [29] 1: 59-73 [The vocabulary of the smithy in OE]

Aitken, W.S.
−1951-2 *A Study of the Old Kentish Glosses in MS. Cotton Vespasian D. vi − with Text* (London M.A. thesis; ASLIB *Index* 2: 146)

Albers, J.
1907 *Der syntaktische Gebrauch der Präposition* to *in der altenglischen Poesie* (Kiel)

Allen, C.L.
1980 '*Whether* in Old English' *LingI* 11: 789-93

Amosova, N.N.
– 1956 *Etimologicheskie osnovy slovarnogo sostava sovremennogo angliiskogo iazyka* (Moscow) [The etymological basis of the vocabulary of the contemporary English language]

Anderson, E.R.
1970 'Flyting in the *Battle of Maldon*' *NM* 71: 197-202
1972 '*Sæmearh* and Like Compounds: A Theme in Old English Poetry' *Comitatus* 3: 3-10
1973 'The Sun in the *Battle of Brunanburh*, 12b-17a' *N&Q* 218: 362-3
1974-5 '*Beowulf* 2216b-2217: A Restoration' *ELN* 12: 1-5
1975 '*The Husband's Message:* Persuasion and the Problem of *genyre*' *ES* 56: 289-94
1977 'Treasure Trove in *Beowulf:* A Legal View of the Dragon's Hoard' *Mediaevalia* 3: 141-64

Anderson, G.K.
1935 'Some Irregular Uses of the Instrumental Case in Old English' *PMLA* 50: 946-56

Anderson, L.F.
1903 *The Anglo-Saxon Scop*, University of Toronto Studies, Philological Series 1 (Toronto)

Anderson (Arngart), O.S.
1937 *The Seafarer: An Interpretation*, Kungl. Human. Vetenskapssamfundets i Lund, Årsberättelse 1937-1938, I (Lund)
1941 *Old English Material in the Leningrad Manuscript of Bede's Ecclesiastical History*, Skrifter utgivna av Kungl. Human. Vetenskapssamfundets i Lund 31 (Lund)
1941-2 'An Etymological Note' *SN* 14: 247-51

Andrew, S.O.
1936 'Relative and Demonstrative Pronouns in Old English' *Language* 12: 283-93

Andrews, C.M.
1892 *The Old English Manor: A Study in English Economic History* (Baltimore)

Anklam, E.
1908 *Das englische Relativ im 11. und 12. Jahrhundert* (Berlin)

Anonymous
1929 [Untitled paragraph: discussion of OE *husl,* etymology and cognates] *N&Q* 157: 326
1942 'Forest Word: *frith' N&Q* 182: 303-4 / 183: 87, 148, 357-8
1956 'Robert of Gloucester's *Chronicle:* Some Additions to the *OED' N&Q* 201: 279-81

Anscombe, A.
1925 'Lancelot: Derivation' *N&Q* 148: 32-3, 142

Anttila, R.
1970 *'Soon* "again" ' *Sprache* 16: 171-4

Århammar, N.
1964 'Altsächs. *skion* m. "Wolke" und altengl. *scēo* (?)' *Jahrbuch des Vereins für niederdeutsche Sprachforschung* 87: 24-8

Armentrout, R.E.
1978 *The Development of Subordinating Conjunctions in English* (Pennsylvania State diss.; *DAI* 39: 846A)

Armitage, E.S.
1912 *The Early Norman Castles of the British Isles* (New York)

Arngart, O.S.
1943 'English *craft* "a vessel" and Some Other Names for Vessels' *ES* 25: 161-9
1945-6 'The Word *shilling' SN* 18: 105-14
1946 'Some Notes on Cynewulf's *Elene' ES* 27: 19-21
1972 'On the *Ingtūn* Type of English Place Name' *SN* 44: 263-73
1977 'Further Notes on the *Durham Proverbs' ES* 58: 101-4
1979a *'The Seafarer:* A Postscript' *ES* 60: 249-53
1979b 'Old English *hund,* "a territorial hundred"?' *NB* 67: 26-33
1979c 'Adverbial Phrases with *thing' NM* 80: 46-7

1979d 'The Word *wolverine*' *N&Q* 224: 494-5
1979e '*Domus Godebiete*' *SN* 51: 125-6

Arnoid, I.V.
— 1959 *Leksikologiia angliiskogo iazyka* (Moscow) [Lexicography in the English language]

Arnoldson, T.W.
*1915 *Parts of the Body in Older Germanic and Scandinavian* (Chicago; repr. New York, 1971)

Arntz, H.
1943-4a 'Die anglofriesischen *sceattas*' *Beibl.* 54-5: 67-82
1943-4b 'Der Beginn anglofriesischer Münzprägung' *Beibl* 54-5: 118-25

Ars, E.
—1958 'Sushchestvitel'nye so znacheniem deistvuiushchego litsa na -*ere* i -*estre* v drevneangliiskom iazyke' Riga, Ped. Institut, *Uchenye zapiski* 9: 27-44 [Nouns with the meaning of the agent in -*ere* and -*estre* in OE]
— 1964 'K istorii slovoobrazovatel'noi modeli *nomen agentis* s suffiksom -*er(e)* v drevne- i sredneangliiskikh iazykakh' *XXIV Nauchnometodicheskaia konferentsiia*, Riga, Latviiskii gos. Universitet, FilN, TD: 19-20 [On the history of word-formation model *nomen agentis* with the suffix -*er(e)* in Old and Middle English]

Ashdown, M.
1930 '*Beowulf*, ll. 1543ff.' *MLR* 25: 78

Askeberg, F.
1944 *Norden och Kontinenten i gammal tid: Studier i forngermansk Kulturhistoria* (Uppsala) Ch. 4, 'Vikingarna': 114-83

b

Bacquet, P.
1975 'From Doubt to Negativity: Remarks on the Particle *ne* in Old English' in A. Joly and T. Fraser, eds., *Studies in English Grammar* (Paris): 13-15

Bäck, H.
1934 *The Synonyms for* child, boy, girl *in Old English: An Etymological-Sema-siological Investigation,* LSE 2 (Lund; repr. Nendeln/Liechtenstein 1967)

Bähr, D.
1959 *Ae.* aeþele *und* freo, *ihre Ableitungen und Synonyma im Alt- und Mittelenglischen: Wortgeschichtliche Studien zum Wandel des englischen Freiheitsbegriffes im Mittelalter* (Berlin diss.)
1971 'Altenglisch *isig* (*Beowulf,* Zeile 33)' *ZAA* 19: 409-12

Baetke, W.
1942 *Das Heilige im Germanischen* (Tübingen)

Bagramova, N.V.
− 1970 'Obstoiatel'stva prichiny, vyrazhennye predlozhno-imennymi soche-taniiami s predlogom *thurh* v drevneangliiskom iazyke' Leningrad, Ped. Institut, *Uchenye zapiski* 469: 1-7 [Adverbs of manner, expressed in preposition-noun combinations with the preposition *þurh* in OE]

Bailes, J.-L.
1952 '*OED marrow* SB.2' *N&Q* 197: 166-7

Bailey, H.W. and Ross, A.S.C.
1961 'Path' *TPS* (1961): 107-42

Baird, J.L.
1967 'The Uses of Ignorance: *Beowulf* 435, 2330' *N&Q* 212: 6-8
1968 '*for metode: Beowulf* 169' *ES* 49: 418-23
1970 'Unferth the *þyle*' *MÆ* 39: 1-12

Baker, P.S.
1978 *Studies in the Old English Canon of Byrhtferth of Ramsey* (Yale diss.; *DAI* 41: 3569A)
1980 'The Old English Canon of Byrhtferth of Ramsey' *Speculum* 55: 22-37
1981 'The Ambiguity of *Wulf and Eadwacer*' *SP* 78: 39-51

Baker, S.A.
1963 '*Weal* in the Old English *Ruin*' *N&Q* 208: 328-9

Ball, C.J.E.

1960a '*Incge Beow.* 2577' *Anglia* 78: 403-10

1960b 'Old Kentish *wig* and Middle English *owy*' *RES* n.s. 11: 52-3

1965 '*Beowulf* 987' *Archiv* 201: 43-6

1970a 'Questions of Old English Lexicography' in A. Cameron, R. Frank, and J. Leyerle, eds., *Computers and Old English Concordances* (Toronto): 89-94

1970b 'The Language of the *Vespasian Psalter* Gloss: Two Caveats' *RES* n.s. 21: 462-5

Baltensberger, H.

1920 *Eid, Versprechen und Treuschwur bei den Angelsachsen* (Zurich diss.)

Bammesberger, A.

– 1965a *Deverbative* jan-*Verba des Altenglischen, vergleichend mit den übrigen altgermanischen Sprachen dargestellt* (Munich diss.)

1965b 'Old English *gycer* and Gothic *jukuzi*' *Language* 41: 416-19

1967a 'Old English *brecþa* and -*brecþ*' *Language* 43: 452-6

1967b 'Altenglisch *blectha* "Aussatz"' *MSzS* 22: 5-6

1967c 'Die Nominalbildungen zur indogermanischen Wurzel **ǵeus-* in den altgermanischen Sprachen' *ZvS* 81: 213-16

1968a 'Altenglisch *suht* und -*siht*' *MSzS* 23: 5-6

1968b 'Altenglisch *frēo* "frei"' *NSpr* n.s. 17: 257-8

1968c 'Althochdeutsch *hlosēn*' *ZvS* 82: 298-303

1969a 'Gibt es ae. *fyllað* m. "Fülle"?' *Anglia* 87: 392-3

1969b 'Germanic **-hug-di-z*' *Language* 45: 532-7

1969c 'Zur Runeninschrift auf dem Sax von Steindorf' *MSzS* 24: 7-10

1969d 'Das Genus von ae. -*swyrd* "Schwur"' *MSzS* 25: 5-6

1969e 'Die kurzsilbigen femininen i-Stämme im Altenglischen' *Sprache* 15: 46-52

1969f 'Der Ansatz ae. *feogað* "Hass"' *Sprache* 15: 62

1970a 'Av. *mimara-*, lat. *memor* und ae. *gemimor*' *MSzS* 28: 5-8

1970b 'Gibt es ein Abstraktsuffix urgermanisch **-idō*?' *ZvS* 84: 94-7

1971a 'Urgermanisch **funsaz*' *Sprache* 17: 46-9

1971b 'Zu altenglisch -*faerae* in *Bedas Sterbespruch*' *ZvS* 85: 276-9

1972a 'Zur Vorgeschichte von westsächsisch -*sīene*/-*sȳne* und anglisch *gesēne*' *Anglia* 90: 427-36

1972b 'Altenglisch *hligan*' *MSzS* 30: 5-7

1972c 'Altenglisch *gedægeþ* in Napier XLIV' *ZvS* 86: 190-92

1972d 'Altenglisch *hlæfþe*' *ZvS* 86: 307-11

1973a 'Altenglisch *geoht* und *geiht*' *IF* 77 (1972): 100-2

1973b 'Zu altenglisch *berofan* in Genesis 2078b' *Sprache* 19: 205-7

1973c 'Altenglisch *gethyngu*' *MSzS* 31: 5-9
1973d 'Altenglisch *brosnian* und *molsnian*' *MSzS* 31: 11-13
1973e 'Das anglische Verb *lioran/leoran*' *ZvS* 87: 272-82
1974a 'Einige versteckte Weiterbildungen von altenglisch *ǣwisc(e)*' *Sprache* 20: 130-33
1974b 'Altenglisch *gedræg* und *gedreag*' *ZvS* 88: 139-46
1975a 'Zu *Exodus* 145b' *Anglia* 93: 140-44
1975b 'Altenglisch *agetan*' *Archiv* 212: 313-16
1975c 'Altenglisch *stulor*' *MSzS* 33: 5-6
1975d 'Gotisch *hnasqus** und altenglisch *hnesce*' *Sprache* 21: 188-91
1975e 'Die Flexion der altenglischen Abstrakta auf -*(ð)u*' *ZvS* 89: 283-90
1976a 'Gotisch *awepi*' *MSzS* 34: 5-7
1976b 'Zum Ansatz von altenglisch *bedæcc(e)an*' *MSzS* 35: 5-6
1976c 'Altenglisch *gamban* "Tribut" ' *Sprache* 22: 53-4
1976d 'Altenglisch *sneowan/snowan* und gotisch *sniwan*' *ZvS* 90: 258-61
1977a 'Two Old English Glosses' *ES* 58: 1-3
1977b 'Zur Herkunft von ae. *ondrǣdan* und *andrysne*' *BGdSL* 99: 206-12
1978a 'On the Gloss to Matthew 26.8 in the *Lindisfarne Gospels*' in M.A. Jazayery, E.C. Polomé, and W. Winter, eds., *Linguistic and Literary Studies in Honor of Archibald A. Hill*, vol. III, *Historical and Comparative Linguistics*, Trends in Linguistics: Studies and Monographs 9 (The Hague, Paris, and New York): 9-12
1978b 'Old English *broc* and Middle Irish *broc(c)*' *Bulletin of the Board of Celtic Studies* 27: 552-4
1979a *Beiträge zu einem etymologischen Wörterbuch des Altenglischen: Berichtigungen und Nachträge zum altenglischen etymologischen Wörterbuch von Ferdinand Holthausen*, AF 139 (Heidelberg)
1979b 'Zum Vokalismus von altenglisch -*nǣman*' *Anglia* 97: 420-28
1979c 'Die westgermanischen Entsprechungen zu urgerm. **uz(-)*' *BGdSL* 101: 30-35
1979d 'Vieil irlandais *sacart* et vieil anglais *sacerd*' *Etudes celtiques* 16: 187-9
1980a 'Three *Beowulf* Notes' *ES* 61: 481-4
1980b 'Altenglische Komposita mit *hild(e)-*' *MSzS* 39: 5-10
1981a 'Vier altenglische Interpretamenta des Épinal-Erfurt Glossars' *Anglia* 99: 383-9
1981b 'Die Betonung der Nominalen **ga*-Komposita im Urgermanischen' *BGdSL* 103: 377-91

Bandy, S.C.
1971 '*Beowulf:* The Defense of Heorot' *Neoph* 56: 86-91
1973 'Cain, Grendel, and the Giants of *Beowulf*' *PLL* 9: 235-49

Banks, R.A.
1968 *A Study of the Old English Versions of the Lord's Prayer, the Creeds, the Gloria, and some Prayers found in British Museum MS. Cotton Galba A. XIV, together with a New Examination of the Place of Liturgy in the Literature of Anglo-Saxon Magic and Medicine* (London diss.; ASLIB *Index* 18: 306) Glossary: 543-726

Banning, A.
*1886 *Die epischen Formeln im Beowulf* (Marburg diss.)

Barley, N.F.
1974 'Old English Colour Classification: Where do Matters Stand?' *ASE* 3: 15-28

Barnes, R.
1960 'Horse Colors in Anglo-Saxon Poetry' *PQ* 39: 510-12

Barney, S.A.
1977 *Word-Hoard: An Introduction to Old English Vocabulary* (New Haven and London)

Barnouw, A.J.
1902 'Die Schicksale der Apostel doch ein unabhängiges Gedicht' *Archiv* 108: 371-5

Barry, P.
1936 'Old English *priusa* "tabanus bovinus" ' *MLN* 51: 331-5

Bartels, A.
1913 *Rechtsaltertümer in der angelsächsischen Dichtung* (Kiel diss.)

Baskervill, W.M.
1887 'Other Notes on the *Andreas*' *MLN* 2:151-2
1891 'The Etymology of English *tote*' *MLN* 6: 180-81

Batchelor, C.C.
1937 'The Style of the *Béowulf:* A Study of the Composition of the Poem' *Speculum* 12: 330-42

Bately, J.M.
1970 'King Alfred and the Old English Translation of Orosius' *Anglia* 88: 433-60

1980 'The Compilation of the Anglo-Saxon Chronicle, 60 B.C. to A.D. 890: Vocabulary as Evidence' *PBA* 64 (1978): 93-129

Battaglia, F.J.
1964-5 'Notes on *Maldon:* Towards a Definitive *ofermod*' *ELN* 2: 247-9

Bauer, G.
1963 'Über Vorkommen und Gebrauch von ae. *sin*' *Anglia* 81: 323-34

Bauschatz, P.C.
1975 'Urth's Well' *Journal of Indo-European Studies* 3: 53-86

Bazell, C.E.
1968 'Notes on Old English Metre and Morphology' in H.E. Brekle and L. Lipka, eds., *Wortbildung, Syntax, und Morphologie: Festschrift zum 60. Geburtstag von Hans Marchand,* Janua linguarum, series maior 36 (The Hague and Paris): 17-19

Beaty, J.O.
1934 'The Echo-Word in *Beowulf* with a Note on the *Finnsburg Fragment*' *PMLA* 49: 365-73

Bechler, K.
1909 *Das Präfix* to *im Verlaufe der englischen Sprachgeschichte* (Königsberg diss.)

Beck, H.
1965 *Das Ebersignum im Germanischen: Ein Beitrag zur germanischen Tier-Symbolik,* Q&F, N.F. 16 (Berlin)
1968 'Waffentanz und Waffenspiel' in H. Birkhan and O. Gschwantler, eds., *Festschrift für Otto Höfler zum 65. Geburtstag* (Vienna): 1-16
1975 'Philologische Bemerkungen zu "Bauer" im Germanischen' in R. Wenskus, H. Jankuhn, and K. Grinda, eds., *Wort und Begriff* Bauer, Abhandlungen der Akademie der Wissenschaften in Göttingen, phil.-hist. Klasse, III. Folge, Nr. 89 (Göttingen): 58-72

Beck, H. and Strunk, K.
1972 'Germanisch *armaz und vedisch *árma-* (I und II)' in H. Backes, ed., *Festschrift für Hans Eggers zum 65. Geburtstag* (Tübingen): 18-41

Becker, W.
1969 *Studien zu Aelfrics Homiliae Catholicae* (Marburg diss.)

Beckers, H.
1968 *Die Wortsippe* *hail- *und ihr sprachliches Feld im Altenglischen* (Münster diss.; Cologne)

Beer, H.
1939 Führen *und* Folgen, Herrschen *und* Beherrschtwerden *im Sprachgut der Angelsachsen: Ein Beitrag zur Erforschung von Führertum und Gefolgschaft in der germanischen Welt*, Sprache und Kultur der germanischen und romanischen Völker, Anglistische Reihe 31 (Breslau)

Behre, F.
1944-5 'English *gal(e), gol, goal' SN* 17: 265-83

Belden, H.M.
1897 *The Prepositions* in, on, to, for, fore, *and* æt *in Anglo-Saxon Prose: A Study of Case Values in Old English* (Johns Hopkins diss.)
1903 'Perfective *ge-* in Old English *bringan* and *gebringan' EStn* 32: 366-70

Beliaeva, T.M.
1958 'O prichinakh ischeznoveniia glagola *weorthan* iz angliiskogo iazyka' Leningrad, Universitet, *Uchenye zapiski* 262, *Ser. filol. nauk* 50: 12-16 [On the reasons for the disappearance of the verb *weorþan* in English]
−1965 'Glagol'noe slovoobrazovanie v drevneangliiskom iazyke' *Issledovaniia po angliiskoi filologii* 3: 121-33 [Verb formation in OE]

Bel'skaia, I.K.
−1955 *Istoriko-semasiologisheskoe issledovanie gruppy slov, sviazannykh s vyrazheniem poniatiia* chelovek *v angliiskom iazyke* (Moscow, Universitet diss.) [A historical-semasiological investigation of a group of words related to the expression of the concept *man* in English]

Bender, H.H.
1934 'English *strawberry' AJP* 55: 71-4

Benediktsson, H.
1978 'Lo. *mikill*: *mykill' Arkiv för Nordisk Filologi* 93: 48-62

Benham, A.R.
1908 'The Clause of Result in Old English Prose' *Anglia* 31: 197-255

Bennett, J.A.W.
1942 'Old English *hrohian' MÆ* 11: 90

Benning, H.A.

1961 Welt *und* Mensch *in der altenglischen Dichtung: Bedeutungsgeschichtliche Untersuchungen zum germanisch-altenglischen Wortschatz*, Beiträge zur englischen Philologie 44 (Bochum-Langendreer)

1971 *Die Vorgeschichte von neuenglisch* duty: *Zur Ausformung der Pflichtidee im Substantivwortschatz des Englischen*, Linguistica et Litteraria 7 (Frankfurt)

Benveniste, E.

1947-8 'La famille étymologique de *learn*' *EGS* 1: 1-5

1969 *Le Vocabulaire des institutions indo-européennes* (Paris); trans. by E. Palmer, *Indo-European Language and Society*, Miami Linguistic Series 12 (Coral Gables 1973)

Bergener, C.

1928 *A Contribution to the Study of the Conversion of Adjectives into Nouns* (Lund)

Bergsten, N.

1911 *A Study on Compound Substantives in English* (Uppsala)

Berkhout, C.T.

1973 '*Beowulf* 3123b: Under the Malice-Roof'*PLL* 9: 428-31

1973-4 '*Feld dennade* – Again' *ELN* 11: 161-2

1974 'The Problem of OE *holmwudu*' *MS* 36: 429-33

1980-81 'Four Difficult Passages in the Exeter Book *Maxims*' *ELN* 18: 247-51

Berkhout, C.T. and Doubleday, J.F.

1973 'The Net in *Judith* 46b-54a' *NM* 74: 630-34

Bessinger, J.B.

1962 '*Maldon* and the *Óláfsdrápa:* An Historical Caveat' *CL* 14: 23-35; repr. in *Brodeur Festschrift* (1963): 23-35

1974 'Homage to Caedmon and Others: A Beowulfian Praise Song' *Pope Festschrift*: 91-106

Best, K

*1905 *Die persönlichen Konkreta des Altenglischen nach ihren Suffixen geordnet* (Strassburg diss.)

Bethurum, D.
1932 'Stylistic Features of the Old English Laws' *MLR* 27: 263-79
1950 'Six Anonymous Old English Codes' *JEGP* 49: 449-63

Beysel, K.
1927 *Die Namen der Blutsverwandtschaft im Englischen*, Giessener Beiträge
zur Erforschung der Sprache und Kultur Englands und Nordamerikas 3
(Breslau): 89-152

Bierbaumer, P.
1974 'Ae. *fornetes folm:* Eine Orchideenart' *Anglia* 92: 172-6
1975 *Der botanische Wortschatz des Altenglischen*, 1. Teil: *Das Læcebōc*,
Grazer Beiträge zur englischen Philologie 1 (Bern and Frankfurt)
1976 *Der botanische Wortschatz des Altenglischen*, 2. Teil: *Lācnunga*,
Herbarium Apuleii, Peri Didaxeon, Grazer Beiträge zur englischen Philologie 2 (Bern, Frankfurt, and Munich)
1979a *Der botanische Wortschatz des Altenglischen*, 3. Teil: *Der botanische*
in altenglischen Glossen, Grazer Beiträge zur englische Philologie 3 (Frankfurt, Bern, and Las Vegas)
1979b 'Zu den altenglischen Psalterglossen *hwit stow* und *hwit tor*' *Anglia*
97: 168-71
1979c 'Altenglisch *seonuwealtian* – Ein "Ghost Word"?' *Anglia* 97: 429-30

Binchy, D.A.
1970 *Celtic and Anglo-Saxon Kingship* (Oxford)

Björkman, E.
1900-2 *Scandinavian Loan-Words in Middle English*, SEP 7, 11 (Halle;
repr. New York 1969)
1905 'Ae. *weg-lā, weg-lā-weg*, me. *wei-la-wei*, etc.' *Archiv* 114: 164
1906 'Zu den altenglischen Insektennamen' *Archiv* 117: 364-6
1907 'Zum altenglischen Gedicht von der Schlacht bei Brunanburh' *Archiv*
118: 384-6
1910 'Tvänne germanska etymologier' in *Festskrift tillegnad Karl Ferdinand*
Johansson på hans 50-årsdag den 16 Sept. 1910 (Göteborg): 1-15
1913 'Miszellen 1: Zu den *festermen* des Ælfric' *Beibl* 24: 281-3
1914-15 'Merc. *onsien* "facies" ' *EStn* 48: 115-23
1916 'Zur englischen Wortkunde' *Anglia* 39: 357-71
1917-19 'Wortgeschichtliche Kleinigkeiten' *Beibl* 28 (1917) 62-4, 92-4,
184-9, 251-4, 274-80, 313-17 / 29 (1918) 179-80, 235-43, 304-12,
336-44 / 30 (1919) 318-20
1919 'Zu einigen Namen im *Beowulf*' *Beibl* 30: 170-80

1920 'Hæðcyn und Hákon' *EStn* 54: 24-34

Bjork, R.E.
1980 'Unferth in the Hermeneutic Circle: A Reappraisal of James L. Rosier's "Design for Treachery: The Unferth Intrigue"' *PLL* 16: 133-41

Blackburn, F.A.
1896 'Note on Alfred's *Cura pastoralis*' *MLN* 11: 58
1897 'The Christian Coloring in the *Beowulf*' *PMLA* 12: 205-25

Blake, N.F.
1962a 'Some Problems of Interpretation and Translation in the OE *Phoenix*' *Anglia* 80: 50-62
1962b 'The Heremod Digressions in *Beowulf*' *JEGP* 61: 278-87
1962c 'Two Notes on the Exeter Book' *N&Q* 207: 45-7
1965 '*The Battle of Maldon*' *Neophil* 50: 332-45
1975-6 'The Flyting in the *Battle of Maldon*' *ELN* 13: 242-5
1977 *The English Language in Medieval Literature* (London and Totowa)

Blakeley, L.
1947-8 'Accusative-Dative Syncretism in the *Lindisfarne Gospels*' *EGS* 1: 6-31
1958 '*Riddles* 22 and 58 of the Exeter Book' *RES* n.s. 9: 241-52

Bliss, A.J.
1979 '*Beowulf*, lines 3074-3075' in M. Salu and R.T. Farrell, eds., *J.R.R. Tolkien, Scholar and Storyteller: Essays in Memoriam* (Ithaca and London): 41-63
1981 'Auxiliary and Verbal in *Beowulf*' *ASE* 9: 157-82

Bloomfield, L.
1929 'Notes on the Preverb *ge-* in Alfredian English' in *Klaeber Festschrift*: 79-102
1930 'OHG *eino*, OE *ana* "solus" ' in J.T. Hatfield et al., eds., *G.O. Curme Volume of Linguistic Studies* (Baltimore): 50-59
1937 'Notes on Germanic Compounds' *Acta Jutlandica* 9: 303-7

Bloomfield, M.W.
1949-51 '*Beowulf* and Christian Allegory: An Interpretation of Unferth' *Traditio* 7: 410-15
1962 'Patristics and Old English Literature: Notes on Some Poems' *CL* 14: 36-43; repr. in *Brodeur Festschrift* (1963): 36-43

Bode, W.
1886 *Die Kenningar in der angelsächsischen Dichtung: Mit Ausblicken auf andere Litteraturen* (Strassburg diss.; Darmstadt and Leipzig)

Bödtker, A.T.
1908 *Critical Contributions to Early English Syntax: First Series,* Videnskabs-Selskabets Skrifter II, hist-filos. Klasse 6 (Christiania)
1909 'French Words in English after 1066' *MLN* 24: 214-17
1912 '*Of* and the Genitive Case in Late Old English' *EStn* 45: 465-7

Bolton, W.F.
1959-60 'Connectives in the *Seafarer* and the *Dream of the Rood*' *MP* 57: 260-62
1968 '*The Dream of the Rood* 9b: *engel = nuntius?*' *N&Q* 213: 165-6
1969 'Byrhtnoð in the Wilderness' *MLR* 64: 481-90
1974 'A Further Echo of the Old English *Genesis* in Milton's *Paradise Lost*' *RES* n.s. 25: 58-61
1977 'Alcuin and Old English Poetry' *YES* 7: 10-22

Bonjour, A.
1955 'On Sea Images in *Beowulf*' *JEGP* 54: 111-15; repr. in *Twelve Beowulf Papers, 1940-1960: With Additional Comments* (Neuchatel and Geneva 1962): 115-19

Bonser, W.
1926a 'The Dissimilarity of Ancient Irish Magic from that of the Anglo-Saxons' *Folk-Lore* 37: 271-88
1926b 'Magical Practices against Elves' *Folk-Lore* 37: 350-63
1951-2 'Anglo-Saxon Medical Nomenclature' *EGS* 4: 13-19
1963 *The Medical Background of Anglo-Saxon England,* Publications of the Wellcome Historical Medical Library n.s. 3 (London)

Borowski, B.
1925 'Funktion, Affekt, Gliederzahl, und Laut: Beiträge aus dem Englischen' in *Germanica: Eduard Sievers zum 75. Geburtstage, 25 November 1925* (Halle): 273-312

Bosse, R.B.
1973 'Aural Aesthetic and the Unity of the *Seafarer*' *PLL* 9: 3-14

Both, M.
*1909 *Die konsonantischen Suffixe altenglischer Konkreta und Kollektiva* (Kiel diss.)

Bouman, A.C.
1951 'Een drietal Etymologieen: *aibr, eolete, garsecg' Neophil* 35: 238-41

Bourcier, G.
*1977 *Les propositions relatives en vieil-anglais* (Paris)

Boyd, P.
1942 'Boundary Dykes' *N&Q* 182: 273

Boyd, W.J.P.
1967 'Aldrediana VII: Hebraica' *EPS* 10: 1-32
1975a *Aldred's Marginalia: Explanatory Comments in the Lindisfarne Gospels*, Exeter Medieval English Texts and Studies [4] (Exeter)
1975b 'Aldrediana XXV: *Ritual* Hebraica' *EPS* 14: 1-57

Bracher, F.
1937 'Understatement in Old English Poetry' *PMLA* 52: 915-34

Bradler, H.
1950 *Eine Biographie des altenglischen Wortes* ymbgang *ergänzt durch Vergleiche zu anderen germ. Sprachen* (Vienna diss.)

Bradley, H.
1881 'Esher' *N&Q* ser. 6, 3: 255
1884 Review of *A New English Dictionary on Historical Principles*, in *Academy* 25: 141-2
1887a 'The Etymology of *shire' Academy* 31: 239
1887b 'Etymological Notes' *Academy* 31: 326-7
1888 'The First *Riddle* of the Exeter Book' *Academy* 33: 197-8; repr. in R. Bridges, ed., *The Collected Papers of Henry Bradley* (Oxford 1928): 208-10
1889a Review of J. Earle, *A Handbook to Land-Charters and other Saxonic Documents*, in *Academy* 35: 28-9
1889b 'The Etymology of the Word *God' Academy* 35: 432
1889c 'The Old Northumbrian Glosses in MS. Palatine 68' *Academy* 36: 154
1889d 'The Etymology of *neorxnawang' Academy* 36: 254
1891a 'Old English *efenehþ' Academy* 40: 15
1891b '*Efennehðu' Academy* 40: 198

1904 'The Song of the Nine Magic Herbs ("Neunkräutersegen")' *Archiv* 113: 144-5
1910 'English Place-Names' *E&S* o.s. 1: 7-41; repr. in R. Bridges, ed., *The Collected Papers of Henry Bradley* (Oxford 1928): 80-109
1911 'Two *Riddles* of the Exeter Book' *MLR* 6: 433-40
1916 'Some Emendations in Old English Texts' *MLR* 11: 212-15
1917a '*Tręson* in the *Anglo-Saxon Chronicle*' *MLR* 12: 72-4
1917b 'At-after' *MLR* 12: 74-6
1922 'The Alleged Old English Word *streat*' *TLS* Dec. 21: 860

Bradley, H., and Sisam, K.
1919 'Textual Notes on the Old English *Epistola Alexandri*' *MLR* 14: 202-5

Brady, C.
1940 '*Innweorud earmanrices*' *Speculum* 15: 454-9
1952a 'The Synonyms for *sea* in *Beowulf*' in L.R. Lind, ed., *Studies in Honor of Albert Norey Sturtevant*, University of Kansas Humanistic Series 29 (Lawrence): 22-46
1952b 'The Old English Nominal Compounds in -*rád*' *PMLA* 67: 538-71
1979 '"Weapons" in *Beowulf:* An Analysis of the Nominal Compounds and an Evaluation of the Poet's Use of Them' *ASE* 8: 79-141

Braekman, W.L.
1980 'Notes on Old English Charms' *Neophil* 64: 461-9

Brandl, A.
1921 'Zur Vorgeschichte der "Weird Sisters" im *Macbeth*' in M. Förster and K. Wildhagen, eds., *Texte und Forschungen zur englischen Kulturgeschichte: Festgabe für Felix Liebermann* (Halle): 252-70

Brasch, C.
1910 *Die Namen der Werkzeuge im Altenglischen: Eine kulturhistorisch-etymologische Untersuchung* (Kiel diss.; Leipzig)

Braude, J.
1932 *Die Familiengemeinschaften der Angelsachsen*, Rechtsgeschichtliche Abhandlungen 3 (Leipzig)

Braune, W.
1918 'Althochdeutsch und Angelsächsisch' *BGdSL* 43: 361-445

Bremmer, R.H.
1979 'Old Frisian *dom* "crowd, multitude"?' *Us Wurk, Tydskrift foar Frisistyk* 28: 45-50

Brett, C.
1919 'Notes on Passages of Old and Middle English' *MLR* 14: 1-9
1927 'Notes on Old and Middle English' *MLR* 22: 257-64

Bridier, Y.
1972 'La Fonction sociale du *Horn* chez les Anglo-Saxons' *EA* 25: 74-7

Brie, M.
1910 'Über die ags. Bezeichnung des Wortes *zauberer*' *EStn* 41: 20-27

Bright, J.W.
1886 'The Etymology of *endemes(t)*' *MLN* 1: 19-20
1887 'The Etymology of *firmetton* and *frimdig*' *AJP* 8: 471-2
1888a 'The Anglo-Saxon *bâsnian* and *wrâsen*' *MLN* 3: 37
1888b '*Thraf-caik*' *MLN* 3: 69-70
1889 'The Etymology of *gospel*' *MLN* 4: 104-5
1890 'Lexical Notes' *MLN* 5: 121
1891 'An Emendation in the Anglo-Saxon Gospels: Luke i,5: *of Abian tune*' *MLN* 6: 7-8
1895 'Notes on the *Beowulf*' *MLN* 10: 43-4
1902 'Notes on the Cædmonian *Exodus*' *MLN* 17: 212-13
1912a 'On the Anglo-Saxon Poem *Exodus*' *MLN* 27: 13-19
1912b 'An Idiom of the Comparative in Anglo-Saxon' *MLN* 27: 181-3
1916a 'Anglo-Saxon *umbor* and *seld-guma*' *MLN* 31: 82-4
1916b '*Beowulf* 489-90' *MLN* 31: 217-23

Britton, G.C.
1953 'Heroic Poetry' *TLS* Feb. 27: 137
1961 'Aldrediana IV: The *e*- and *i*- Diphthongs' *EGS* 7: 1-19
1965 'The Characterization of the Vikings in the *Battle of Maldon*' *N&Q* 210: 85-7
1967 '*Bealuwara weorc* in the *Dream of the Rood*' *NM* 68: 273-6
1969 'Aldrediana XII: *æ-e*' *EPS* 12: 1-34

Brockman, B.
1974 '"Heroic" and "Christian" in *Genesis A:* The Evidence of the Cain and Abel Episode' *MLQ* 35: 115-28

Brodeur, A.G.

1959 *The Art of Beowulf* (Berkeley; repr. 1969) Appendix B: 'Check-List of Compounds Formed on the Same Base-Words in *Beowulf* and in Other Poems': 254-71

1968 'A Study of Diction and Style in Three Anglo-Saxon Narrative Poems' in A.H. Orrick, ed., *Nordica et Anglica: Studies in Honor of Stefan Einarsson* (The Hague and Paris): 97-114

Brøndegaard, V.J.

1979 'Ein angelsächsischer Pflanzenname: *openars(e)' Sudhoffs Archiv: Zeitschrift für Wissenschaftgeschichte* 63: 190-93

Bromwich, J.

1950 'Who was the Translator of the Prose Portion of the *Paris Psalter?*' in *Chadwick Memorial Volume:* 290-303

Brooke, C.

1963 *The Saxon and Norman Kings* (London; repr. Glasgow 1977)

Brooks, K.R.

1948-9 'Old English *wopes hring' EGS* 2: 68-74

1949-50 'Two Textual Emendations in the Old English *Andreas' EGS* 3: 61-4

1952-3 'Old English *ēa* and Related Words' *EGS* 5: 15-66

Brorström, S.

1971 'A Historical Survey of Prepositions Expressing the Sense "for the duration of"'*ES* 52: 105-16

Brown, A.K.

1972 *'Heifer' Neophil* 56: 79-85

1973a 'Some Further Etymologies of *heifer' Neophil* 57: 94

1973b *'Neorxnawang' NM* 74: 610-23

1975 'Bede, a Hisperic Etymology, and Early Sea Poetry' *MS* 37: 419-32

1978 'The English Compass Points' *MÆ* 47: 221-46

1980 'The Firedrake in *Beowulf' Neophil* 64: 439-60

Brown, C.

1919 *'Beowulf* 1080-1106' *MLN* 34: 181-3

1938 *'Beowulf* and the Blickling Homilies and Some Textual Notes' *PMLA* 53: 905-16

1940 *'Poculum mortis* in Old English' *Speculum* 15: 389-99

Brown, E.M.
1892 'Anglo-Saxon *gien, giena*' *MLN* 7: 125-6

Brown, G.H.
1973-4 '*Bēowulf* 1278b: *sunu þeod wrecan*' *MP* 72: 172-4

Brown, M.D.
1952 *A Study of the Vocabulary of Archbishop Wulfstan* (Nottingham M.A. thesis; ASLIB *Index* 2: 153)

Brown, R.A.
1969 'An Historian's Approach to the Origins of the Castle in England' *Archaeological Journal* 126: 131-46

Bruce-Mitford, R.
1952 'The Sutton Hoo Ship Burial' in R.H. Hodgkin, ed., *A History of the Anglo-Saxons* (London): II, 749-56
1974 *Aspects of Anglo-Saxon Archaeology: Sutton Hoo and Other Discoveries* (London)

Brunner, H.
1897 'Ae. *dryhtinbeag*' *Archiv* 98: 398

Bryan, W.F.
1920 '*Beowulf* Notes' *JEGP* 19: 84-5
1929 'Epithetic Compound Folk-Names in *Beowulf*' in *Klaeber Festschrift*: 120-34
1930-31 '*Ǣrgōd* in *Beowulf* and Other Old English Compounds of *ǣr*' *MP* 28: 157-61

Buckalew, R.E.
1978 'Leland's Transcript of Ælfric's *Glossary*' *ASE* 7: 149-64

Buckhurst, H.T.M.
1929 'Terms and Phrases for the Sea in Old English Poetry' in *Klaeber Festschrift*: 103-19

Büchner, G.
1968 *Vier altenglische Bezeichnungen für vergehen und verbrechen, firen, gylt, man, scyld* (Berlin diss.)

Bugge, S.
1888 'Zur altgermanischen Sprachgeschichte: Germanisch *ug* aus *uw*' *BGdSL*
13: 504-15

Bullough, D.A.
1968 'Anglo-Saxon Institutions and Early English Society' *Annali della
fondazione italiana per la storia amministrativa* 2: 647-59
1972 'The Educational Tradition in England from Alfred to Ælfric: Teaching
utriusque linguae' *Settimane di studio del Centro Italiano di studi sull'alto
medioevo* 19: 453-94

Burchfield, R.W.
1955 '*Beowulf* 219: *ymb an tid*' *MLR* 50: 485-7

Burlin, R.B.
1974 'Inner Weather and Interlace: A Note on the Semantic Value of Structure in *Beowulf*' in *Pope Festschrift:* 81-9

Burnham, J.M.
1911 *Concessive Constructions in Old English Prose*, YSE 39 (New York)

Burrow, J.
1965 '*The Wanderer:* Lines 73-87' *N&Q* 210: 166-8
1980 'Layamon's *Brut* 10642: *wleoteð*' *N&Q* 255: 2-3

Bush, J.D.
1921 'A Note on *Beowulf* 1600-1605' *MLN* 36: 251

Byers, J.R.
1965 'On the Decorating of Heorot' *PMLA* 80: 299-300

Bynon, T.
1967 'Concerning the Etymology of English *path*' *TPS* (1966): 67-87

ſ

C., B.H.
1861 *'Fulluht:* The Anglo-Saxon Baptism' *N&Q* ser. 2, 12: 523-4

C., H.C.
1851 'A Saxon Bell-House' *N&Q* ser. 1, 4: 178
1853 'Derivation of *lad* and *lass*' *N&Q* ser. 1, 7: 256-7 / 8: 210
1861 *'Fulluht:* The Anglo-Saxon Baptism' *N&Q* ser. 2, 12: 393

Caie, G.D.
1969 *The Theme of Pride in Old English Poetry* (McMaster M.A. thesis)
1976 *The Judgment Day Theme in Old English Poetry,* Publications of the Department of English, University of Copenhagen 2 (Copenhagen)
1978 'The Old English *Daniel:* A Warning against Pride' *ES* 59: 1-9

Calder, D.G.
1971 'Setting and Mode in the *Seafarer* and the *Wanderer*' *NM* 72: 264-75
1972 'The Vision of Paradise: A Symbolic Reading of the Old English *Phoenix*' *ASE* 1: 167-81

Caldwell, R.A.
1973 *'Beowulf* vv. 413b-414' *MÆ* 42: 131

Caluwé-Dor, J. De
1969 'Towards an Etymology of the Verb *to lie*' *ES* 50: 80-82
1977 'A propos de l'etymologie du verbe anglais *to come*' in S. De Vriendt and C. Peeters, eds., *Linguistics in Belgium, Linguistiek in Belgie, Linguistique en Belgique* (Brussels): I, 14-22

Cameron, A.F.
1968 *The Old English Nouns of Colour: A Semantic Study* (Oxford diss.; ASLIB *Index* 19: 339)
1969 'Old English *unbleoh* Again' *Neophil* 53: 299-302

Cameron, K.
1973 'Early Field-Names in an English-Named Lincolnshire Village' in F. Sandgren, ed., *Otium et Negotium: Studies in Onomatology and Library Science Presented to Olof von Feilitzen,* Acta bibliothecæ regiæ Stockholmiensis 16 (Stockholm): 38-43

Campanile, E.
1970 'Elementi lessicali di origine inglese nel *Vocabularium Cornicum*' *Studi e saggi linguistici* 10: 193-201

1974 'Minima Cornica' *Zeitschrift für celtische Philologie* 33: 23-7

Campbell, A.
1933 'Old English *reord*' *MLR* 28: 231-3

Campbell, B.R.
1969 'The *superne gar* in the *Battle of Maldon*' *N&Q* 214: 45-6

Campbell, C.D.
1905 *The Names of Relationship in English: A Contribution to English Semasiology* (Strassburg diss.)

Campbell, J.J.
1950 *The Differences in Vocabulary in the Manuscripts of the Old English Version of Bede's Ecclesiastical History* (Yale diss.)
1951 'The Dialect Vocabulary of the OE Bede' *JEGP* 50: 349-72
1952 'The OE Bede: Book III, Chapters 16 to 20' *MLN* 67: 381-6
1955 'The Harley Glossary and "Saxon Patois"' *PQ* 34: 71-4

Candelaria, F.
1963-4 '*Garsecg* in *Beowulf*' *ELN* 1: 243-4

Carlson, A.M.
1978 'A Diachronic Treatment of English Quantifiers' *Lingua* 46: 295-328

Carlson, S.M.
1967 'The Monsters of *Beowulf*: Creations of Literary Scholars' *Journal of American Folklore* 80: 357-64

Carr, C.T.
1939 *Nominal Compounds in Germanic*, St. Andrews University Publications 41 (London)
1948-9 'OE *fitel*, OLG *fitil*, OHG *fizzel*, ON *-fjǫtli*' *EGS* 2: 56-8

Cassidy, F.G.
1963 'The Edged Teeth' in *Brodeur Festschrift*: 227-36
1970 'A Symbolic Word-Group in *Beowulf*' in J. Mandel and B.A. Rosenberg, eds., *Medieval Literature and Folklore Studies: Essays in Honour of Francis Lee Utley* (New Brunswick, N.J.): 27-34, 345-8
1972a '*Beowulf: icge* and *incge* Once More' in E.S. Firchow et al., eds., *Studies for Einar Haugen Presented by Friends and Colleagues*, Janua linguarum, series maior 59 (The Hague and Paris): 115-18

1972b 'Old English *gārsecg* — An Eke-Name?' *Names* 20: 95-100

Cawley, A.C.
1948-9 'Notes on Old English' *EGS* 2: 75-80

Chadwick, H.M.
1905 *Studies on Anglo-Saxon Institutions* (Cambridge; repr. New York 1963)

Chadwick, N.K.
1959 'The Monsters and *Beowulf*' in P. Clemoes, ed., *The Anglo-Saxons: Studies in Some Aspects of their History and Culture Presented to Bruce Dickins* (London): 171-203

Chaney, W.A.
1962 'Grendel and the *gifstol:* A Legal View of Monsters' *PMLA* 77: 513-20

Chase, D.E.
1976 *A Semantic Study of Old English Words for* warrior (New York diss.; *DAI* 37: 5807A)

Chickering, H.D.
1971 'The Literary Magic of *wið færstice*' *Viator* 2: 83-104

Child, C.G.
1893 '*Stapol* = *patronus* (Sp. *padron*, Port. *padrão*)' *MLN* 8: 252-3
1906 '*Beowulf* 30, 53, 132, 2957' *MLN* 21: 175-7, 198-200

Chrimes, S.B.
1952 *An Introduction to the Administrative History of Mediaeval England* (Oxford)

Christiani, B.
*1938 *Zwillingsverbindungen in der altenglischen Dichtung* (Königsberg diss.; Würzburg)

Christophersen, P.
1939 *The Articles: A Study of their Theory and Use in English* (Copenhagen and London): 82-108

Chupryna, O.G.
1979 'Stanovlenie torgovo-denezhnoi leksiki v angliiskom iazyke' *Vestnik*

Moskovskogo Univ. ser. filologiia 1979 no. 1: 51-60 [The development of the trade and money vocabulary in English]

Clark, C.
1952-3 'Studies in the Vocabulary of the *Peterborough Chronicle,* 1070-1154' *EGS* 5: 67-89
1957 'Gender in the *Peterborough Chronicle,* 1070-1154' *ES* 38: 109-15, 174
*1976a 'Some Early Canterbury Surnames' *ES* 57: 294-309
1976b 'People and Languages in Post-Conquest Canterbury' *Journal of Medieval History* 2: 1-33

Clark, G.
1968 '*The Battle of Maldon:* A Heroic Poem' *Speculum* 43: 52-71
1979 'The Hero of *Maldon:* Vir pius et strenuus' *Speculum* 54: 257-82

Clark, R.P.
1976 'A New Kenning in *Beowulf: ealuscerwen'* *Scholia satyrica* 2: 35-6

Clark Hall, J.R.
1910 'A Note on *Beowulf* 1142-1145' *MLN* 25: 113-14

Classen, E.
1915 'OE *nicras (Beowulf* 422, 575, 845, 1427)' *MLR* 10: 85-6

Clemoes, P.
1971 'Cynewulf's Image of the Ascension' in *Whitelock Festschrift:* 293-304

Closs (Traugott), O.E.E.
*1964 *A Grammar of Alfred's Orosius* (California, Berkeley diss.; *DA* 25: 1899)

Clover, C.J.
1980 'The Germanic Context of the Unferþ Episode' *Speculum* 55: 444-68

Coates, R.
1979 'Old English *steorf* in Sussex Placenames' *Beiträge zur Namenforschung* 14: 320-24

Coens, M.
1956 'Aux origines de la céphalophorie: Un fragment retrouvé d'une ancienne passion de S. Just, martyr de Beauvais' *Analecta Bollandiana* 74: 86-114

Coleridge, H.
1859 'On the Scandinavian Element in the English Language' *TPS* (1859): 18-31

Colgrave, B.
1937a *'Scŭrheard' MLR* 32: 281
1937b 'Some Notes on *Riddle* 21' *MLR* 32: 281-3

Collinder, B.
1932 'Wortgeschichtliches aus dem Bereich der germanisch-finnischen und germanisch-lappischen Lehnbeziehungen' *Acta philologica Scandinavica* 7: 193-225

Collins, D.C.
1959 'Kenning in Anglo-Saxon Poetry' *E&S* n.s. 12: 1-17

Collins, R.L.
1970 Six Words in the *Blickling Homilies'* in *Meritt Festschrift:* 137-41

Colman, R.V.
1981 *'Hamsocn:* Its Meaning and Significance in Early English Law' *American Journal of Legal History* 25: 95-110

Conant, J.B.
1973 'Runic *alu* − A New Conjecture' *JEGP* 72: 467-73

Condren, E.I.
1973 *'Unnyt* Gold in *Beowulf* 3168' *PQ* 52: 296-9

Cook, A.S.
1888a 'The Cliff of the Dead' *Academy* 34: 355
1888b 'Notes on Old English Words' *MLN* 3: 6-7
1889a 'The Old Northumbrian Glosses in MS. Palatine 68' *Academy* 36: 89
1889b 'The Old English Word *synrust'* *MLN* 4: 129
1892 'Old English *scúrheard' MLN* 7: 253
1896 'An Anglo-Saxon Gloss' *MLN* 11: 160
1902 'Old English Notes' *MLN* 17: 209-10
1906 'Cynewulf, *Christ* 1320' *MLN* 21: 8
1925a 'Bitter Beer-Drinking' *MLN* 40: 285-8
1925b *'Beowulf* 159-163' *MLN* 40: 352-4
1926a 'The Beowulfian *maðelode' JEGP* 25: 1-6
1926b 'Hellenic and Beowulfian Shields and Spears' *MLN* 41: 360-63

1926c 'Augustine's Journey from Rome to Richborough' *Speculum* 1: 375-97
1928 '*Beowulf* 1039 and the Greek ἀρχι-' *Speculum* 3: 75-81

Cook, M.J.
*1962 *Developing Techniques in Anglo-Saxon Scholarship in the Seventeenth Century as They Appear in the Dictionarium Saxonico-Latino-Anglicum of William Somner* (Toronto diss.)

Cooke, W.G.
1971 '*Hronas* and *hronfixas*' *N&Q* 216: 245-7

Corso, L.
1980 'Some Considerations of the Concept *nið* in *Beowulf*' *Neophil* 64: 121-6

Cortelyou, J. van Z.
1906 *Die altenglischen Namen der Insekten, Spinnen- und Krustentiere,* AF 19 (Heidelberg; repr. Amsterdam 1969)

Cosijn, P.J.
1877 '*Beowulf* 1694' *Taalkundige Bijdragen* 1: 286
1880 '*Geþawenian*' *BGdSL* 7: 454-6
1881 'Anglosaxonica' *TNTL* 1: 143-58
1882 'Zum *Beowulf*' *BGdSL* 8: 568-74
1887 '*Beran*' *MLN* 2: 5
1888 '*Niel, wiel*' *TNTL* 8: 243-7
1893 '*Fara*' *TNTL* 11: 83-8
1894-8 'Anglosaxonica' *BGdSL* 19 (1894): 441-61 / 20 (1895): 98-116 / 21 (1896): 8-26 / 23 (1898): 109-30

Cosmos, S.
1975 'Old English *limwæstm* (*Christ and Satan* 129)' *N&Q* 220: 196-8

Cowgill, W.
1960 'Gothic *iddja* and Old English *ēode*' *Language* 36: 483-501

Craigie, W.A.
1906 'The Etymology of *awl*' *TPS* (1903-6): 261-4
1924 'The Meaning of *ambyre wind*' *Philologica* 2: 19-20
1925 'A Rare Use of the Preposition *to*' *MLR* 20: 184-5
1935 'Survival of Old English *eax, æx*' *AS* 10: 233

Cramp, R.J.

1957 *Some Aspects of Old English Vocabulary in the Light of Recent Archaeological Evidence* (Oxford diss.; ASLIB *Index* 8: 128)

1958 '*Beowulf* and Archaeology' *Medieval Archaeology* 1: 57-77

Cravens, M.J.

1932 *Designations and Treatment of the Holy Eucharist in Old and Middle English before 1300* (Catholic U. of America diss.)

Crawford (Roberts), J.

1963 'Evidences for Witchcraft in Anglo-Saxon England' *MÆ* 32: 99-116

1967 '*Scirwered: Beowulf* 496a' *N&Q* 212: 204-5

Crawford, S.J.

1926 '*Ealu-scerwen*' *MLR* 21: 302-3

1928 '*Beowulf,* ll. 168-9' *MLR* 23: 336

1931 'Beowulfiana' *RES* o.s. 7: 448-50

Creed, R.P.

1957 'The *andswarode*-system in Old English Poetry' *Speculum* 32: 523-8

1958 '*Genesis* 1316' *MLN* 73: 321-5

1975 'Widsith's Journey through Germanic Tradition' in *McGalliard Festschrift:* 376-87

Crépin, A.

1969 *Poétique vieil-anglaise: Désignations du Dieu chrétien* (Paris diss.; Amiens)

1976 'Bede and the Vernacular' in G. Bonner, ed., *Famulus Christi: Essays in Commemoration of the Thirteenth Centenary of the Birth of the Venerable Bede* (London): 170-92

Cronne, H.A.

1949 'The Royal Forest in the Reign of Henry I' in H.A. Cronne, T.W. Moody, and D.B. Quinn, eds., *Essays in British and Irish History in Honour of James Eadie Todd* (London): 1-23

Crosby, H.L.

1940 'Two Notes on *Beowulf*' *MLN* 55: 605-6

Cross, J.E.

1955 'Notes on Old English Texts' *Neophil* 39: 203-6

1956 ' "Ubi sunt" Passages in Old English — Sources and Relationship'

Vetenskaps-Societetens i Lund Årsbok: 25-44

1957a 'On Sievers-Brunner's Interpretation of the *Ruin,* line 7, *forweorone geleorene' EGS* 6: 104-6

1957b ' "The Dry Bones Speak" — A Theme in Some Old English Homilies' *JEGP* 56: 434-9

1959 'On the Allegory in the *Seafarer* — Illustrative Notes' *MÆ* 28: 104-6

1961 'On the Genre of the *Wanderer' Neophil* 45: 63-75

1962a *Latin Themes in Old English Poetry* (Lund diss.)

1962b 'Aspects of Microcosm and Macrocosm in Old English Literature' *CL* 14: 1-22; repr. in *Brodeur Festschrift* (1963): 1-22

1963 *Ælfric and the Mediaeval Homiliary — Objection and Contribution,* Scripta minora, Regiae societatis humaniorum litterarum Lundensis, Studier utg. av Kungl. Humanistiska Vetenskapssamfundet i Lund 1961-62 (Lund)

1964 'The "coeternal beam" in the OE *Advent Poem (Christ I),* ll. 104-129' *Neophil* 48: 72-81

1965a 'Oswald and Byrhtnoth: A Christian Saint and a Hero who is Christian' *E&S* 46: 93-109

1965b 'Gregory, *Blickling Homily* X, and Ælfric's *Passio S. Mauricii* on the World's Youth and Age' *NM* 66: 327-30

1967 'The Conception of the Old English *Phoenix*' in Creed *Essays:* 129-52

1968 'More Sources for Two of Ælfric's *Catholic Homilies' Anglia* 86: 59-78

1969a '*Halga hyht* and Poetic Stimulus in the *Advent Poem (Christ I)* 50-70' *Neophil* 53: 194-9

1969b 'On the *Blickling Homily* for Ascension Day (No. XI)' *NM* 70: 228-40

1969c 'The Metrical Epilogue to the Old English Version of Gregory's *Cura pastoralis' NM* 70: 381-6

1969d 'Ælfric — Mainly on Memory and Creative Method in Two *Catholic Homilies' SN* 41: 135-55

1971a 'Source and Analysis of Some Ælfrician Passages' *NM* 72: 446-53

1971b 'Lexicographical Notes on the Old English *Life of St. Giles* and the *Life of St. Nicholas' N&Q* 202: 369-72

1972 'The Literate Anglo-Saxon — On Sources and Disseminations' *PBA* 58: 3-36

1974a 'Mainly on Philology and the Interpretative Criticism of *Maldon*' in *Pope Festschrift:* 235-53

1974b 'The Poem in Transmitted Text — Editor and Critic' *E&S* n.s. 27: 84-97

1975 '*Blickling Homily* XIV and the *Old English Martyrology* on John the Baptist' *Anglia* 93: 145-60

1977 ' "Legimus in ecclesiasticis historicis": A Sermon for All Saints, and its Use in Old English Prose' *Traditio* 33: 101-35

1978 'Mary Magdalen in the *Old English Martyrology:* The Earliest Extant "Narrat Josephus" Variant of her Legend' *Speculum* 53: 16-25
1979 'Cynewulf's Traditions about the Apostles in *Fates of the Apostles*' *ASE* 8: 163-75
1981 'Old English *leasere*' *N&Q* 226: 484-6

Cruz, J.M. de la
– 1968-9 *Origins and Development of the Phrasal Verb to the End of the Middle English Period* (Belfast, Queen's University diss.)
1972 'The Latin Influence on the Germanic Development of the English Phrasal Verb' *EPS* 13: 1-42
1973 'The Origins of the Germanic Phrasal Verb' *IF* 77 (1972): 73-96
1975 'Old English Pure Prefixes: Structure and Function' *Linguistics* 145: 47-81

Curry, J.L.
1966 'Approaches to a Translation of the Anglo-Saxon *The Wife's Lament*' *MÆ* 35: 187-98

Curtis, J.L.
1946 *The Vocabulary of Medical* craftas *in the Old English Leechbook of Bald* (North Carolina, Chapel Hill diss.)

D

Dahl, I.
1938 *Substantival Inflexion in Early Old English: Vocalic Stems,* LSE 7 (Lund; repr. Nendeln/Liechtenstein 1968)

Dahl, T.
1936 *Form and Function: Studies in Old and Middle English Syntax* (Copenhagen)

Dam, J. van
1957 *The Causal Clause and Causal Prepositions in Early Old English Prose* (Amsterdam diss.; Groningen and Djakarta)

Danchev, A.
− 1967 *The Syntactic Functions of the Preposition* mid *in Old English Poetry and Prose,* I Annuaire de l'Université de Sofia, Faculté des lettres, 61, 2 (Sofia): 51-130
1969-70 *The Parallel Use of the Synthetic Dative, Instrumental, and Periphrastic Prepositional Constructions in Old English,* Annuaire de l'Université de Sofia, Faculté des lettres, 63, 2 (Sofia): 39-99

Dane, J.A.
1980 'The Structure of the Old English *Solomon and Saturn II' Neophil* 64: 592-603

Daniels, J.
1904-5 'Anglosaxonica' *TNTL* 23 (1904): 99-101 / 24 (1905): 218-24

Daunt, M.
1916 *'The Seafarer,* ll. 97-102' *MLR* 11: 337-8
1918 'Some Difficulties of the *Seafarer* Reconsidered' *MLR* 13: 474-9
1959 'Minor Realism and Contrast in *Beowulf*' in *Mélanges de linguistique et de philologie: Fernand Mossé in Memoriam* (Paris): 87-94
1966 'Some Modes of Anglo-Saxon Meaning' in C.E. Bazell et al., eds., *In Memory of John Rupert Firth* (London): 66-78

Davidson, H.R.E.
1962 *The Sword in Anglo-Saxon England: Its Archaeology and Literature* (Oxford)

Davies, J.
*1857 'On the Connexion of the Keltic with the Teutonic Languages, and Especially with the Anglo-Saxon' *TPS* (1857): 39-93

Davis, N.
1953 *'Hippopotamus* in Old English' *RES* n.s. 4: 141-2

Davison, B.K.
1967 'The Origins of the Castle in England' *Archaeological Journal* 124: 201-11

Dawson, R.M.
1962 'The Structure of the Old English Gnomic Poems' *JEGP* 61: 14-22

Dean, C.
1965-6 *'Weal wundrum heah, wyrmlicum fah* and the Narrative Background of the *Wanderer' MP* 63: 141-3

Denisova, O.K.
— 1960 'K voprosu ob istorii razvitiia gruppy prilagatel'nykh oboznachiush-chikh poniatie razmera *vysokii-nizkii* v drevneangliiskii period' Irkutsk, Ped. Institut, *Uchenye zapiski* 4: 3-45 [On the problem of the historical development of a group of adjectives denoting the sense of the dimension *high* or *low* in OE]

Dent, A.
1965 'OE *hors-ōme' N&Q* 210: 446

Derolez, R.
1946 '— and that Difficult Word, *garsecg* (Gummere)' *MLQ* 7: 445-52
1948 'Some Notes on OE *firgenstream'* in *Album Prof. Dr. Frank Baur* (Antwerp): I, 182-91
1955 'De Oudengelse Aldhelmglossen in HS. 1650 van de Koninklijke Bibliotheek te Brussel' *Handelingen der Zuidnederlandse Maatschappij voor Taal- en Letterkunde en Geschiedenis* 9: 37-50
1958 'Periodisering en continuïteit of: "When did Middle English begin?" (K. Malone)' in *Album Edgard Blancquaert* (Tongeren): 77-84
1959 'Aldhelmus Glosatus III' *ES* 40: 1-6
1960 'Aldhelmus Glosatus IV: Some *hapax legomena* among the Old English Aldhelm Glosses' *SGG* 2: 81-95
1970 'Some Notes on the *Liber scintillarum* and its Old English Gloss' in *Meritt Festschrift:* 142-51
1971 'The Orientation System in the Old English Orosius' in *Whitelock Festschrift:* 253-68
1974 *Götter und Mythen der Germanen,* trans. J. von Wattenwyl (Wiesbaden) [German trans. of *De Godsdienst der Germanen* (Roermond 1959)]

Derolez, R. and Schwab, U.
1980-81 *'Logŏor,* ein altenglisches Glossenwort' *SGG* 21: 95-125

De Roo, C.H.
1979 'Two Old English Fatal Feast Metaphors: *ealuscerwen* and *meoduscerwen' English Studies in Canada* 5: 249-61
1980 'Old English *sele' Neophil* 64: 113-20

Deutschbein, M.
1901 'Dialektisches in der ags. Uebersetzung von Bedas *Kirchengeschichte' BGdSL* 26: 169-244

Devleeschouwer, J.
1974 'Note sur l'origine du nom germanique de la main' *Orbis* 23: 130-41

Dick, E.S.
1965 *Ae.* dryht *und seine Sippe: Eine wortkundliche, kultur- und religionsgeschichtliche Betrachtung zur altgermanischen Glaubensvorstellung vom wachstümlichen Heil,* Neue Beiträge zur englischen Philologie 3 (Münster)

Dickins, B.
1926 'The Peterborough Annal for 1137' *RES* o.s. 2: 341-3
1933 'English Names and Old English Heathenism' *E&S* o.s. 19: 148-60
1943 'Yorkshire Hobs' *Transactions of the Yorkshire Dialect Society* 7, pt. 43 (1942): 9-23
1973 *'Fagaduna* in Orderic (A.D. 1075)' in F. Sandgren, ed., *Otium et Negotium: Studies in Onomatology and Library Science Presented to Olof von Feilitzen,* Acta bibliothecæ regiæ Stockholmiensis 16 (Stockholm): 44-5

Diekstra, F.N.M.
1971 *'The Wanderer* 65b-72: The Passions of the Mind and the Cardinal Virtues' *Neophil* 55: 73-88

Dieter, F.
1888 'Altengl. *ymbeaht* = got. *andbahts' EStn* 11: 492
1896 'Altenglisch *healstán' Anglia* 18: 291-2

Dieth, E.
1955 *'Hips:* A Geographical Contribution to the *she* Puzzle' *ES* 36: 209-17

Dietrich, F.
1853 *'Hycgan* und *hopian' ZfdA* 9: 214-22

Dike, E.B.
*1933-4 'Our Oldest Obsoletisms' *EStn* 68: 339-50
*1935 'Obsolete English Words: Some Recent Views' *JEGP* 34: 351-65

Dishington, J.
1976 'Functions of the Germanic *ē-* Verbs: A Clue to their Formal Pre-history' *Language* 52: 851-65

Doane, A.N.
1966 'Heathen Form and Christian Function in the *Wife's Lament' MS* 28: 77-91
1973 ' "The Green Street of Paradise": A Note on Lexis and Meaning in Old English Poetry' *NM* 74: 456-65
1977 *'Genesis B* 317a: *sum heard gewrinc' PQ* 56: 404-7
1979 *'Elene* 610a: *Rexgeniðlan' PQ* 58: 237-40

Dobbie, E.V.K.
1952 *'Mwatide, Beowulf* 2226' *MLN* 67: 242-5

Dobnigg, E.
1950 *Biographie von as.* sælig (Vienna diss.)

Dobrunova, T.V.
– 1972 'Semanticheskaia struktura gruppy slov, vyrazhaiushchei ponatie *strakh* v drevneangliiskom iazyke' *Angliiskaia filologiia* 3: 194-202 [Semantic structure of a group of words expressing the concept of *fear* in OE]

Dodgson, J.M.
1968 'ME *cronebery' N&Q* 213: 88-9

Doig, J.F.
1981-2 *'Beowulf* 3069b: Curse or Consequence?' *ELN* 19: 3-6

Dollenz, A.M.
1950 *Lat.* benedicere, benedictio *in der germanischen Kirchensprache unter besonderer Berücksichtigung des Angelsächsischen* (Vienna diss.)

Donahue, C.
1965 '*Beowulf* and Christian Tradition: A Reconsideration from a Celtic Stance' *Traditio* 21: 55-116

Dorskii, S.L.
— 1958 'Nekotorye voprosy suffiksatsii i polusuffiksatsii otvlechennykh imen sushchestvitel'nykh v drevneangliiskom iazyke' Minsk, Belorusskii gos. Universitet, *Trudy po iazykoznaniiu* 1: 307-58 [Some problems of suffixation and semi-suffixation of abstract nouns in OE]
— 1960 *Slovoobrazovanie otvlechennykh imen sushchestvitel'nykh v drevneangliiskom iazyke (suffiksal'noe i polusuffiksal'noe)* (Minsk) [Word-formation of abstract substantives in OE (process of suffixation and semi-suffixation)]

Downer, L.J.
1972 *Leges Henrici primi* (Oxford)

Dowsing, A.
1979 'Some Syntactic Structures Relating to the Use of Relative and Demonstrative ðæt and *se* in Late Old English Prose' *NM* 80: 289-303

Dragland, S.L.
1977 'Monster-Man in *Beowulf*' *Neophil* 61: 606-18

Drago, A.
1969 'Le glosse anglosassoni di Lindisfarne al Vangelo di S. Marco' *Rendiconti dell'Istituto Lombardo Accademia di Scienza e Lettere* 103: 619-33

Droege, G.B.
1975 'OE *grindan* – OFris. **grinda* 'to grind': an English-Frisian Isogloss Within Germanic' *Us Wurk* 24: 12-18

Drosdowski, G.
1950 *Studien zur Bedeutungsgeschichte angelsaechsischer Zeitbegriffswörter* (Berlin diss.)

DuBois, A.E.
1934-5 '*Beowulf*, 1107 and 2577: Hoards, Swords, and Shields' *EStn* 69: 321-8
1935 '*Beowulf* 489-490' *MLN* 50: 89-90
1954 '*Gifstol*' *MLN* 69: 546-9
1955a '*Hafelan hydan, Beowulf* ll. 446, 1372' *MLN* 70: 3-5

1955b *'Stod on stapole' MLQ* 16: 291-8

Dubs, K.E.
1975 *'Hæleð:* Heroism in the *Dream of the Rood' Neophil* 59: 614-15
1976 *'Niobedd:* Bed of Death and Rebirth' *AN&Q* 14: 145-6

Duckert, A.R.
1972 *'Erce* and Other Possibly Keltic Elements in the Old English Charm for Unfruitful Land' *Names* 20: 83-90

Düwel, K.
1970 'Germanische Opfer und Opferriten im Spiegel altgermanischer Kultworte' in H. Jankuhn, ed., *Vorgeschichtliche Heiligtümer und Opferplätze in Mittel- und Nordeuropa,* Abhandlungen der Akademie der Wissenschaften in Göttingen, phil.-hist. Klasse, III. Folge, Nr. 74 (Göttingen): 219-39

Dumville, D.N.
1979 'The *ætheling:* A Study in Anglo-Saxon Constitutional History' *ASE* 8: 1-33

Dunning and Bliss
1969 See under Reference Works 2

Dunstan, A.C.
1925 *'Beowulf,* ll. 223-4' *MLR* 20: 317-18

Dusenschön, F.
1907 *Die Präposition* æfter, æt, *und* be *in der altenglischen Poesie* (Kiel diss.)

E

Earl, J.W.
1979a 'Beowulf's Rowing-Match' *Neophil* 63: 285-90
1979b 'The Necessity of Evil in *Beowulf*' *SAB* 44: 81-98

Earle, J.
*1880 *English Plant Names from the Tenth to the Fifteenth Century* (Oxford)

Eastwood, J.
1861 '*Fulluht:* The Anglo-Saxon Baptism' *N&Q* ser. 2, 12: 524

Ebbinghaus, E.A.
1976 'Old English *agu* "pica"' *GL* 16: 187-90
1977 'The Etymology of OE *mælsceafa*' *GL* 17: 92-3

Eckhardt, E.
1903 'Die angelsächsischen Deminutivbildungen' *EStn* 32: 325-66

Egan, R.B.
1977 'Gothic *hroþeigs*' *Orbis* 26: 120-23

Egorova, T.A.
−1954 'K istorii prefiksatsii kak sposoba slovoobrazovaniia v angliiskom
iazyke' Leningrad, Ped. Institut im. Gertsena, *Uchenye zapiski* 93: 79-98
[On the history of prefixes as the means of word-building in English]
1955 'K voprosu ob otnoshenii slovoobrazovaniia k grammatike (Sochetaniia
glagol'nykh osnov s prostranstvennymi ot nikh pristavkami v drevneangliiskom iazyke)' Leningrad, Ped. Institut im. Gertsena, *Uchenye zapiski*
111: 132-4 [On the problem of the relationship of word-formation to
grammar (the combination of the verb bases with spatial prefixes in OE)]

Ehrensperger, E.C.
1931 'Dream Words in Old and Middle English' *PMLA* 46: 80-89

Ehrhart, M.J.
1975 'Tempter as Teacher: Some Observations on the Vocabulary of the Old
English *Genesis B*' *Neophil* 59: 435-46

Ehrismann, G.
1890 'Ags. *twégen, bégen* und einige germanische Verwandtschaftsbegriffe'
Germania 35: 168-9
1895 'Etymologien II' *BGdSL* 20: 46-65
1897 'An. *gabba*, ags. *gabbian*' *BGdSL* 22: 564-6

Einarsson, S.

1934 'Old English *beot* and Old Icelandic *heitstrenging*' *PMLA* 49: 975-93

1937 'Old and Middle English Notes' *JEGP* 36: 183-7

1938 'Two Scandinavisms in the *Peterborough Chronicle*' *JEGP* 37: 18-20

1949 '*Beowulf* 249: *wlite* = Icelandic *litr*' *MLN* 64: 347

1952 'Old English *ent:* Icelandic *enta*' *MLN* 67: 554-5

1960 '*Kyning-wuldor* and *mann-skratti*' *MLN* 75: 193-4

Einenkel, E.

1899-1901 'Das Indefinitum' *Anglia* 21 (1899): 1-20, 289-99, 509-20 / 22
(1899): 489-98 / 23 (1901): 109-22 / 24 (1901): 343-80

1903-4 'Das englische Indefinitum' *Anglia* 26 (1903): 461-572 / 27 (1904):
1-202

1905-12 'Zum "englischen Indefinitum"' *Anglia* 28 (1905): 127-39, 493-
503 / 29 (1906): 542-4 / 30 (1907): 135-6 / 31 (1908): 545-8 / 33
(1910): 530-31 / 34 (1911): 270-71 / 35 (1912): 424-5, 539-40 / 36
(1912): 139-40

1912 'Der Ursprung der Fügung *a good one*' *Anglia* 36: 539-44

1914 'Nochmals zur Fügung *a good one*' *Anglia* 38: 193-212

1916 'Bemerkungen zum vorstehenden' *Anglia* 39: 275-6

Ekwall, E.

1909 'Engl. *shoal* "shallow"' *Beibl* 20: 209-12

1912 *On the Origin and History of the unchanged Plural in English*, Lunds
Universitets Årsskrift. N.F. Afd. 1, Bd. 8, Nr. 3 (Lund and Leipzig)

1918 'A Few Notes on English Etymology and Word-History' *Beibl* 29:
195-201

1920 'Zu zwei keltischen Lehnwörtern im Altenglischen' *EStn* 54: 102-10

1936 'The Etymology of the Word *tinker*' *ES* 18: 63-7

1943 'Old English *ambyrne wind*' in *Mélanges de philologie offerts à M.
Johan Mélander* (Uppsala): 275-84

1943-4 'Old English *forræpe*' *SN* 16: 33-8

1957 'A Hundred-Name' *RES* n.s. 8: 408-9

Eliason, N.E.

1935 '*Wulfhlið* (*Beowulf*, l. 1358)' *JEGP* 34: 20-23

1952 'The "Improvised Lay" in *Beowulf*' *PQ* 31: 171-9

1952-3 '*Beowulf* Notes' *Anglia* 71: 438-55

1963 'The *þyle* and *scop* in *Beowulf*' *Speculum* 38: 267-84

1965 'The Thryth-Offa Digression in *Beowulf*' in *Magoun Festschrift:*
124-38

1978 'Beowulf, Wiglaf, and the Wægmundings' *ASE* 7: 95-105

1979 'Beowulf's Inglorious Youth' *SP* 76: 101-8
1980 'The Burning of Heorot' *Speculum* 55: 75-83

Ellegård, A.
1953 *The Auxiliary* do: *The Establishment and Regulation of its Use in English,* Gothenburg Studies in English 2 (Stockholm)

Eller, A.L.
1978 *Semantic Ambiguity as a Structural Element in Beowulf* (State University of New York, Binghamton diss.; *DAI* 39: 2924A)

Ellert, E.E.
1946 *The Etymology and Semantic Development of Words of Family Relationship in the Germanic Languages* (North Carolina, Chapel Hill diss.)

Elliott, C.O.
1956 *Studies in Some Words in the Anglo-Saxon Gloss to the Lindisfarne Gospels* (Birmingham M.A. thesis; ASLIB *Index* 7: 147)

Elliott, C.O. and Ross, A.S.C.
*1972 'Aldrediana XXIV: The Linguistic Peculiarities of the Gloss to St. John's Gospel' *EPS* 13: 49-72

Elliott, R.W.V.
1953a 'Cynewulf's Runes in *Christ II* and *Elene*' *ES* 34: 49-57
1953b 'Cynewulf's Runes in *Juliana* and *Fates of the Apostles*' *ES* 34: 193-204
1955 'The Runes in the *Husband's Message*' *JEGP* 54: 1-8
1962 'Byrhtnoth and Hildebrand: A Study in Heroic Technique' *CL* 14: 53-70; repr. in *Brodeur Festschrift* (1963): 53-70

Elmeyer von Vestenbrugg, R.
—1958 *Studien zum Darstellungsbereich und Wortschatz des Beowulf-Epos* (Graz diss.)

Emerson, O.F.
1892 'On a Passage in the *Peterborough Chronicle*' *MLN* 7: 254-5
1899 'The Legend of Joseph's Bones in Old and Middle English' *MLN* 14: 166-7
1916 'Miscellaneous Notes' *MLR* 11: 458-62
1917 '*Trẹson* in the *Chronicle* Again' *MLR* 12: 490-92

1919 'Notes on Old English' *MLR* 14: 205-9
1923 'Notes on Old English' *Archiv* 145: 254-8; *MLN* 38: 266-72
1926a 'The Crux in the *Peterborough Chronicle*' *MLN* 41: 170-72
1926b 'Originality in Old English Poetry' *RES* o.s. 2: 18-31

Engblom, V.
1938 *On the Origin and Early Development of the Auxiliary* do, LSE 6
 (Lund)

Enkvist, N.E.
1957 *The Seasons of the Year: Chapters on a Motif from Beowulf to the
 Shepherd's Calendar,* Societas scientiarum Fennicae, Commentationes
 humanarum litterarum 22, 4 (Helsinki)
1972 'Old English Adverbial *þā* — An Action Marker?' *NM* 73: 90-96

Erades, P.A.
1967 'A Romance Congener of OE *symbel*' *ES* 48: 25-7

Erdmann, A.
1871 *Essay on the History and Modern Use of the Verbal Forms in* -ing *in
 the English Language,* Part I: *Old Anglo-Saxon Period* (Stockholm)
1891 'Bidrag till *īni*-stammarnes historia i fornnordiskan' *ANF* 7: 75-85

Erhardt-Siebold, E. von
1947 'Old English *Riddle* No. 57: OE **cā* "jackdaw"' *PMLA* 42: 1-8
1950 'Old English *Riddle* 23 "bow", OE *boga*' *MLN* 65: 93-6

Erickson, J.
1973 '*An* and *na þæt an* in Late Old English Prose: Some Theoretical
 Questions of Derivation' *ArL* n.s. 4: 75-88
1975 'The *Deor* Genitives' *ArL* n.s. 6: 77-84
1977 'Subordinator Topicalization in Old English' *ArL* n.s. 8: 99-111

Ericson, E.E.
1930-31 'Old English *swa* in Worn-Down Correlative Clauses' *EStn* 65: 343-50
1931 'The Use of Old English *swa* as a Pseudo-Pronoun' *JEGP* 30: 6-20, 473
1932 *The Use of* swa *in Old English,* Hesperia, Ergänzungsreihe 12
 (Göttingen and Baltimore)

Erlemann, E.
1902 *Das landschaftliche Auge der angelsächsischen Dichter* (Berlin diss.)

Ettmüller, L.
1872 'Beiträge zur Kritik der Eddalieder' *Germania* 17: 1-18

Evans, D.R.
1963 'The Sequence of Events in *Beowulf,* ll. 207-16' *MÆ* 32: 214-16

Evans, R.
1979 'Worcester Glosses in an Old English Homily' *N&Q* 224: 393-5

f

Faiss, K.
1967 Gnade *bei Cynewulf und seiner Schule: Semasiologisch-onomasiologische Studien zu einem semantischen Feld,* SEP N.F. 12 (Tübingen)
1969 'Old English Verbs in *-sian:* Bemerkungen zur Lars-G. Hallanders Studie' *Language and Style* 2: 233-43
1970 '*Gnade* und seine Kontexte in der altenglischen *Genesis:* Ein Beitrag zum Problem der altenglischen Dichtersprache' *Linguistics* 56: 5-30
1978 *Verdunkelte Compounds im Englischen: Ein Beitrag zu Theorie und Praxis der Wortbildung,* Tübinger Beiträge zur Linguistik 104 (Tübingen)

Falk, H.
1912 'Altnordisches Seewesen' *Wörter und Sachen* o.s. 4: 1-122
*1914 *Altnordische Waffenkunde,* Videnskapsselskapets Skrifter 2, hist-fil. Kl. 6 (Oslo)

Fanagan, J.M.
1976 '*Wulf and Eadwacer:* A Solution to the Critics' Riddle' *Neophil* 60: 130-37

Farina, D.P.
1967 '*Wædum geweorðod* in the *Dream of the Rood*' *N&Q* 212: 4-6

Farr, J.M.
1905 *Intensives and Reflexives in Anglo-Saxon and Early Middle-English* (Baltimore)

Farrell, R.T.
1966 'Eight Notes on Old English *Exodus*' *NM* 67: 364-75
1968 'The Structure of Old English *Daniel*' *NM* 69: 533-59
1972 *Beowulf, Swedes, and Geats* (London; also in *SBVS* 18, 3: 226-86)
1974 See under Reference Works 2

Faull, M.L.
1975 'The Semantic Development of Old English *wealh*' *Leeds Studies* n.s. 8: 20-44

Fay, E.W.
1918 'Etymological Notes' *JEGP* 17: 423-5

Fehr, B.
1909 *Die Sprache des Handels in Altengland: Wirtschafts- und kultur-*

geschichtliche Beiträge zur englischen Wortforschung (St. Gallen diss.)
1910 'Zur Etymologie von ae. *massere' Anglia* 33: 133-6, 403-4
1923 'Zur Etymologie von ne. *doe' Beibl* 34: 59-60

Feldman, T.P.
1975 'Terminology for *kingship* and *god* in *Beowulf' Literary Onomastic Studies* 2: 100-15

Fell, C.E.
1975 'Old English *beor' Leeds Studies* n.s. 8: 76-95

Ferguson, P.F.
1978-9 *'Exodus* 107b-111a' *ELN* 16: 1-4

Ferrel, C.C.
1893 *Teutonic Antiquities in the Anglo-Saxon* Genesis (Leipzig diss.; Halle)

Fiedler, H.G.
1942 'The Oldest Study of Germanic Proper Names' *MLR* 37: 185-92

Fijn van Draat, P.
1902 'The Loss of the Prefix *ge-* in the Modern English Verb and Some of its Consequences' *EStn* 31: 353-84

Finberg, H.P.R.
1964 *Lucerna: Studies of Some Problems in the Early History of England* (London and New York)
1972 'Anglo-Saxon England to 1042' in H.P.R. Finberg, ed., *The Agrarian History of England and Wales* vol. I (Cambridge): 385-525

Finkenstaedt, T.
1963 You *und* thou: *Studien zur Anrede im Englischen (mit einem Exkurs über die Anrede im Deutschen)* Q&F 134 (Berlin)

Finnegan, R.E.
1981 'God's *handmægen* versus the Devil's *cræft* in *Genesis B' ESA* 7: 1-14

Fischer, Albert
1908 *Der syntaktische Gebrauch der Partikeln* of *und* from *in Ælfric's Heiligenleben und in den Blickling-Homilien* (Leipzig)

Fischer, Andreas
1981 *Engagement, Wedding, and Marriage in Old English* (Basel diss.)

Fischer, O.
1979 'A Comparative Study of Philosophical Terms in the Alfredian and Chaucerian Boethius' *Neophil* 63: 622-39

Fischer, W.
1944 'Zur Etymologie von ae. *docga*, ne. *dog*, und einigen anderen Tiernamen' *Anglia* 68: 321-38

Flasdieck, H.M.
1923 'Zu ae. *ongean* u. ä.' *Beibl* 34: 271-2
1929 'Anglosaxonica' *Beibl* 40: 342-5
1933 'Ae. *ēow*' *Anglia* 57: 208-15
1935 'Untersuchungen über die germanischen schwachen Verben III. Klasse (unter besonderer Berücksichtigung des Altenglischen)' *Anglia* 59: 1-192
1936 'Die reduplizierenden Verben des Germanischen (unter besonderer Berücksichtigung des Altenglischen)' *Anglia* 60: 241-365
1936-7 'Das altgermanische Verbum Substantivum unter besonderer Berücksichtigung des Altenglischen' *EStn* 71: 321-49
1937a 'Das Verbum *wollen* im Altgermanischen (unter besonderer Berücksichtigung des Altenglischen)' *Anglia* 61: 1-42
1937b 'Ae. *dōn* und *gān*' *Anglia* 61: 43-64
1937-8 'Nachschrift' *EStn* 72: 158-60
1950 'OE *nefne:* A Revaluation' *Anglia* 69: 135-71
1951a 'Nochmals ae. *nefne*' *Anglia* 70: 46
1951b 'Studien zur Laut- und Wortgeschichte' *Anglia* 70: 225-84
1952 *Zinn und Zink: Studien zur abendländischen Wortgeschichte,* Buchreihe der Anglia 2 (Tübingen)

Fleischhacker, R. von
1891 'On the Old English Nouns of More than One Gender' *TPS* (1888-90): 235-54

Fleming, J.
1962 'A Note on the Word *nephew*' *N&Q* 207: 167

Förster, M.
1902 'Das lateinisch-altenglische Fragment der Apokryphe von Jamnes und Mambres' *Archiv* 108: 15-28
1908 'Beiträge zur altenglischen Wortkunde aus ungedruckten volkskund-

lichen Texten' *EStn* 39: 321-55

1913 *Der Vercelli-Codex* CXVII *nebst Abdruck einiger altenglischer Homilien der Handschrift* (Halle); VIII. 'Lexikalisches': 148-79

1914 'Altenglisch *ȳre* der Singular zu *ōran* "Ör"' *Archiv* 132: 397-9

1921 'Keltisches Wortgut im Englischen: Eine sprachliche Untersuchung' in M. Förster and K. Wildhagen, eds., *Texte und Forschungen zur englischen Kulturgeschichte: Festgabe für Felix Liebermann* (Halle): 119-242

1922 'Englisch-Keltisches' *EStn* 56: 204-39

1923a 'Herrn Otto Schlutter zur Antwort' *Anglia* 47: 185-8

1923b 'Das *Whitlead-teauer*-Rezept' *Beibl* 34: 115-6

1932 'Ae. *bam handum twam awritan*' *Archiv* 162: 230

1935-6 'Altenglisch *stōr*, ein altirisches Lehnwort' *EStn* 70: 49-54

1937 'Ae. *hrider, hriddern*, und *hriddel* im Lichte altbritischer Entlehnungen' *Anglia* 61: 341-50

1937-8 'König Eadgars Tod († 975)' *EStn* 72: 10-13

1941a *Der Flussname* Themse *und seine Sippe: Studien zur Anglisierung keltischer Eigennamen zur Lautkronologie des Altbritischen,* Sitzungsberichte der Bayerischen Akademie der Wissenschaften, phil.-hist. Abt., Jahrgang 1941, Bd. 1 (Munich)

1941b 'Die spätae. deiktische Pronominalform *þæge* und ne. *they*' *Beibl* 52: 274-80

1942a 'Zu den ae. Texten aus MS. Arundel 155' *Anglia* 66: 52-5

1942b 'Die Bedeutung von ae. *gebisceopian* und seiner Sippe' *Anglia* 66: 255-62

1942c 'Nochmals ae. *þæge*' *Beibl* 53: 86-7

1942d 'Zu ae. *beard* und *bearm*' *Beibl* 53: 141-2

1942e 'Die liturgische Bedeutung von ae. *traht*' *Beibl* 53: 180-84

Fogelman, R.H.

1965 *Semantic Systems in Anglo-Saxon Poetry* (Virginia, Charlottesville diss.; *DA* 26: 7304)

Fogg, W.F.

1928 'OE *mægeþ* in *Hali Meidenhad*' *MLN* 43: 527-9

Foley, J.M.

1976 '*Riddle* I of the Exeter Book: The Apocalyptical Storm' *NM* 77: 347-57

Forsberg, R.

1961 'Old English *scipsteall*' *SN* 33: 128-32

1979 'An Edition of the Anglo-Saxon Charter Boundaries of Berkshire' *SN* 51: 139-51

Fortescue-Aland, J.

1714 'The Preface' in Sir John Fortescue, *The Difference Between an Absolute and Limited Monarchy as it More Particularly Regards the English Constitution* (London): iii-lxxxii

Foster, R.

1975 'The Use of *þa* in Old and Middle English Narratives' *NM* 76: 404-14

Foster, T.G.

1892 *Judith: Studies in Metre, Language and Style with a View to Determining the Date of the Old English Fragment and the Home of its Author*, Q&F 71 (Strassburg): 1-103

Fourquet, J.

1941-2 'Anglo-saxon *éode, dyde,* et la théorie du prétérit faible' *SN* 14: 420-26

Fowkes, R.A.

1943 'Two Germanic Etymologies' *JEGP* 42: 269-70
1945 'Germanic Etymologies' *JEGP* 44: 208-9

Fowler, D.C.

1954 'An Unusual Meaning of *win* in Chaucer's *Troilus and Criseyde*' *MLN* 69: 313-15

Fowler, P.J.

1981 'Farming in the Anglo-Saxon Landscape: An Archaeologist's Review' *ASE* 9: 263-80

Fowler, R.

1967 'A Theme in the *Wanderer*' *MÆ* 36: 1-14

Frank, R.

1972 'Some Uses of Paronomasia in Old English Scriptural Verse' *Speculum* 47: 207-26

Frankis, P.J.

1959 'Beowulf and the One That Got Away' *NM* 60: 173-5
1973 'The Thematic Significance of *enta geweorc* and Related Imagery in the *Wanderer*' *ASE* 2: 253-69

Franson, J.K.
1976 'An Anglo-Saxon Etymology for Milton's *Haemony' AN&Q* 14: 18-19

Franz, W.
−1921 'Grammatisches' *Zeitschrift für französischen und englischen Unterricht* 20: 120-23

Frary, L.G.
1929 *Studies in the Syntax of the Old English Passive with Special Reference to the use of* wesan *and* weorðan, Language Dissertations 5 (Baltimore)

Fraser, T.K.H.
1975 'The Preverbs *for-* and *fore-* in Old English' in A. Joly and T. Fraser, eds., *Studies in English Grammar* (Paris): 19-28
1980 'Les Rôles du préverbe en vieil-anglais' in D. Buschinger, ed., *Actes du Colloque des 29 et 30 Avril 1977: Linguistique et philologie (applications aux textes médiévaux)*, Université de Picardie Centre d'études médiévales (Paris): 79-94

French, W.H.
1952 '*The Wanderer* 98: *wyrmlīcum fāh' MLN* 67: 526-9

Frey, C.
1977 'Lyric in Epic: Hrothgar's Depiction of the Haunted Mere (*Beowulf* 1357b-76a)' *ES* 58: 296-303

Frey, E.
1967 *Die Verben des Transportfelds bei Chaucer und König Alfred dem Grossen: Untersuchung über das nebeneinander sprachlicher Begriffe im semantischen Feld* (Zurich)

Fricke, R
1886 *Das altenglische Zahlwort: Eine grammatische Untersuchung* (Göttingen diss.)

Frings, T. and Unwerth, W. von
1910 'Miscellen zur ags. Grammatik' *BGdSL* 36: 559-62

Fritzsche, A.
1879 'Das angelsächsische Gedicht *Andreas* und Cynewulf' *Anglia* 2: 441-96

Fröhlich, J.

1951 *Der* indefinite Agens *im Altenglischen, unter besonderer Berücksichtigung des Wortes* man, SAA 25 (Zurich diss.; Bern)

Fry, D.K.

1981-2 'Launching Ships in *Beowulf* 210-216 and *Brunanburh* 32b-36' *MP* 79: 61-6

Fry, D.P.

1860-63 'On the Last Syllable in the Words *knowledge, revelach,* and *wedlock*' *TPS* (1860-61): 75-89 / (1862-3): 33-47

Fujiwara, Y.

– 1978a 'Ko eigo settoji no bunseki' *Kumamoto Daigaku KyōikuGakubu Kiyō* 27, 9: 185-96 [Analysis of prefixes in OE]
– 1978b 'Ko eigo ni okeru fukugō dōshi' *Ōtsuka Review* 14, 8: 63-7 [Compound verbs in OE]

Fulk, R.D.

1978 'Old English *icge* and *incge*' *ES* 59: 255-6

Fulton, E.

1901 'The Anglo-Saxon *Daniel* 320-325' *MLN* 16: 61-2

Funke, O.

1914 *Die gelehrten lateinischen Lehn- und Fremdwörter in der altenglischen Literatur von der Mitte des X. Jahrhunderts bis um das Jahr 1066* (Halle)
1958 'Altenglische Wortgeographie (Eine bibliographische Überschau)' in K. Brunner, H. Koziol, and S. Korninger, eds., *Anglistische Studien: Festschrift zum 70. Geburtstag von Prof. Dr. Fr. Wild,* WBEP 66 (Vienna): 39-51; repr. in SAA 56 (1965): 5-15

Furuhjelm, Å.

1931 'A Note on a Passage in *Beowulf*' *NM* 32: 107-9
1933 'Beowulfiana' *Anglia* 57: 317-20

G

G., C.W.
1850 'Aelfric's *Colloquy*' *N&Q* ser. 1, 1: 248-9

Gaaf, W. van der
1904 'Some Remarks on *þencan* and its ME and Mod. E. Representatives' *EStn* 34: 52-62
1931 '*Beon* and *habban* Connected with an Inflected Infinitive' *ES* 13: 176-88
1932 'To Laugh to Scorn' *ES* 14: 20-21
1934 'The Connection between Verbs of Rest (*lie, sit,* and *stand*) and Another Verb, Viewed Historically' *ES* 16: 81-99

Gamillscheg, E.
1968 'Zur Geschichte der lateinischen Lehnwörter im Westgermanischen' in H.E. Brekle and L. Lipka, eds., *Wortbildung, Syntax, und Morphologie: Festschrift zum 60. Geburtstag von Hans Marchand,* Janua linguarum, series maior 36 (The Hague and Paris): 82-92

Gardner, J.
1975 'Guilt and the World's Complexity: The Murder of Ongentheow and the Slaying of the Dragon' in *McGalliard Festschrift*: 14-22

Gardner, T.J.
1966 'Old English *gārsecg*' *Archiv* 202: 431-6
1968 *Semantic Patterns in Old English Substantival Compounds* (Heidelberg diss.; Hamburg)
1969 '*þreaniedla* and *þreamedla:* Notes on Two Old English Abstracta in *-la(n)*' *NM* 70: 255-61
1972 'The Application of the Term "kenning"' *Neophil* 56: 464-8

Garrett, R.M.
1909 *Precious Stones in Old English Literature,* Münchener Beiträge zur romanischen und englischen Philologie 47 (Leipzig)

Gatty, A.
1851 'A Saxon Bell-House' *N&Q* ser. 1, 4: 102

Geisness, T.
−1902 *Comparative Study of Words denoting Joy and Grief in the Gothic, Old English, and Old Saxon, with Reference to Corresponding Words and Expressions in Greek and Latin* (Minnesota diss.)

Geldner, J.

1906 *Untersuchung einiger altenglischer Krankheitsnamen* (Würzburg diss.; Braunschweig)

Gericke, B.

1934 *Die Flexion des Personalpronomens der 3. Person im spätags.*, Palaestra 193 (Leipzig)

Gerould, G.H.

1910 'Studies in the *Christ*' *EStn* 41: 1-19
1916 'Cynewulf's *Christ* 678-679' *MLN* 31: 403-4

Gerritsen, J.

1954 '*þurh þreata geþræcu*' *ES* 35: 259-62
1962 'A Ghost-Word: *crucet-hus*' *ES* 42: 300-1

Gerstein, M.R.

1975 'Germanic *warg:* The Outlaw as Werwulf' in G.J. Larson, ed., *Myth in Indo-European Antiquity* (Berkeley): 131-56

Giacalone-Ramat, A.

1976 'A proposito dei composti germanici con *ga-*' in A.M. Davies and W. Meid, eds., *Studies in Greek, Italic, and Indo-European Linguistics offered to Leonard R. Palmer* (Innsbruck): 65-76

Gibson, M.J.

1935 'Survival of Old English *eax, æx*' *AS* 10: 155-6

Gibson, W.S.

1853 '*Drengage*' *N&Q* ser. 1, 7: 137-8

Gill, W.W.

1945 '*Chat* as a dialect Word' *N&Q* 189: 172

Gillam, D.M.E.

1961 'The Use of the Term *æglæca* in *Beowulf* at lines 893 and 2592' *SGG* 3: 145-69
1962 'The Connotations of OE *fæge:* With a Note on Beowulf and Byrhtnoth' *SGG* 4: 165-201
1964 'A Method for Determining the Connotations of OE Poetic Words' *SGG* 6: 85-101

Gingher, R.S.
1975 'The Unferth Perplex' *Thoth* 14: 19-28

Girvan, R.
1935 *Beowulf and the Seventh Century: Language and Content* (London; repr. University Paperbacks 350, 1971)

Glogauer, E.
1922 *Die Bedeutungsübergänge der Konjunktionen in der angelsächsischen Dichtersprache,* Neue anglistische Arbeiten 6 (Leipzig)

Gneuss, H.
1955 *Lehnbildungen und Lehnbedeutungen im Altenglischen* (Berlin)
1968 *Hymnar und Hymnen im englischen Mittelalter: Studien zur Überlieferung, Glossierung, und Übersetzung lateinischer Hymnen in England, mit einer Textausgabe der lateinisch-altenglischen Expositio hymnorum,* Buchreihe der Anglia 12 (Tübingen): 167-93
1972 'The Origin of Standard Old English and Æthelwold's School at Winchester' *ASE* 1: 63-83
1976a *Die Battle of Maldon als historisches und literarisches Zeugnis,* Bayerische Akademie der Wissenschaften, phil.-hist. Klasse, Sitzungsberichte, Jahrgang 1976, Heft 5 (Munich)
1976b '*The Battle of Maldon* 89: Byrhtnoð's *ofermod* Once Again' *SP* 73: 117-37

Gober, W.G.
1972 '*Andreas,* lines 360-362' *NM* 73: 672-4

Godden, M.R.
1980 'Ælfric's Changing Vocabulary' *ES* 61: 206-23

Götz, D.
1971 *Studien zu den verdunkelten Komposita im Englischen,* Erlanger Beiträge zur Sprach- und Kunstwissenschaft 40 (Nürnberg)

Goetz, H.-G.
1964 *Geschichte des Wortes* rūn (rune) *und seiner Ableitungen im Englischen* (Göttingen)

Golden, J.
1976 'A Typological Approach to the *gifstol* of *Beowulf* 168' *NM* 77: 190-204

Goldsmith, M.E.

1954 *'The Seafarer* and the Birds' *RES* n.s. 5: 225-35

1962 'The Christian Perspective in *Beowulf' CL* 14: 71-90; repr. in *Brodeur Festschrift* (1963): 71-90

1967 'Corroding Treasure: A Note on the Old English *Rhyming Poem,* lines 45-50' *N&Q* 212: 169-71

1970 *The Mode and Meaning of Beowulf* (London)

1975 'The Enigma of the *Husband's Message'* in *McGalliard Festschrift:* 242-63

Gorbachevich, V.A.

−1956 *Iz istorii razvitiia leksicheskoi gruppy glagolov znania i proizvodnych ot nich imen sushchestvitel'nych v angliiskom iazyke,* Pedagogicheskii institut inostrannych iazykov (Leningrad) [On the historical development of the lexical group of verbs of knowledge and their derived substantives in English]

Gordon, E.V.

1935 *'Wealhþeow* and Related Names' *MÆ* 4: 169-75

Gordon, I.L.

1954 'Traditional Themes in the *Wanderer* and the *Seafarer' RES* n.s. 5: 1-13

Gorelova, N.E.

−1967 'Smyslovoe razvitie glagolov *shine* i *to light* v drevne- i sredneangliiskie periody' Moscow, Ped. Institut, *Uchenye zapiski* 293: 35-43 [The semantic development of the verbs *shine* and *to light* in the Old and Middle English periods]

Gorrell, J.H.

1895 'Indirect Discourse in Anglo-Saxon' *PMLA* 10: 342-485

Gottlieb, E.

1931 *A Systematic Tabulation of Indo-European Animal Names with Special Reference to their Etymology and Semasiology,* Language Dissertations 8 (New York)

Gottlieb, S.A.

1965 'The Metaphors of *Wanderer,* lines 53a-55a' *NM* 66: 145-8

Gottweiss, R.

1905 'Die Syntax der Präpositionen *æt, be, ymb* in den Ælfric-Homilien und

andern Homilien-Sammlungen unter Hinweis auf romanischen Sprach-
gebrauch' *Anglia* 28: 305-93

Gottzmann, C.L.
1977 '*Sippe*' *Sprachwissenschaft* 2: 217-58

Gough, J.V.
1973 'Old English *cuman* and *niman*' *ES* 54: 521-5

Gracheva, N.A.
—1974 'O metodike ogranicheniia leksiko-semanticheskoi gruppy glagolov,
vyrazhaiushchikh ponatie *drozhat* v drevneangliiskom iazyke' Leningrad,
Universitet, *Voprosy filologii* 4: 55-63 [On the methodology of the
restricting of a lexical-semantic group of verbs expressing the concept
shiver in OE]

Gradon, P.
1947-8 'A Contribution to Old English Lexicography' *SN* 20: 199-202

Graf, L.
1909 *Landwirtschaftliches im altenglischen Wortschatze: Nebst einer Untersuchung über die festländische Heimat der germanischen Besiedler Brit-
anniens* (Breslau diss.)

Gramm, W.
1938 *Die Körperpflege der Angelsachsen: Eine kulturgeschichtlich-
etymologische Untersuchung*, AF 86 (Heidelberg)

Grandinger, M.M.
1933 *Die Bedeutung des Adjektivs* good *in der religiösen Literatur der
Angelsachsen* (Munich diss.; Landshut)

Gray, L.H.
1945 '*Man* in Anglo-Saxon and Old High German Bible-Texts' *Word* 1: 19-32

Green, A.
1917 'An Episode in Ongenþeow's Fall' *MLR* 12: 340-43

Green, B.K.
1976 'The Twilight Kingdom: Structure and Meaning in the *Wanderer*'
Neophil 60: 442-51

1977 *'Spes viva:* Structure and Meaning in the *Seafarer'* in B.S. Lee, ed.,
   An English Miscellany Presented to W.S. Mackie (Cape Town): 28-45

Green, D.H.
1965 *The Carolingian Lord: Semantic Studies on Four Old High German
   Words:* balder, frô, truhtin, hêrro (Cambridge)
1968 'Old English *dryht* − A New Suggestion' *MLR* 63: 392-406

Greenfield, S.B.
1952 'Of Locks and Keys − Line 19a of the OE *Christ'* *MLN* 67: 238-40
1953a 'The Theme of Spiritual Exile in *Christ I' PQ* 32: 321-8
1953b *'The Wife's Lament* Reconsidered' *PMLA* 68: 907-12
1954 'Attitudes and Values in the *Seafarer' SP* 51: 15-20
1955 'The Formulaic Expression of the Theme of Exile in Anglo-Saxon
   Poetry' *Speculum* 30:200-6
1966 *'Beowulf* 207b-228: Narrative and Descriptive Art' *N&Q* 211: 86-90
1969 *'Min, sylf,* and "Dramatic Voices in the *Wanderer* and the *Seafarer"'*
   JEGP 68: 212-20
1972 *The Interpretation of Old English Poems* (London and Boston)
1974 *'Gifstol* and Goldhoard in *Beowulf'* in *Pope Festschrift:* 107-17
1977-8 'Old English Words and Patristic Exegesis − *hwyrftum scriþað:*
   A Caveat' *MP* 75: 44-8
1979a 'Esthetics and Meaning and the Translation of Old English Poetry'
   in D.G. Calder, ed., *Old English Poetry: Essays on Style* (Berkeley, Los
   Angeles, and London): 91-110
1979b 'The Extremities of the Beowulfian Body Politic' in M.H. King and
   W.M. Stevens, eds., *Saints, Scholars and Heroes: Studies in Medieval
   Culture in Honour of Charles W. Jones* (Collegeville, Minn.): 1-14
1980 'Old English *Riddle* 39 Clear and Visible' *Anglia* 98: 95-100

Greenfield, S.B. and Evert, R.
1975 *'Maxims II:* Gnome and Poem' in *McGalliard Festschrift:* 337-54

Gretsch, M.
1973 *Die Regula Sancti Benedicti in England und ihre altenglische Übersetzung,* Texte und Untersuchungen zur englischen Philologie 2 (Munich)
1974 'Æthelwold's Translation of the *Regula Sancti Benedicti* and its Latin
   Exemplar' *ASE* 3: 125-51

Greule, A.
1980 'Neues zur Etymologie von nhd. *Pfad' ZvS* 94: 208-17

Grienberger, T. von
1904a 'Zu *Beowulf*' *Anglia* 27: 331-2
1904b 'Zu den Inschriften des Clermonter Runenkästchens' *Anglia* 27: 436-49
1910 'Bemerkungen zum *Beowulf*' *BGdSL* 36: 77-101
1922 '*Widsið*' *Anglia* 46: 347-82

Grierson, P.
1954 'Carolingian Europe and the Arabs: The Myth of the Mancus' *Revue belge de philologie et d'histoire* 32: 1059-74
1961 'La fonction sociale de la monnaie en Angleterre aux VIIe-VIIIe siècles' in *Moneta e scambi nell'alto medioevo,* Settimane di Studio del Centro Italiano di Studi sull'Alto Medioevo 8 (Spoleto): 341-85
1972 *English Linear Measures: An Essay in Origins* (Reading)

Griffith, D.D.
1955 '*Stod on stapole:* Addendum' *MLQ* 16: 298-9

Grimm, J.
1841 '*Garsecg*' *ZfdA* 1: 578
1852 '*Sagara*' *ZvS* 1: 206-10

Grimm, P.
1912 *Beiträge zum Pluralgebrauch in der altenglischen Poesie* (Halle-Wittenberg diss.; Halle)

Grinda, K.R.
1975 *Arbeit und Mühe: Untersuchungen zur Bedeutungsgeschichte altenglischer Wörter* (Munich)
1979 'Die Hide und verwandte Landmasse im Altenglischen' in H. Beck, D. Denecke, and H. Jankuhn, eds., *Untersuchungen zur eisenzeitlichen und frühmittelalterlichen Flur in Mitteleuropa und ihrer Nutzung: Bericht über die Kolloquien der Kommission für die Altertumskunde Mittel- und Nordeuropas in den Jahren 1975 und 1976,* Teil 1, Abhandlungen der Akademie der Wissenschaften in Göttingen, phil.-hist. Klasse, III. Folge, Nr. 115 (Göttingen): 92-133

Grønbech, V.
1931 *The Culture of the Teutons,* trans. W. Worster (London and Copenhagen) [English trans. of *Vor folkeæt i oldtiden I-IV* (Copenhagen 1909-12)]

Grosz, O.J.H.
1969-70 'The Island of Exiles: A Note on *Andreas* 15' *ELN* 7: 421-2
1970 'Man's Imitation of the Ascension: The Unity of *Christ II*' *Neophil* 54: 398-408

Grube, F.W.
1934 'Cereal Foods of the Anglo-Saxons' *PQ* 13: 140-58
1935 'Meat Foods of the Anglo-Saxons' *JEGP* 34: 511-29
1963a 'Old English Food and Food Names' *Northwest Missouri State College Studies* 27: Feb., 3-28
1963b 'Old English Vegetable Terms' *Northwest Missouri State College Studies* 27: May, 3-30

Gruber, L.C.
1974 'Motion, Perception, and *oþþæt* in *Beowulf*' in L.C. Gruber and D. Loganbill, eds., *In Geardagum: Essays on Old English Language and Literature* (Denver): 31-7
1979 '*Hwaer cwom andgiet:* Translating the *Maxims*' in L.C. Gruber and D. Loganbill, eds., *In Geardagum 3: Essays on Old English Language and Literature* (Denver): 55-65

Grubl, E.D.
1948 *Studien zu den angelsächsischen Elegien* (Marburg)

Grüner, R.
1972 *Die Verwendung der unbestimmten substantivischen Zeitbegriffswörter in der altenglischen Dichtersprache* (Zurich diss.)

Grundy, G.B.
1922 'On the Meanings of Certain Terms in the Anglo-Saxon Charters' *E&S* o.s. 8: 37-69
1943 'The Development of the Meanings of Certain Anglo-Saxon Terms' *Archaeological Journal* 99: 67-98

Günther, V. and Wartburg, W. von
1960 'Das angelsächsische Element im französischen Wortschatz' in W. Iser and H. Schabram, eds., *Britannica: Festschrift für Hermann M. Flasdieck* (Heidelberg): 113-28

Guest, E.
1854a 'On English Pronouns Indeterminate' *PPS* 1 (1842-4): 151-60
1854b 'On a Curious *tmesis,* which is Sometimes met with, in Anglo-Saxon

and Early English Syntax' *PPS* 5 (1850-52): 97-101

1854c 'On Certain Foreign Terms, Adopted by our Ancestors, prior to their
Settlement in the British Islands' *PPS* 5 (1850-52): 169-74, 185-9

Guinet, L.
1978 'Otlinga Saxonia: Etude philologique' *Annales de Normandie* 28: 3-8

Gummere, F.B.
1883 'On the English Dative-Nominative of the Personal Pronoun' *AJP* 4:
283-90
[1889] 'On the Symbolic Use of the Colors Black and White in Germanic
Tradition' *Haverford College Studies* 1: 112-62

Gur'eva, Iu. F.
— 1964 'Parnye narechiia v angliiskom iazyke drevnego i srednego periodov'
Moscow, Ped. Institut, *Uchenye zapiski* 210: 178-87 [Paired (similar stem)
adverbs in the Old and Middle English periods]

Gusmani, R.
1972 'Anglosassone *myltestre* "meretrix"' *StG* (Roma) 10: 157-67

Gutch, U.
— 1979 *Altenglisch* cnawan, cunnan, witan-*Neuenglisch* know: *Eine bedeutungsgeschichtliche Untersuchung* (Berlin diss.)

Gutenbrunner, S.
1936 'Der Malvenname ags. *geormenlēaf*' *ZfM* 12: 40-42

ħ

Haessler, L.

1935a *Old High German* biteilen *and* biskerien, Language Dissertations 19 (Philadelphia)

1935b 'Old English *bebeodan* and *forbeodan*' *Language* 11: 211-15

Hagenlocher, A.

1975 *Schicksal im Heliand: Verwendung und Bedeutung der nominalen Bezeichnungen,* Niederdeutsche Studien 21 (Cologne and Vienna)

Hahn, E.A.

1961 '*Wæs Hrunting nama*' *Language* 37: 476-83

Hall, J.R.

1975 '*Geongordom* and *hyldo* in *Genesis B:* Serving the Lord for the Lord's Favor' *PLL* 11: 302-7

1976 '*Friðgedal: Genesis A* 1142' *N&Q* 221: 207-8

1977a '*Genesis A,* 1698b' *Expl* 35: 16-17

1977b 'Perspective and Wordplay in the Old English *Rune Poem*' *Neophil* 61: 453-60

1980-81 'Old English *Exodus* 344b-351a: The Leader and the Light' *ELN* 18: 163-6

Hallander, L.-G.

1966 *Old English Verbs in* -sian: *A Semantic and Derivational Study,* Stockholm Studies in English 15 (Stockholm)

1970 'Contributions to Old English Lexicography I: *hwamm-hwemm*' *ES* 51: 497-507

1973 'Old English *dryht* and its Cognates' *SN* 45: 20-31

Halsey, J.J.

1893 '*Anelipeman*' *MLN* 8: 127

Halvorson, N.O.

1932 *Doctrinal Terms in Aelfric's Homilies,* University of Iowa Humanistic Series 5 (Iowa City)

Hamp, E.P.

1972 '*Doom* and *do*' *Lingua Posnaniensis* 16: 87-90

1975 'Western Indo-European Notes' *IF* 79 (1974): 156-7

1976 'Etymologies: OE *feower,* OHG *niun*' *Michigan Germanic Studies* 2: 1-2

1977 'Old English *leod-*' *ES* 58: 97-100

Handley, R.R.
- 1973 *A Study of the Twelfth-Century Manuscript, British Museum Cotton Vespasian D. XIV, based on Editions of Selected non-Ælfrician Pieces* (Oxford diss.; ASLIB *Index* 24: 239)

Hanning, R.W.
1973 'Sharing, Dividing, Depriving — The Verbal Ironies of Grendel's Last Visit to Heorot' *TSLL* 15: 203-13

Hanscom, E.D.
1906 'The Feeling for Nature in Old English Poetry' *JEGP* 5: 439-63

Hansen, A.
1913 *Angelsächsische Schmucksachen und ihre Bezeichnungen: Eine kultur-geschichtlich-etymologische Untersuchung* (Kiel diss.)

Harbert, B.
1974 'King Alfred's *æstel*' *ASE* 3: 103-10

Harder, H.
1932 'Zur Deutung von ags. *kiismeel*' *Archiv* 161: 87-8
1935 'Ein ags. Sternbildname' *Archiv* 168: 235-7
1939 'Zur Herkunft von ahd. *thuris*, ags. *þyrs*, aisl. *purs*' *Archiv* 175: 90

Hardy, A.
1969 'The Christian Hero Beowulf and Unferð *þyle*' *Neophil* 53: 55-69
1979 'Historical Perspective and the *Beowulf* Poet' *Neophil* 63: 430-49

Harmer, F.E.
1950 '*Chipping* and *market*: A Lexicographical Investigation' in *Chadwick Memorial Volume*: 335-60
1952 *Anglo-Saxon Writs* (Manchester): 73-82

Harris, J.
1976 '*Stemnettan: Battle of Maldon*, line 122a' *PQ* 55: 113-17
1977 'A Note on *eorðscræf/eorðsele* and Current Interpretations of the *Wife's Lament*' *ES* 58: 204-8

Harrison, T.P.
1892 *The Separable Prefixes in Anglo-Saxon* (Johns Hopkins diss.; repr. College Park 1970)

Harstrick, A.

1890 *Untersuchung über die Praepositionen bei Alfred dem Grossen* (Kiel)

Hart, J.M.

1886-7 'Anglo-Saxonica' *MLN* 1 (1886): 88-9/ 2 (1887): 141-3

1892 'The Anglo-Saxon *gīen, gīena*' *MLN* 7: 61-2

1893 '*Scūrheard*' *MLN* 8: 61

1899 'Schlutter's Old English Etymologies' *MLN* 14: 11-16

1899-1903 'Allotria' *MLN* 14 (1899): 158-9/ 17 (1902): 231-2/ 18 (1903): 117-18

1907 'OE *werg, werig* "accursed"; *wergan* "to curse"' *MLN* 22: 220-22

1912 '*Beowulf* 168-9' *MLN* 27: 198

Hartmann, K.A.M.

1882 'Ist Koenig Aelfred der Verfasser der alliterierenden Uebertragung der *Metra* des Boetius?' *Anglia* 5: 411-50

Hasegawa, H.

—1976 '*Beowulf* ni okeru *wyrd* ni tsuite' *Nihon Daigaku Nōjū Igakubu Ippan Kyōyō Kenkyū Kiyō* 12,3: 50-58 [On *wyrd* in *Beowulf*]

Hatto, A.T.

1957 'Snake-Swords and Boar-Helms in *Beowulf*' *ES* 38: 145-60, 257-9

Hauer, S.R.

1977-8 'Structure and Unity in the Old English Charm *Wið Færstice*' *ELN* 15: 250-57

Haugen, E.

1976 *The Scandinavian Languages: An Introduction to their History* (London)

Haupt, P.

1906 'Some Germanic Etymologies' *AJP* 27: 154-65

Hayashi, H.

1976 '*Gafolgelda* and *gebur* in Ine 6,3' *Hōseishi-kenkyū* 26: 4-8 [English], 45-85 [Japanese]

Heiss, J.

1900 'A.S. *dennode*' *MLN* 15: 242-3

Helbig, L.
1960 *Altenglische Schlüsselbegriffe in den Augustinus- und Boethius-Bearbeitungen Alfreds des Grossen* (Frankfurt diss.)

Helder, W.
1977 'Beowulf and the Plundered Hoard' *NM* 78: 317-25

Heller, L.G.
1973 'Late Indo-European Water Deity as Spearman: Greek *triton* and Old English *gārsecg*' *Names* 21: 75-7

Helm, K.
1950 'Der angelsächsische Flursegen' *Hessische Blätter für Volkskunde* 41: 34-44

Helten, W. van
1909 'As. *under bac* bzw. *undar baka*, ags. *under bæc*' *ZdW* 11: 239-40

Heltveit, T.
1967 *Studies in English Demonstrative Pronouns: A Contribution to the History of English Morphology* (Oslo)

Hemken, E.
1906 *Das Aussterben alter Substantiva im Verlaufe der englischen Sprachgeschichte* (Kiel diss.)

Hempl, G.
1889 'The Etymology of OE *ǣbre, ǣfre*, E *ever*' *MLN* 4: 209
1891a 'Old English *efenehð(u)*' *Academy* 39: 612 / 40: 1
1891b 'The Etymology of "yet", OE *giet*' *Academy* 40: 564
1892 'The Anglo-Saxon *gīen(a), gīet(a)*' *MLN* 7: 123-6
1893 'Is *book* from the Latin?' *Anglia* 15: 220-22
1894a 'The Etymology of *thill, fill*' *MLN* 9: 72-3
1894b 'The Etymology of *nymðe, nemne*, etc.' *MLN* 9: 157-8
1897 'G *skalks*, NHG *schalk*, etc., G *kalkjo*, ON *skækja*, OHG *karl*, NHG *kerl, kegel*, etc.' *JGP* 1: 342-7
1899 'The Semasiology of *epistamai, verstehen, understand, unterstehen, gestehen, unternehmen, undertake*, etc.' *MLN* 14: 233-4
1901a 'Etymologies' *AJP* 22: 426-31
1901b 'OE *rǣsn, ren, ærn, hræn, hærn*' *Anglia* 24: 386-9
1902 'Old English *hǣrfest*' *JGP* 4: 47-9

Hendrickson, J.R.
*1948 Old English Prepositional Compounds in Relationship to their Latin Originals, Language Monographs 43 (Pennsylvania diss.; Philadelphia)

Henel, H.
1931 '*Stānboga* im *Beowulf*' *Anglia* 55: 273-81
1934 'Planetenglaube in Ælfrics Zeit' *Anglia* 58: 292-317
1942 'Notes on Byrhtferth's *Manual*' *JEGP* 41: 427-43

Henelius, E.
1963 *Orden för* lukt *i forn- och medelengelska (till c. 1400): Ett 'semantiskt fält'* (Åbo diss.)

Henning, R.
1893 'Ags. *birel*' *ZfdA* 37: 317-19

Henry, P.L.
1961 '*Beowulf* Cruces' *ZvS* 77: 140-59
1966 *The Early English and Celtic Lyric* (London and New York)

Herben, S.J.
1937 'A Note on the Helm in *Beowulf*' *MLN* 52: 34-6
1939 '*The Ruin*' *MLN* 54: 37-9

Herbermann, C.-P.
1974 *Etymologie und Wortgeschichte: Die indogermanische Sippe des Verbums* strotzen, Marburger Beiträge zur Germanistik 45 (Marburg)

Hermann, J.P.
1974-5 'The Green Rod of Moses in the OE *Exodus*' *ELN* 12: 241-3
1975 'The Theme of Spiritual Warfare in the Old English *Elene*' *PLL* 11: 115-25
1976-7a 'The Selection of Warriors in the Old English *Exodus,* lines 233-240a' *ELN* 14: 1-5
1976-7b '*Solomon and Saturn (II),* 339a: *niehtes wunde*' *ELN* 14: 161-4
1977-8 '*The Dream of the Rood,* 19a: *earmra ærgewinn*' *ELN* 15: 241-4

Heusler, A.
1923 *Die altgermanische Dichtung* (Berlin-Neubabelsberg)

Hieatt, C.B.
1974 '*The Fates of the Apostles:* Imagery, Structure, and Meaning' *PLL* 10:

115-25
1976 'The Harrowing of Mermedonia: Typological Patterns in the Old
English *Andreas' NM* 77: 49-62

Hietsch, O.
*1950 *A Contribution to the Study of Nominal Compounds and Compound
Elements in the Vocabulary of Old English Poetry* (Durham diss.; ASLIB
Index 1: 353)

Hill, B.
1955 'Notes on Five Difficult Glosses to the *Lindisfarne Gospels' MLR* 50:
487-8
1957 'Four Anglo-Saxon Compounds' *RES* n.s. 8: 162-6

Hill, T.D.
1966 'Two Notes on Patristic Allusion in *Andreas' Anglia* 84: 156-62
1968 'Punishment According to the Joints of the Body in the Old English
Soul and Body II' N&Q 213: 409-10
1970 'Notes on the OE *Maxims I* and *II' N&Q* 215: 445-57
1970-71 '*Byrht word* and *hælendes heafod:* Cristological Allusion in the Old
English *Christ and Satan' ELN* 8: 6-9
1971a '*Hwyrftum scriþað: Beowulf*, line 163' *MS* 33: 379-81
1971b 'Further Notes on the Eschatology of the Old English *Christ III'*
NM 72: 691-8
1972 'The Old World, the Levelling of the Earth, and the Burning of the Sea:
Three Eschatological Images in the Old English *Christ III' N&Q* 217: 323-4
1974 'The *fyrst ferhðbana:* Old English *Exodus* 399' *N&Q* 219: 204-5
1975 'The Fall of Angels and Man in the Old English *Genesis B'* in
McGalliard Festschrift: 279-90
1976 'Hebrews, Israelites, and Wicked Jews: An Onomastic Crux in *Andreas*
161-7' *Traditio* 32: 358-61
1979 'The Return of the Broken Butterfly: *Beowulf*, line 163, Again' *Mediaevalia* 5: 271-81
1980 'The *virga* of Moses and the Old English *Exodus'* in J.D. Niles, ed.,
Old English Literature in Context (Cambridge and Totowa): 57-65, 165-7
1981 'The Age of Man and the World in the Old English *Guthlac A' JEGP*
80: 13-21

Hilliard, R.
1972 *A Reexamination of the Separable Verb in Selected Anglo-Saxon Prose
Works* (Memorial U. of Newfoundland diss.; *DAI* 34: 7192A)

Hinderling, R.

1967 *Studien zu den starken Verbalabstrakta des Germanischen,* Q&F 24
[148] (Berlin)

Hittle, E.

1901 *Zur Geschichte der altenglischen Präpositionen* mid *und* wið *mit
Berücksichtigung ihrer beiderseitigen Beziehungen,* AF 2 (Heidelberg;
repr. Amsterdam 1973)

Hoffman, R.L.

1965 'Guðrinc astah: Beowulf 1118b' *JEGP* 64: 660-67

Hoffmann, K.

1968 'Ved. *santya-* und ahd. *samfti,* ags. *sêfte' MSzS* 23: 29-38

Hofmann, D.

1955 *Nordisch-englische Lehnbeziehungen der Wikingerzeit,* Bibliotheca
Arnamagnæana 14 (Copenhagen)
1957 'Untersuchungen zu den altenglischen Gedichten *Genesis* und *Exodus'
Anglia* 75: 1-34
1961 *Die K-Diminutiva im Nordfriesischen und in verwandten Sprachen,*
Niederdeutsche Studien 7 (Cologne)
1972-3 'Fries. *tiuche,* deutsch *zeche,* griech. *dikē* und Verwandte' *Us Wurk*
21-2: 55-75

Hofstetter, W.

1979 'Der Erstbeleg von ae. *pryte/pryde' Anglia* 97: 172-5

Hohenstein, C.

1912 *Das altengl. Präfix* wið(er)- *im Verlauf der engl. Sprachgeschichte mit
Berücksichtigung der andern germ. Dialekte* (Kiel diss.)

Hollander, L.M.

1917 'Beowulf 33' *MLN* 32: 246-7

Hollister, C.W.

1962 *Anglo-Saxon Military Institutions on the Eve of the Norman Conquest*
(Oxford)

Hollmann, E.

−1937 *Untersuchungen über Aspekt und Aktionsart unter besonderer Berücksichtigung des Altenglischen* (Jena diss.; Würzburg)

Hollowell, I.M.
1976 'Unferð the þyle in Beowulf' SP 73: 239-65
1978 'Scop and woðbora in OE Poetry' JEGP 77: 317-29
1980 'Was Widsið a scop?' Neophil 64: 583-91

Holmes, U.T., Jr.
1938 'Old French mangon, Anglo-Saxon mancus, Late Latin mancussus, mancosus, mancessus, etc.' PMLA 53: 34-7

Hols, E.J.
1970 Grammatical Roles of Three Sets of Prepositions in Beowulf and King Horn (Iowa diss.; DAI 31: 4748A)

Holthausen, F.
1888a 'Miscellen' BGdSL 13: 367-72
1888b 'Nachtrag' BGdSL 13: 590
1889 'Zu Anglia XII, 530, 2' Anglia 12: 606
1899 'Zu Sweet's Oldest English Texts' Anglia 21: 231-44
1902 'Zur altsächsischen und jüngeren altenglischen Genesis' Beibl 13: 266
1903 'Wǽgbora' Beibl 14: 49
1903-55 'Etymologien' Beibl 14 (1903): 336 / 15 (1904): 350-51; BGdSL 45 (1921): 297-300; IF 14 (1903): 339-42 / 17 (1904-5): 293-6 / 20 (1906-7): 316-32 / 25 (1909): 147-54 / 30 (1912): 47-9 / 35 (1915): 132-3 / 60 (1952): 277-81 / 62 (1955): 151-7; ZvS 47 (1916): 307-12 / 50 (1920): 141-3
1904a 'Englische Etymologien' Archiv 113: 36-48
1904b 'Anglosaxonica' Beibl 15: 70-73, 349-50
1905 'Zur Quellenkunde und Textkritik der altengl. Exodus' Archiv 115: 162-3
1908-32 'Worterklärungen' Archiv 121 (1908): 291-5; GRM 18 (1930): 150-52 / 20 (1932): 65-8; Wörter und Sachen 2 (1910): 211-13
1910 'Erwiderung' Beibl 21: 319-20
1913 'Altenglische Etymologien' IF 32: 340-41
1913-30 'Wortdeutungen' BGdSL 48 (1924): 458-71; GRM 16 (1928): 164-5 / 17 (1929): 471-3; IF 32 (1913): 333-9 / 39 (1921): 62-74 / 48 (1930): 254-67
* 1915-19 'Vom Aussterben der Wörter' GRM 7: 184-96
1917-24 'Beiträge zur englischen Wortkunde' Beibl 28 (1917): 272-4 / 29 (1918): 250-56 / 32 (1921): 17-23, 61-8 / 34 (1923): 273-80, 342-52 / 35 (1924): 237-56
1918 'Etymologisches' ZvS 48: 237-9
1923 'Zu altenglischen Dichtungen' Beibl 34: 89-91

1928a 'Etymologica' *GRM* 16: 238-9
1928b 'Zur germanischen Wortkunde' *GRM* 16: 239-40
1931 *'Onsæl meoto' Beibl* 42: 249-50
1934 'Altenglisches' *Beibl* 45: 19
1939-44 'Zur altenglischen Wortkunde' *Beibl* 50 (1939): 190-91 / 53 (1942): 272-4 / 54-5 (1943-4): 82-5
*1941-2 'Zum altenglischen Wortschatz' *Beibl* 52 (1941): 40-41 / 53 (1942): 35-7
1943-4a 'Zur englischen Wortkunde' *Beibl* 54-5: 132-4
1943-4b 'Zu engl. *on* und *shrift' Beibl* 54-5: 176
1951 'Beiträge zur englischen Etymologie' *Anglia* 70: 1-21
1954-6 'Wortkundliches' *ZvS* 71 (1954): 49-62 / 72 (1955): 198-208 / 73 (1956): 95-103

Holzknecht, K.J.
1923 *Literary Patronage in the Middle Ages* (Philadelphia)

Hooper, N.
1978 'Anglo-Saxon Warfare on the Eve of the Conquest: A Brief Survey' in R.A. Brown, ed., *Proceedings of the Battle Conference on Anglo-Norman Studies* I (Ipswich and Totowa): 84-93

Hoops, J.
1897 'Etymologie von *helm* "steuerruder"' *BGdSL* 22: 435-6
1903 'Alte *k*-Stämme unter den germanischen Baumnamen' *IF* 14: 478-85
1905 *Waldbäume und Kulturpflanzen im germanischen Altertum* (Strassburg)
1908 'Zur Etymologie von ne. *lady' EStn* 39: 467
1912 *'Felge* und *falge:* Eine glossographische Untersuchung zur Altertumskunde' *BGdSL* 37: 313-24
1920 'Das Verhüllen des Haupts bei Toten, ein angelsächsisch-nordischer Brauch' *EStn* 54: 19-23
1924 'Angelsächsisch *blæd' NM* 25: 109-17
1925 *'Werder, Rasen,* und *Wiese:* Eine Untersuchung zur germanischen Wortgeschichte' in W. Dibelius, H. Hecht, and W. Keller, eds., *Anglica: Untersuchungen zur englischen Philologie: Alois Brandl zum siebzigsten Geburtstage überreicht,* Palaestra 147 (Leipzig): 67-79
1929 'Altenglisch *geap, horngeap, sægeap' EStn* 64: 201-11
1930-1 'Altenglisch *ealuscerwen, meoduscerwen' EStn* 65: 177-80
1931-2 'Altenglisch *ealuscerwen* und kein Ende' *EStn* 66: 3-5
1932 *Kommentar zum Beowulf* (Heidelberg; repr. Darmstadt 1965)
1933 'Nochmals ae. *orc' Anglia* 57: 110-11
1950 *'Right* and *left* in the Germanic Languages' *EG* 5: 81-96

Hoops, R.
1935-6 'Ae. *nefa* (Zur Sachsenchronik a. 534)' *EStn* 70: 429-31

Hopper, H.P.
— 1956 *A Study of the Function of the Verbal Prefix* ge- *in the Lindisfarne Gospel of St. Matthew* (George Washington Univ. diss.)

Horgan, A.D.
1963 '*Beowulf* lines 224-5' *EPS* 8: 24-9
1979 'The Structure of the *Seafarer*' *RES* n.s. 30: 41-9
1980 'Patterns of Variation and Interchangeability in some Old English Prefixes' *NM* 81: 127-30

Horn, W.
1920a 'Zur altenglischen Wortgeschichte' *Archiv* 140: 106
1920b 'Sprachgeschichtliche Bemerkungen' *EStn* 54: 69-79
1921a *Sprachkörper und Sprachfunktion*, Palaestra 135 (Leipzig; 2nd ed. 1923)
1921b 'Zu *IF* 39, 72: ae. *bēocere*' *IF* 39: 230
1929a 'Got. *swa* "so"' *Archiv* 155: 68
1929b 'Ae. *tō*' *Archiv* 155: 249
1935-6 'Altenglisch *hwæþere* "dennoch"' *EStn* 70: 46-8

Hotchner, C.A.
1942 'A Note on *dux vitae* and *lifes lattiow*' *PMLA* 57: 572-5

Howlett, D.R.
1974 'Form and Genre in *Beowulf*' *SN* 46: 309-25
1975 'Alfred's *æstel*' *EPS* 14: 65-74

Howren, R.
1956 'A Note on *Beowulf* 168-9' *MLN* 71: 317-18

Hubbard, F.G.
1918 '*Beowulf* 1598, 1996, 2026; Uses of the Impersonal Verb *geweorþan*' *JEGP* 17: 119-24

Hübener, G.
1936 'Beowulf's *seax*, the Saxons, and an Indian Exorcism' *RES* o.s. 12: 429-39

Hüllweck, A.
1887 *Ueber den Gebrauch des Artikels in den Werken Alfreds des Grossen* (Berlin diss.)

Huffines, M.L.
1974 'OE *āglǣce:* Magic and Moral Decline of Monsters and Men' *Semasia* 1: 71-81

Hughes, G.
1977 'Beowulf, Unferth, and Hrunting: An Interpretation' *ES* 58: 385-95

Huld, M.E.
1979 'English *witch' Michigan Germanic Studies* 5: 36-9

Hull, A.P.
1955 *A Semantic and Etymological Study of Certain Germanic Words for Naturally-Occurring Streams of Fresh Water* (Virginia diss.; *DA* 15: 1850)

Hulme, W.H.
1897 'The Anglo-Saxon *geðæf' MLN* 12: 64

Huppé, B.F.
1970 *The Web of Words: Structural Analyses of the Old English Poems Vainglory, The Wonder of Creation, The Dream of the Rood, and Judith* (Albany)

Hurnard, N.D.
1949 'The Anglo-Norman Franchises' *EHR* 64: 289-327, 433-60

Ihrig, R.M.
1916 *The Semantic Development of Words for* walk, run *in the Germanic Languages,* Linguistic Studies in Germanic 4 (Chicago)

Imelmann, R.
1912 'Zu *neorxnawang' Anglia* 35: 428
1931-2 '*Beowulf* 489 f., 600, 769' *EStn* 66: 321-45

Ingersoll, S.M.
1971 '*Scūr-heard:* A New Dimension of Interpretation' *MLN* 86: 378-80
1978 *Intensive and Restrictive Modification in Old English,* AF 124 (Heidelberg)

Irving, E.B., Jr.
1957 'Latin Prose Sources for Old English Verse' *JEGP* 56: 588-95
1959 'On the Dating of the Old English Poems *Genesis* and *Exodus' Anglia* 77: 1-11
1966 '*Ealuscerwen:* Wild Party at Heorot' *TSL* 11: 161-8
1967 'Image and Meaning in the Elegies' in Creed *Essays:* 153-66
1972 'New Notes on the Old English *Exodus' Anglia* 90: 289-324

Isaacs, N.D.
1962 'Battlefield Tour: Brunanburg' *NM* 63: 236-44; repr. in N.D. Isaacs, *Structural Principles in Old English Poetry* (Knoxville 1968): 118-26
1963 'Six *Beowulf* Cruces' *JEGP* 62: 119-28
1965 'Still Waters Run *undiop' PQ* 44: 545-9; repr. in N.D. Isaacs, *Structural Principles in Old English Poetry* (Knoxville 1968): 83-9
1967 'The Convention of Personification in *Beowulf*' in Creed *Essays:* 215-48
1968 'The Exercise of Art, Part I: *The Rhyming Poem,* Part II: *The Order of the World*' in N.D. Isaacs, *Structural Principles in Old English Poetry* (Knoxville): 56-82

Isshiki, M.
*1958 'The Kennings in Beowulf' in K. Araki et al., eds., *Studies in English Grammar and Linguistics: A Miscellany in Honour of Takanobu Otsuka* (Tokyo): 257-73

Itoh, T.
−1969 '*The Peterborough Chronicle (1070-1154)* ni okeru Auxiliaries' *Bungaku Ronsō* 38, 3: 83-112 [Auxiliaries in the *Peterborough Chronicle (1070-1154)*]

J

Jacobs, H.
1911 *Die Namen der profanen Wohn- und Wirtschaftsgebäude und Gebäudeteile im Altenglischen: Eine kulturgeschichtliche u. etymologische Untersuchung* (Kiel diss.)

Jacobs, N.
1971 'OE *wered* "drink," *werod* "sweet"' *N&Q* 216: 404-7
1974 'Middle English *cleo* "hill"' *N&Q* 219: 44-6

Jacobsen, J.
1908 *Der syntaktische Gebrauch der Präpositionen* for, geond, of, *und* ymb *in der ae. Poesie* (Kiel)

Jacobson, S.
1979 'Adverb Generation in a Historical Perspective' in M. Rydén and L.A. Björk, eds., *Studies in English Philology, Linguistics, and Literature presented to Alarik Rynell, 7 March 1978,* Acta universitatis Stockholmiensis 46 (Stockholm): 64-73

Jacoby, M.
1974 Wargus, vargr *'Verbrecher,' 'Wolf,' eine sprach- und rechtsgeschichtliche Untersuchung,* Acta universitatis Upsaliensis, Studia Germanistica Upsaliensia 12 (Uppsala)

Jaeschke, K.
1931 *Beiträge zur Frage des Wortschwundes im Englischen,* Sprache und Kultur der germanischen und romanischen Völker, Anglistische Reihe 7 (Breslau)

Jelinek, V.
1956 'Three Notes on *Beowulf*' *MLN* 71: 239-42

Jellinghaus, H.
*1898 'Angelsächsisch-neuenglische Wörter, die nicht niederdeutsch sind' *Anglia* 20: 463-6

Jenks, E.
1898 *Law and Politics in the Middle Ages, with a Synoptic Table of Sources* (London)

Jennings, L.G.
*1968 *The Old English Noun in Present English* (Pennsylvania diss.; *DA* 29: 2243A)

Jensen, E.
1978-9 'Narrative Voice in the Old English *Wulf*' *ChauR* 13: 373-83

Jensen, J.
*1913 *Die I. und II. Ablautsreihe in der ae. Wortbildung* (Kiel diss.)

Jente, R.
1921 *Die mythologischen Ausdrücke im altenglischen Wortschatz: Eine kulturgeschichtlich-etymologische Untersuchung,* AF 56 (Heidelberg)

Jespersen, O.
1925 'Prop-Word and Numeral' *Beibl* 36: 154-5
1927 'The Ending -*ster*' *MLR* 22: 129-36

Jiriczek, O.L.
1912 '*Scepen* in Caedmons Hymnus Hs. N' *IF* 30: 279-82
1929 'Zur Bedeutung von ae. *stede-heard* (*Judith* 223)' *EStn* 64: 212-18

Johannessohn, M.
1943 'Die Behandlung des neutestamentlichen *kai idou* (*et ecce*) in einigen älteren und jüngeren germanischen Bibelübersetzungen' *ZvS* 68: 1-32

Johannisson, T.
1939 *Verbal och postverbal Partikelkomposition i de germanska Spraken, mit einer Zusammenfassung in deutscher Sprache* (Lund)
1941-2 'Altenglisch *incūð* und *oncȳð(ð)*' *SN* 14: 214-20

Johansen, H.
1935 *Zur Entwicklungsgeschichte der altgermanischen Relativsatz-konstruktionen* (Copenhagen)

Johansson, K.F.
1899 'Über aisl. *eldr,* ags. *æled* "feuer" usw.' *ZfdPh* 31: 285-302

John, E.
1960 *Land Tenure in Early England: A Discussion of Some Problems* (Leicester; 2nd impr. 1964)
1966 *Orbis Britanniae and Other Studies* (Leicester)

1979 'Edward the Confessor and the Norman Succession' *EHR* 94: 241-67

Johnson, W.C., Jr.
1974 '"Deep Structure" and Old English Poetry: Notes Towards a Critical Model' in L.C. Gruber and D. Loganbill, eds., *In Geardagum: Essays on Old English Language and Literature* (Denver): 12-18
1976-7 'Pushing and Shoving in *Beowulf:* A Semantic Inquiry' *ELN* 14: 81-7

Jolliffe, J.E.A.
1935 'English Book-Right' *EHR* 50: 1-21
1937 *The Constitutional History of Medieval England* (London; 4th ed. 1961)

Joly, A.
1967 '*Ge-* préfixe lexicale en vieil anglais' *Canadian Journal of Linguistics* 12: 78-89
1972 'La négation dite "expletive" en vieil anglais et dans d'autres langues indo-européennes' *Etudes anglaises* 25: 30-44

Jones, C.
1967 'The Functional Motivation of Linguistic Change: A Study of the Development of the Grammatical Category of Gender in the Late Old English Period' *ES* 48: 97-111
1969 'A Further Note on the Use of *this* in the Gloss to the *Lindisfarne Gospels* and the *Durham Ritual*' *N&Q* 214: 122-5
1971 'Some Features of the Determiner Usage in the Old English Glosses to the *Lindisfarne Gospels* and the *Durham Ritual*' *IF* 75 (1970): 198-219

Jones, I.F.
1945 '*Chat* as a Dialect Word' *N&Q* 189: 106

Jones, O.F.
1966 'The Etymology of Gothic *undarleijin*' *MLN* 81: 498-500

Jordan, R.
1903 *Die altenglischen Säugertiernamen,* AF 12 (Heidelberg; repr. Amsterdam 1967)
1906 *Eigentümlichkeiten des anglischen Wortschatzes: Eine wortgeographische Untersuchung mit etymologischen Anmerkungen,* AF 17 (Heidelberg; repr. Amsterdam 1967)
1908 'Zu den reduplizierten Präterita: Northumbrisch *speoft, beoft*' *EStn* 38: 28-34

Jost, K.
1909 Beon *und* wesan: *Eine syntaktische Untersuchung,* AF 26 (Heidelberg; repr. Amsterdam 1966)
1950 *Wulfstanstudien,* SAA 23 (Bern): 155-68

Jovy, H.
1900 'Untersuchungen zur altenglischen *Genesisdichtung' BBzA* 5: 1-32

Jungner, H.
1919 'Uppsala-och Vendel-konungarnes mytiska ätte-fäder' *Fornvännen* 14: 79-102

Juzi, G.
1939 *Die Ausdrücke des Schönen in der altenglischen Dichtung: Untersuchung über ein sprachliches Feld* (Zurich diss.)

k

Kabell, A.
1971 'Mittelenglisch *bryniges' Anglia* 89: 117-18

Kärre, K.
1915 *Nomina agentis in Old English, Part I: Introduction, Nomina agentis with l-Suffix, Nomina agentis in -end, with an Excursus on the Flexion of Substantival Present Participles* (Uppsala)
1920 'Zur Etymologie und Bedeutung von altengl. *bord-* und *scild-hreoða' BGdSL* 44: 168-76

Käsmann, H.
1951 Tugend *und* Laster *im Alt- und Mittelenglischen: Eine bezeichnungs-geschichtliche Untersuchung* (Berlin, Freie U. diss.)
1959 'Anmerkungen zum *Middle English Dictionary' Anglia* 77: 65-74
*1961 *Studien zum kirchlichen Wortschatz des Mittelenglischen 1100-1350: Ein Beitrag zum Problem der Sprachmischung,* Buchreihe der Anglia 9 (Tübingen)

Kahrl, S.J.
1971-2 'Feuds in *Beowulf:* A Tragic Necessity?' *MP* 69: 189-98

Karsten, G.E.
1892 'Etymologies' *MLN* 7: 172-3

Karstien, C.
1926-7 'Ags. *nāmon-geāfon' EStn* 61: 1-8

Kartschoke, D.
1977 *'Selfsceaft' ZfdA* 106: 73-82

Kasik, J.C.
1979 'The Use of the Term *wyrd* in *Beowulf* and the Conversion of the Anglo-Saxons' *Neophil* 63: 128-35

Kaske, R.E.
1958 *'Sapientia et fortitudo* as the Controlling Theme of *Beowulf' SP* 55: 423-56; repr. in L.E. Nicholson, ed., *An Anthology of Beowulf Criticism* (Notre Dame): 269-310
1963a 'Hygelac and Hygd' in *Brodeur Festschrift:* 200-6
1963b 'Weland and the *wurmas* in *Deor' ES* 44: 190-91
1964 'The Reading *genyre* in the *Husband's Message,* line 49' *MÆ* 33: 204-6
1967a 'The *eotenas* in *Beowulf'* in Creed *Essays:* 285-310

1967b 'A Poem of the Cross in the Exeter Book: *Riddle* 60 and the
  Husband's Message' Traditio 23: 41-71
1971 *'Beowulf* and the Book of Enoch' *Speculum* 46: 421-31

Kaspers, W.
1922 'Etymologien' *ZvS* 50: 155-7

Kastovsky, D.
1968 *Old English Deverbal Substantives Derived by Means of a Zero
  Morpheme* (Tübingen diss.; Esslingen)
1971 'The Old English Suffix *-er(e)' Anglia* 89: 285-325

Kats, R.
1958 *Razvitie glagol'nogo slovoobrazovaniia s prefiksom* be *v angliiskom
  iazyke* (Leningrad Universitet diss.) [The development of word-formation
  of verbs with the prefix *be-* in English]

Kawamoto, T.
− 1969 'The Verbs of the *Parker Chronicle* from Preface to 891' *Nara Kyōiku
  Daigaku Kiyō (Jinbun Shakai)* 17, 1, 2: 25-53

Keenan, H.T.
1970 *'Exodus* 312, "The Green Street of Paradise"' *NM* 71: 455-60
1973 *'Exodus* 312a: Further Notes on the Eschatological "Green Ground"'
  NM 74: 217-19

Keightley, T.
1854 'Etymologies' *N&Q* ser. 1, 10: 398-9

Keiser, A.
1919 *The Influence of Christianity on the Vocabulary of Old English Poetry*,
  University of Illinois Studies in Language and Literature 5 (Urbana; repr.
  New York 1967)

Keller, M.
1938 *Die Frau und das Mädchen in den englischen Dialekten* (Zurich diss.)

Keller, M.L.
1906 *The Anglo-Saxon Weapon Names Treated Archaeologically and Ety-
  mologically*, AF 15 (Heidelberg; repr. Amsterdam 1967)

Kellermann, G.

1954 *Studien zu den Gottesbezeichnungen der angelsächsischen Dichtung: Ein Beitrag zum religionsgeschichtlichen Verständnis der Germanenbekehrung* (Münster diss.)

Kemble, J.M.

1850 'On a Peculiar Use of the Anglo-Saxon Patronymical Termination *-ing'* *PPS* 4 (1848-50): 1-10

Kennedy, B.H. et al.

1850 'Meaning of *gradely'* *N&Q* ser. 1, 2: 334-5, 361-2

Kent, C.W.

1887 *Teutonic Antiquities in Andreas and Elene* (Leipzig diss.; Halle)
1888 'The Anglo-Saxon *burh* and *byrig'* *MLN* 3: 176-7

Keough, T.

1976 'The Tension of Separation in *Wulf and Eadwacer'* *NM* 77: 552-60

Ker, N.R.

1932a 'Old English *scægan'* *MÆ* 1: 137-8
1932b 'Old English *hrohian'* *MÆ* 1: 208

Kern, H.

1877a 'Hrêdh en Hrêdhgotan' *Taalkundige Bijdragen* 1: 29-46
1877b 'Angelsaksische Kleinigheden' *Taalkundige Bijdragen* 1: 193-209
1877c 'Een paar bedorven plaatsen' *Taalkundige Bijdragen* 1: 210
1879 'Uit de Friesche Wetten' *Taalkundige Bijdragen* 2: 171-209
1897 *'Hengst'* *TNTL* 16: 268-71

Kern, J.H.

1905 'Zu altenglisch *mærsian'* *Anglia* 28: 394-6
1910 'Zur *Cura pastoralis'* *Anglia* 33: 270-76
1913 'Zum Vokalismus einiger Lehnwörter im Altenglischen' *Anglia* 37: 54-61
1917-18 'Altenglische Varia' *EStn* 51 (1917): 1-15 / 52 (1918): 289-98
1923a 'A Few Notes on the *Metra* of Boethius in Old English' *Neophil* 8: 295-300
1923b 'A Ghostword' *Neophil* 8: 301-3

Key, T.H.

1867 'On the German Prefix *ver-* and Allied Forms' *TPS* (1867): 93-105

Khaimovich, B.S.
—1948 *K istorii angliiskikh glagol'nykh prefiksov* (Moscow, Gos. Universitet diss.) [On the history of English verb prefixes]

Khomiakov, V.A.
1964 'A Note on the So-Called "Passive Participles with Active Meaning" in Old English' *JEGP* 63: 675-8

Kieckers, E.
1917-20 'Verschiedenes' *IF* 38: 209-19
1921 'Zu altengl. *specan* und ahd. *spechan* "sprechen"' *BGdSL* 45: 304-5

Kienle, M. von
1933 'Der Schicksalsbegriff im Altdeutschen' *Wörter und Sachen* 15: 81-111

Kiernan, K.S.
1974-5 '*Cwene:* The Old Profession of Exeter *Riddle 95*' *MP* 72: 384-9

Kiessling, N.K.
1967 *New Aspects of the Monsters in Beowulf* (Wisconsin diss.; *DA* 28: 3146A)
1967-8 'Grendel: A New Aspect' *MP* 65: 191-201

Kim, S.
—1975 'The Worcester Marks and Glosses of the Old English Manuscripts: A New Interpretation and Addenda' *English Language and Literature* (Seoul) 56: 131-41

Kintgen, E.R., Jr.
*1970 *Word Echo in Old English Poetry* (Wisconsin diss.; *DAI* 31: 2883A)
*1974 'Echoic Repetition in Old English Poetry, especially the *Dream of the Rood*' *NM* 75: 202-23
1975 'Wordplay in the *Wanderer*' *Neophil* 59: 119-27

Kirby, I.J.
1974 'Old English *ferð*' *N&Q* 219: 443

Kirkland, J.H.
1886 'A Passage in the Anglo-Saxon Poem *The Ruin*, Critically Discussed' *AJP* 7: 367-9

Kirschner, J.
1975 *Die Bezeichnungen für* Kranz *und* Krone *im Altenglischen* (Munich diss.)

Kisbye, T.
1965 'Zur pronominalen Anrede bei Ælfric: Anmerkung zu Th. Finkenstaedts *You und Thou' Archiv* 201: 432-5

Kishida, T.
− 1971 'On Some Features of Preverbs of Old English' *Gakushūin Daigaku Bungakubu Kenkyū Nenpō* 18, 3: 111-46
− 1974 'Ælfric no *First Series of Catholic Homilies* in okeru zenchishi no mondai ten' *Gakushūin Daigaku Bungakubu Kenkyū Nenpō* 21, 3: 167-93 [Problems with prepositions in the first series of Ælfric's *Catholic Homilies*]
− 1976 '*Beowulf* ni okeru zenchishi no mondai ten − zenchishi soshiki no suii o chūshin to shite' *Gakushūin Daigaku Bungakubu Kenkyū Nenpō* 23, 3: 61-98 [Problems of the prepositions in *Beowulf* centring on the changes in structure of the prepositions]

Kitson, P.
1978 'Lapidary Traditions in Anglo-Saxon England, Part I: The Background, The Old English *Lapidary' ASE* 7: 9-60

Kjellmer, G.
1973 *Middle English Words for People,* Gothenburg Studies in English 27 (Stockholm)

Klaeber, F.
1901 'An Emendation in the Old English Version of Bede IV.24' *JGP* 3: 497-500
1902 'Zur altenglischen Bedeutungslehre' *Archiv* 109: 305-13
1904 'Zu altenglischen Dichtungen' *Archiv* 113: 146-9
1904-5 'Emendations in Old English Poems' *MP* 2: 141-6
1905 'Hrothulf' *MLN* 20: 9-11
1906 '*Wanderer* 44; *Rätsel* XII. 3f.' *Beibl* 17: 300-1
1908a 'Jottings on the *Andreas' Archiv* 120: 153-6
1908b 'Zum *Beowulf' EStn* 39: 463-7
1911a 'Zur Texterklärung des *Beowulf' Beibl* 22: 372-4
1911b 'Old Saxon *karm* and *hrōm: Genesis* 254, *Heliand* 2459' *MLN* 26: 141-3
1912 'Die christlichen Elemente im *Beowulf' Anglia* 35: 111-36, 249-70,

453-82 / 36: 169-99

1912-13 'Zu ae. *ræde* "lectio"' *EStn* 46: 330

1916 'Zu ae. *hwonne ær, ðonne (ðon), ær ðe' Anglia* 40: 503-4

1919 'Concerning the Functions of Old English *geweorðan* and the Origin of German *gewähren lassen' JEGP* 18: 250-71

1921 'Zu altengl. *ændian = ær(e)ndian' Beibl* 32: 37-8

1922a 'Zum Bedeutungsinhalt gewisser altenglischer Wörter und ihrer Verwendung' *Anglia* 46: 232-8

1922b 'Die altenglische Bedaübersetzung und der Denkspruch auf Oswald' *Archiv* 144: 251-3

1926 'Zur jüngeren *Genesis' Anglia* 49: 361-75

1927 'Weitere Randglossen zu Texterklärungen' *Beibl* 38: 354-60

1929a 'Altenglische wortkundliche Randglossen' *Beibl* 40: 21-32

1929b '*Belūcan* in dem altenglischen Reisesegen' *Beibl* 40: 283-4

1931 'Eine Randbemerkung zum Schwund von altengl. *weorðan' Beibl* 42: 348-52

1931-2 'Altenglisch *ealuscerwen* und kein Ende' *EStn* 66: 1-3

1932-3 '*Beowulf* 769' *EStn* 67: 24-6

1935a 'Altenglisch *begǣð* "bekennt," "behauptet"' *Archiv* 166: 81-2

1935b 'Zu altenglischen Dichtungen' *Archiv* 167: 36-41

1938 'Bede's Story of Caedmon Again' *MLN* 53: 249-50

1938-9 '*Beowulf* 769 und *Andreas* 1526 ff.' *EStn* 73: 185-9

1940a '*Beowulf* 2041: *beah' Beibl* 51: 206-7

1940b 'Concerning Old English *winterstund' PQ* 19: 146-7

1941 'Eine Randbemerkung zur Nebenordnung und Unterordnung im Altenglischen' *Beibl* 52: 216-19

1943 'Das 9. altenglische *Rätsel' Archiv* 182: 107-8

1943-4 'Zur Texterklärung altenglischer Dichtungen' *Beibl* 54-5: 170-76

1948 'Ein paar Anmerkungen zu den altenglischen *Deor*-Versen' *Archiv* 185: 124-6

1950 'Noch einmal *Exodus* 56-58 und *Beowulf* 1408-1410' *Archiv* 187: 71-2

1955 'Some Notes on OE Poems' *Archiv* 191: 218-20

Klegraf, J.
1972 '*Beowulf* 769: *ealuscerwēn' Archiv* 208: 108-12

Klein, W.F.
1975 'Purpose and the "Poetics" of the *Wanderer* and the *Seafarer*' in *McGalliard Festschrift:* 208-23

Kleman, M.M.
1953 'Three Old English Verbs for *cleanse, purge'* *International Anthropological and Linguistic Review* 1: 179-84

Kluge, F.
1881 'Anglosaxonica' *Anglia* 4: 105-6
1883 'Sprachhistorische Miscellen' *BGdSL* 8: 506-39
1885-95 'Englische Etymologien' *EStn* 8 (1885): 479 / 9 (1886): 505-6 / 10 (1887): 180 / 11 (1888): 511-12 / 20 (1895): 333-5
*1886a *Nominale Stammbildungslehre der altgermanischen Dialecte* (Halle; 3rd ed., ed. L. Sütterlin and E. Ochs, 1926)
*1886b 'Zum altenglischen Sprachschatz: Excerpte aus der Interlinearversion von Bedas *Liber scintillarum'* *EStn* 9: 35-42
1890 'Ae. *gærdas, bocstafas, boc'* *ZfdA* 34: 210-13
1895 'NE. *Proud-Pride'* *EStn* 21: 334-5
1901 'Anglo-Saxon Etymologies' in *An English Miscellany Presented to Dr. Furnivall in Honour of his Seventy-Fifth Birthday* (Oxford): 199-200
1906-7 'Ahd. *zit* = angls. *tima'* *ZdW* 8: 145-6
1918 'Ags. *íren* = ahd. *îsan'* *BGdSL* 43: 516-17
1921 'Griechisch *despoina* = angls. *fǽmne?'* *IF* 39: 127-9
1922 'Zur Lehre von der germ. Anfangsbetonung' *Anglia* 46: 191-2

Klump, W.
1908 *Die altenglischen Handwerkernamen sachlich und sprachlich erläutert,* AF 24 (Heidelberg)

Kniezsa, V.
−1971 'Az. angloszasz kronika' *Anglo es Amerikai Filologiai Tanulmanyok* 1: 5-40

Knobloch, J.
1959 'Der Ursprung von nhd. *Ostern,* engl. *Easter'* *Sprache* 5: 27-45

Koban, C.
*1963 *Substantive Compounds in Beowulf* (Illinois diss.; *DA* 24: 4175)

Kock, E.A.
1902-23 'Interpretations and Emendations of Early English Texts' *Anglia* 25 (1902): 316-28 / 26 (1903): 364-76 / 27 (1904): 218-37 / 42 (1918): 99-124 / 43 (1919): 298-312 / 44 (1920): 97-114, 245-60 / 45 (1921): 105-31 / 46 (1922): 63-96, 173-90 / 47 (1923): 264-73
1918 *Jubilee Jaunts and Jottings: 250 Contributions to the Interpretation*

and Prosody of Old West Teutonic Alliterative Poetry, Lunds Universitets
Årsskrift, N.F., Avd. 1, Bd. 14, Nr. 26 (Lund and Leipzig)
1922 *Plain Points and Puzzles: 60 Notes on Old English Poetry,* Lunds
Universitets Årsskrift, N.F., Avd. 1, Bd. 17, Nr. 7 (Lund and Leipzig)
1929 'Old West Germanic and Old Norse' *Klaeber Festschrift:* 14-20

Köbler, G.
1973 *'Civitas* und *vicus, burg, stat, dorf,* und *wik'* in H. Jankuhn, W.
Schlesinger, and H. Steuer, eds., *Vor- und Frühformen der europäischen
Stadt im Mittelalter,* Abhandlungen der Akademie der Wissenschaften in
Göttingen, phil-hist. Klasse, III. Folge, Nr. 83 (Göttingen): 61-76

Köhler, J.J.
1906 *Die altenglischen Fischnamen,* AF 21 (Heidelberg; repr. Amsterdam
1968)

Kökeritz, H.
1941-2 'Two Interpretations' *SN* 14: 277-80; also in *MLN* 58 (1943): 191-4
1963 'The Anglo-Saxon Unicorn' in A. Brown and P. Foote, eds., *Early
English and Norse Studies Presented to A. Hugh Smith in Honour of his
60th Birthday* (London): 120-26

König, G.
1957 *Die Bezeichnungen für* Farbe, Glanz, *und* Helligkeit *im Altenglischen*
(Mainz diss.)

Koike, K.
— 1975 'Kodai Eigo kenkyū — *The Seafarer* ni arawareru tango o megutte' *Eigo
Eibungaku Ronsō* 6, 10: 13-23 [Research in OE on vocabulary that
appears in the *Seafarer*]
— 1977 'A Study of Old English: The Word *king* in the *Anglo-Saxon Chronicle'
Eigo Eibungaku Ronsō* 7, 3: 30-40
— 1978 'An *Anglo-Saxon Chronicle* ni okeru *king* ni tsuite, British Museum,
Cotton MS., Tiberius B. iv no baai' *Obirin Review* 2, 2: 5-8 [On the case
of *king* in an *Anglo-Saxon Chronicle*]

Kolb, E.
1965a 'Skandinavisches in den nordenglischen Dialekten' *Anglia* 83: 127-53
1965b *'Beowulf* 568: An Emendation' *ES* 46: 322-3

Koo, Zung-Fung Wei

1947 *Old English Living Noun-Suffixes Exclusive of Personal and Place-Names* (Radcliffe diss.)

Korhammer, M.

1976 *Die monastischen Cantica im Mittelalter und ihre altenglischen Inter-linearversionen: Studien und Textausgabe,* Texte und Untersuchungen zur englischen Philologie 6 (Munich): 175-245

1980 'Altenglische Dialekte und der *Heliand' Anglia* 98: 85-94

Korte, D.

1974 *Untersuchungen zu Inhalt, Stil, und Technik angelsächsischer Gesetze und Rechtsbücher des 6. bis 12. Jahrhunderts,* Archiv für vergleichende Kulturwissenschaft 10 (Meisenheim am Glan)

Koskenniemi, I.

1968 *Repetitive Word Pairs in Old and Early Middle English Prose: Expressions of the Type* whole and sound *and* answered and said, *and Other Parallel Constructions,* Annales universitatis Turkuensis, series B, 107 (Turku)

Kotova, Z.I.

— 1962 'Imena sushchestvitel'nye sobiratel'nye v drevneangliiskom iazyke' Leningrad, Ped. Institut im. Gertsena, *Uchenye zapiski* 226: 135-45 [Collective nouns in OE]

Koziol, H.

1937 *Handbuch der englischen Wortbildungslehre* (Heidelberg)

1941 'Zur Wortbildung im Englischen' *Anglia* 65: 51-63

1967 *Grundzüge der englischen Semantik,* WBEP 70 (Vienna)

*1972 *Häufung von Substantiven gleicher Bildungsweise im englischen Schrifttum,* SÖAW 278, 1 (Vienna)

Krackow, O.

*1903 *Die Nominalcomposita als Kunstmittel im altenglischen Epos* (Berlin diss.; Weimar)

Krämer, P.

1968 'Altenglisch *dyde* und altfriesisch *dwa*' in H. Birkhan and O. Gschwantler, eds., *Festschrift für Otto Höfler zum 65. Geburtstag* (Vienna): II, 315-26

Kranz, M.
1973 *A Semantic Analysis of the Verbs Denoting Speech in the Anglo-Saxon Poem Daniel* (Catholic U. of America diss.; *DAI* 33: 6336A)

Krapp, G.P.
1904 'Miscellaneous Notes' *MLN* 19: 232-5
1904-5 'Notes on the *Andreas*' *MP* 2: 403-10

Krieg, M.L.F.
*1975 *Semantic Fields of Color Words in Old French, Old English, and Middle English* (Michigan diss.; *DAI* 37: 1517A)

Kristensson, G.
1969 'Old English **gēol, *golu*' *SN* 41: 130-34
1971 'An Etymological Note: Old English *drȳgan* "to make dry"' *SN* 43: 257-9
1972 'A Note on Old English *slagu* "slag, dross"' *SN* 44: 274-7
1979 'A Piece of Middle English Word Geography' *ES* 60: 254-60

Kroesch, S.
1911 'The Semasiological Development of Words for *perceive*, etc., in the Older Germanic Dialects' *MP* 8: 461-510
1920 'Semantic Notes' *JEGP* 19: 86-93
1928-9 'The Semantic Development of OE *cræft*' *MP* 26: 433-43
1929 'Semantic Borrowing in Old English' in *Klaeber Festschrift:* 50-72

Krogmann, W.
1929a 'Ags. *neorxenawang*' *Anglia* 53: 337-44
1929b '*Mûdspelli*' *GRM* 17: 231-8
1930 'Got. *stafs*' *IF* 48: 268-72
1931 'Ae. *geneorð*' *Anglia* 55: 397-9
1931-2 'Ae. **scerwan*' *EStn* 66: 346
1932a 'Ae. *orcnēas*' *Anglia* 56: 40-42
1932b 'Ae. *īsig*' *Anglia* 56: 438-9
1932c '*Mûdspelli*' *Wörter und Sachen* 14: 68-85
1932-3 '*Ealuscerwen* und *meoduscerwen*' *EStn* 67: 15-23
1933a *Der Name der Germanen: Mit einer Abbildung* (Wismar)
1933b 'Ae. *orc*' *Anglia* 57: 112
1933c 'Ae. *gang*' *Anglia* 57: 216-17
1933d 'Ae. *dyde*' *Anglia* 57: 377-95
1933e '*Orc* und *orcnēas*' *Anglia* 57: 396
1933-4 'Got. *iddja* und ae. *ēode*' *EStn* 68: 155-7

1934a 'Ae. *neorx(e)nawang* "Paradies"' *Anglia* 58: 28-9

1934b 'Ae. *strosle* "Drossel"' *Anglia* 58: 448

1934-5a 'Ae. *geormanlēaf* und der Name der Germanen' *EStn* 69: 161-79

1934-5b 'Ae. *ēolet (Beowulf* 224)' *EStn* 69: 351-7

1935 'Ae. *tō-sōcnung*' *Anglia* 59: 271-2

1935-6a 'Altengl. *āntīd* und seine Sippe' *EStn* 70: 40-45

1935-6b 'Ae. *defu*' *EStn* 70: 321-2

1935-6c 'Ae. *georman-, geormen-*' *EStn* 70: 322-3

1935-6d 'Richtigstellung' *EStn* 70: 323-4

1936a 'Zwei ae. Wortdeutungen' *Anglia* 60: 33-8

1936b 'Ae. Wortdeutungen' *Anglia* 60: 369-73

1936c 'Ae. *geormanlēaf*' *ZfM* 12: 173-81

1937-9 'Altenglisches' *Anglia* 61 (1937): 351-60 / 63 (1939): 67-72, 398-9

1940-41 'Ae. *(n)eorx(e)nawang*' *EStn* 74: 1-18

1953 'Die Bodenständigkeit des *Crist III*' *ZfM* 21: 1-28

1955 '*Neorxna wang* und *Iða vǫllr*' *Archiv* 191: 31-43

Krohmer, W.

1904 *Altenglisch* in *und* on (Berlin diss.)

Kross, T.

1911 *Die Namen der Gefässe bei den Angel-Sachsen* (Kiel diss.; Erlangen)

Krüger, T.

1884 'Zum *Beowulf*' *BGdSL* 9: 571-8

Kühlwein, W.

1967 *Die Verwendung der Feindseligkeitsbezeichnungen in der altenglischen Dichtersprache*, Kieler Beiträge zur Anglistik und Amerikanistik 5 (Neumünster)

1968 *Modell einer operationellen lexikologischen Analyse: Altenglisch blut*, AF 95 (Heidelberg)

1969 'Andreascrux 1241 und Beowulfcrux 849' *BGdSL* 91: 77-81

1971 'Entropie und Redundanz in der angelsächsischen Poesie' *Linguistics* 68: 13-28

Kühn, P.T.

1889 *Die Syntax des Verbums in Ælfrics Heiligenleben* (Leipzig diss.)

Kuhn, H.

1951 'Es gibt kein *balder* "Herr"' in *Erbe der Vergangenheit, Germanistische Beiträge: Festgabe für Karl Helm zum 80. Geburtstag* (Tübingen): 37-45;

repr. in H. Kuhn, *Kleine Schriften* (Berlin 1969-78) II, 332-8

1962 'Angelsächsisch *cōp* "Kappe" und seinesgleichen' in *Festgabe für L.L. Hammerich: Aus Anlass seines siebzigsten Geburtstags* (Copenhagen): 113-24; repr. in *Kleine Schriften* I, 390-99

1972 'Das römische Kriegswesen im germanischen Wortschatz' *ZfdA* 101: 13-53; repr. in *Kleine Schriften* IV, 23-60

Kuhn, S.M.

1943 'The Sword of Healfdene' *JEGP* 42: 82-95

*1947 'Synonyms in the Old English Bede' *JEGP* 46: 168-76

1957 'Some Early Mercian Manuscripts' *RES* n.s. 8: 355-74

1969 '*Beowulf* and the Life of Beowulf: A Study in Epic Structure' in Atwood and Hill *Studies:* 243-64

1977 'Further Thoughts on *brand Healfdenes*' *JEGP* 76: 231-7

1979 'Old English *aglæca* – Middle Irish *ochlach*' in I. Rauch and G.F. Carr, eds., *Linguistic Method: Essays in Honor of Herbert Penzl,* Janua linguarum, series maior 79 (The Hague, Paris, and New York): 213-30

Kuriyagawa, F.

*1930 'Kenningar in *Beowulf*' *English Literature and Philology* (Keio University) 1: 1-8

Kylstra, H.E.

1975 'Ale and Beer in Germanic' in G. Turville-Petre and J.M. Martin, eds., *Iceland and the Mediaeval World: Studies in Honour of Ian Maxwell* (Melbourne): 7-16

l

Lally, T.D.P.
1979 'Thought and Feeling in the *Wanderer*' in L.C. Gruber and D. Logan-bill, eds., *In Geardagum 3: Essays on Old English Language and Literature* (Denver): 46-54

Lambert, C.
1940 'The Old English Medical Vocabulary' *Proceedings of the Royal Society of Medicine* 33: 137-45

Lancaster, L.
1958 'Kinship in Anglo-Saxon Society' *British Journal of Sociology* 9: 230-50, 359-77

Lane, G.S.
1931 *Words for Clothing in the Principal Indo-European Languages*, Language Dissertation 9 (Baltimore)
1933a 'Two Germanic Etymologies' *JEGP* 32: 293-5
1933b 'Germanic Etymologies' *JEGP* 32: 483-7
1933c 'The Germano-Celtic Vocabulary' *Language* 9: 244-64

Langenfelt, G.
1931 'The OE Paradise Lost' *Anglia* 55: 250-65
1936 'The OE Paradise Lost: *neorxnawang*' *Anglia* 60: 374-6

Langenhove, G.Ch. van
1923 'De etymologie van *ontberen*, ohd. *inbëran*, ags. *onberan* en *oðberan*' *Verslagen en Mededeelingen der Koninklijke Vlaamsche Academie voor Taal- en Letterkunde* (Ghent)

Larson, L.M.
1904 *The King's Household in England before the Norman Conquest*, Bulletin of the University of Wisconsin, History Series 1: 55-211

Last, W.
1925 *Das Bahuvrîhi-Compositum im Altenglischen, Mittelenglischen und Neuenglischen* (Greifswald)

Latham, R.E.
1959 'Some Minor Enigmas from Medieval Records' *EHR* 74: 664-71

Lauffer, H.

1976 *Der Lehnwortschatz der althochdeutschen und altsächsischen Pruden-tiusglossen,* Münchener germanistische Beiträge 8 (Munich)

Lawrence, W.W.

1902 '*The Wanderer* and *The Seafarer*' *JGP* 4: 460-80
1907-8 'The Banished Wife's Lament' *MP* 5: 387-405

Lefèvre, P.

*1883 'Das altenglische Gedicht vom heiligen Guthlac' *Anglia* 6: 181-240

Lehmann, H.

1885 *Brünne und Helm im angelsächsischen Beowulfliede: Ein Beitrag zur germanischen Alterthumskunde* (Leipzig)
1886 'Über die Waffen im angelsächsischen Beowulfliede' *Germania* 31: 486-97

Lehmann, W.

1906a *Das Präfix* uz- *besonders im Altenglischen, mit einem Anhang über das präfigierte westgerm.* *ō- (*ā-): Ein Beitrag zur germanischen Wort-bildungslehre,* Kieler Studien zur englischen Philologie N.F. 3 (Kiel)
1906b 'Zum ae. Wortschatz' *Beibl* 17: 296-300
1907a 'Anmerkungen zum ae. Sprachschatz' *Archiv* 119: 184-9, 433-5
1907b 'Anglosaxonica minora' *Beibl* 18: 298-301
1907c 'Zu ae. *collon-crōh,* ahd. *coller-wurz* "nymphaea"' *ZdW* 9: 23-6, 161

Lehmann, W.P.

1955 'The Finnsburg Fragment 34a: *hwearflacra hrær*' *University of Texas Bulletin: Studies in English* 34: 1-5
1959 '*Beowulf* 33: *īsig*' *MLN* 74: 577-8
1964 'On the Etymology of *black*' in W. Betz, E.S. Coleman, and K. North-cott, eds., *Taylor Starck Festschrift* (The Hague): 56-61
1967 '*Atertanum fah*' in W.W. Arndt, F.E. Coenen, P.W. Brosman, and W.P. Friederich, eds., *Studies in Historical Linguistics in Honor of George Sherman Lane,* University of North Carolina Studies in Germanic Languages and Literatures 58 (Chapel Hill): 221-32
1969a '*Skrǫggr:* An Exercise in Etymology' in C. Gellinek, ed., *Festschrift für Konstantin Reichardt* (Bern): 103-8
1969b 'On Posited Omissions in the *Beowulf*' in Atwood and Hill *Studies:* 220-29

Leisi, E.

1952-3 'Gold und Manneswert im *Beowulf' Anglia* 71: 259-73

1959 'Aufschlussreiche altenglische Wortinhalte' in H.T. Gipper, ed., *Sprache Schlüssel zur Welt: Festschrift für Leo Weisgerber* (Düsseldorf): 309-18

Leitzmann, A.

1906 'Ags. *neorxna-wong' BGdSL* 32: 60-66

Lenaghan, R.T.

1961 'A Note on OE *melcan' N&Q* 206: 6

Lendinara, P.

1973 'Un'Allusione ai Giganti: *Versi Gnomici Exoniensi* 192-200' *AION-SG* 16: 85-98

1975a *'Poculum mortis:* una nota' *AION-SG Filologia Germanica* 18: 131-41

1975b 'E se ꝑ stesse per *bana?* Una nuova interpretazione dell' *Enigma* n. 17 del Codice Exoniense' *AION-SG Filologia Germanica* 18: 161-81

1976 'Ags. *wlanc:* Alcune annotazioni' *AION-SG Filologia Germanica* 19: 53-81

1978 'Un incantesimo del *Læcebōc' AION-SG Filologia Germanica* 21: 7-15

1980 'Ags. *fahame' AION Filologia Germanica* 23: 191-6

Lenz, P.

1886 *Der syntactische Gebrauch der Partikel* ge *in den Werken Alfred des Grossen* (Heidelberg diss.; Darmstadt)

Lenze, J.

1909 *Das Praefix* bi- *in der altenglischen Nominal- und Verbalkomposition mit gelegentlicher Berücksichtigung der anderen germanischen Dialekte* (Kiel diss.)

Lerner, L.D.

1951 'Colour Words in Anglo-Saxon' *MLR* 46: 246-9

Lewis, A.S.

1924 [Untitled paragraph on *tota*] *N&Q* 147: 272

Leydecker, C.

*1910 *Angelsächsisches in althochdeutschen Glossen* (Bonn diss.)

*1911 *Über Beziehungen zwischen ahd. und ags. Glossen* (Bonn)

Liberman, A.
1978 'Germanic *sendan* "to make a sacrifice"' *JEGP* 77: 473-88

Lidén, E.
1905-6 'Altenglische Miszellen' *IF* 18: 407-16
1906 'Neue altenglische Miszellen' *IF* 19: 359-70
1908 'Beiträge zur altenglischen Wortkunde' *EStn* 38: 337-43
1934 'Zur alten tieranatomischen Terminologie' *ZvS* 61: 14-28

Liebermann, F.
1896 'Die englische Gilde im achten Jahrhundert' *Archiv* 96: 333-40
1897 'Altenglisch *homola* "Verstümmelter" *orige* "unsichtbar"' *Archiv* 98:
   127-8
1899 'Die angelsächsische Verordnung über die Dunsæte' *Archiv* 102: 267-96
1900 'Matrosenstellung aus Landgütern der Kirche London, um 1000'
   Archiv 104: 17-24
1901a *Ueber die leges Henrici primi* (Halle)
1901b 'Über die Leis Willelme' *Archiv* 106: 113-38
1902a '*Streoneshealh*' *Archiv* 108: 368
1902b 'Die Abfassungszeit von "Rectitudines singularum personarum" und
   ags. *aferian*' *Archiv* 109: 73-82
1905a 'Das angelsächsische *Rätsel* 56: "Galgen" als Waffenständer' *Archiv*
   114: 163-4
1905b 'Kentisch *hionne* "Hirnhaut"' *Archiv* 115: 177-8
1905c 'Ags. *rihthamscyld:* echtes Hoftor' *Archiv* 115: 389-91
1907a '*Outlaw* und *Danelaw*' *Archiv* 118: 130-32
1907b 'Ags. *innanburgware*' *Archiv* 118: 132
1907c 'Zu ags. *forlætan*' *Archiv* 119: 174-5
1908 'Angelsächsisch *færbena*' *Archiv* 120: 337-40
1909 'Angelsächsisch *boldgetæl* "Provinz"' *Archiv* 123: 400-1
1911 'Angelsächsisch *drinclean*' *Archiv* 127: 196
1913a *The National Assembly in the Anglo-Saxon Period* (Halle)
1913b 'Mancus als Goldmünze' *Archiv* 131: 153
1921 'Die altengl. Glosse *ling: simulabo*' *Archiv* 142: 254
1922a '"Speer" figürlich für "Blutrache"' *Archiv* 143: 248
1922b 'Altenglands Kammer und Halle' *Archiv* 143: 248
1922c 'Ags. *for neode* "durch (unter) Zwang"' *Archiv* 144: 91
1922d 'Ags. *oftorfian*' *Archiv* 144: 251
1922e 'Ags. *teon* "erfolgreich verklagen, prozessual besiegen"' *Archiv* 144:
   253
1922f '*Færbena* ags. "Bauer"' *Archiv* 144: 254
1924 'Angelsächsisch *lidwicas*' *Archiv* 147: 249-50

1925 'Das Gedicht von König Eadmund I, a. 942' *Archiv* 148: 96
1927a 'Ags. *oððe* "und"' *Archiv* 151: 79-80
1927b 'Ags. *hydesace* "Fellsack"' *Archiv* 151: 80
1927c 'Ælfreds *dulmun* aus Isidor' *Archiv* 151: 80
1927d 'Zwei Stellen übers Ordal der Angelsachsen' *Archiv* 151: 81

Liedtke, E.
*1910 *Die numerale Auffassung der Kollektiva im Verlaufe der englischen Sprachgeschichte* (Königsberg diss.)

Liggins, E.M.
1955 *The Expression of Causal Relationship in Old English Prose* (London diss.; ASLIB *Index* 5: 131)

Liljegren, S.B.
1941-2 'Some Notes on the OE Poem *The Seafarer*' *SN* 14: 145-59

Limar', L.S.
1965 *K voprosu o roli pristavok i vidovom znachenii glagolov (Na materiale drevneangliiskogo iazyka)* (Moscow, Gos. ped. Institut inostrannykh iazykov im. Morisa Toreza diss.) [On the problem of the role of prefixes and of aspectual meaning in verbs (based on OE material)]

Lindelöf, U.
1912 'Keltisches *min*, f. *os* im Altenglischen' *Anglia* 35: 540
1914 'Altnordhumbrisches *gimungo* "Hochzeit"' *Beibl* 25: 180-81

Lindeman, F.O.
1967 'Gotisch *iddja* und altenglisch *ēode*' *IF* 72 (1967-8): 275-86

Lindemann, J.W.R.
1965 'Old English Preverbal *ge-*: A Re-Examination of Some Current Doctrines' *JEGP* 64: 65-83
1970 *OE Preverbal ge-: Its Meaning* (Charlottesville)

Lindheim, B. von
1949 'OE *drēam* and its Subsequent Development' *RES* o.s. 25: 193-209
1951a 'Traces of Colloquial Speech in OE' *Anglia* 70: 22-42
1951b 'Neue Wege der Bedeutungsforschung' *Neuphilologische Zeitschrift* 3: 101-14
1958-69 'Die weiblichen Genussuffixe im Altenglischen' *Anglia* 76 (1958): 479-504 / 87 (1969): 64-5

1964a 'Problems of Old English Semantics' in G.I. Duthie, ed., *English Studies Today, 3rd series* (Edinburgh): 67-77
1964b 'Problems and Limits of Textual Emendation' in D. Riesner and H. Gneuss, eds., *Festschrift für Walter Hübner* (Berlin): 3-15
1970 'Das altenglische Deminutivsuffix *-incel*' *BGdSL* 92: 43-50
1972 'Das Suffix *-bære* im Altenglischen' *Archiv* 208: 310-20

Lindkvist, K.-G.
1978 At *versus* on, in, by: *On the Early History of Spatial* at *and Certain Primary Ideas Distinguishing* at *from* on, in, by, Stockholm Studies in English 49 (Stockholm)

Lindner, F.
1873 *Ueber das Präfix* a *im Englischen* (Rostock)

Lindow, J.
1976 *Comitatus, Individual and Honor: Studies in North Germanic Institutional Vocabulary,* University of California Publications in Linguistics 83 (Berkeley)

Lindström, P.E.
1895 'Zur Etymologie von *preost*' *EStn* 20: 147-8

Lingard, J.
1845 *The History and Antiquities of the Anglo-Saxon Church, Containing an Account of its Origin, Government, Doctrines, Worship, Revenues, and Clerical and Monastic Institutions,* rev. ed., 2 vols. (London)

Linke, G.
1937 'Zu ae. *blægettan* = "blöken, schreien"' *Archiv* 172: 64-5
1938 'Zur Präposition *betweoh* und zum Zahlwort *tuwa* im ags. Beda' *Archiv* 173: 71-2
1938-9 '*Standeð* und *stent* und dergleichen in ags. sicher fixierten Hss.' *EStn* 73: 321-30
*1939 'Grammatische und phraseologische Tautologie im ae. Beda' *Archiv* 175: 98-101

Lipp, F.R.
1969 'Contrast and Point of View in the *Battle of Brunanburh*' *PQ* 48: 166-77

Little, A.G.
1889 'Gesiths and Thegns' *EHR* 4: 723-9

Lockwood, W.B.
1965 'Das altdeutsche Glossenwort *dun(n)* und Verwandtes' *ZvS* 79: 294-300
1973 'More English Etymologies' *ZAA* 21: 414-23
1977 'Some British Bird Names' *TPS* (1975): 173-86
1979 'Some Expressions for the Setting Sun' *MÆ* 48: 102-4

Löfvenberg, M.T.
1944-5 'An Etymological Note' *SN* 17: 259-64
1956 'Old English *twicele*' *Stockholm Studies in Modern Philology* 19: 125-8

Loewe, R.
1918a 'Angelsächsisch *ece*' *ZvS* 48: 99-100
1918b 'Angelsächsisch *geréfa*' *ZvS* 48: 100-1

Logeman, H.
1889a 'Stray Gleanings' *Anglia* 12: 528-31, 606
1889b 'The Northumbrian *ebolsung*' *MLN* 4: 76-7
1909 'The *mægð* that Wulfstan Found among the Estonians' *EStn* 40: 464-5

Lorz, A.
1908 *Aktionsarten des Verbums im Beowulf* (Würzburg diss.)

Lotspeich, C.M.
1931 'Notes on the Personal Pronouns in Germanic' *JEGP* 30: 150-51
1938 'The Type OE *lōca hwā*, ME *looke who*' *JEGP* 37: 1-2
1941 'Old English Etymologies' *JEGP* 40: 1-4

Loyn, H.R.
1953 'The Term *ealdorman* in the Translations prepared at the Time of King Alfred' *EHR* 68: 513-25
1955 '*Gesiths* and *thegns* in Anglo-Saxon England from the Seventh to the Tenth Century' *EHR* 70: 529-49
1971 'Towns in Late Anglo-Saxon England: The Evidence and Some Possible Lines of Enquiry' in *Whitelock Festschrift:* 115-28
1974 'Kinship in Anglo-Saxon England' *ASE* 3: 197-209

Lucas, A.M.
1969 'The Narrator of the *Wife's Lament* Reconsidered' *NM* 70: 282-97

Lucas, P.J.
1969a '*Exodus* 480: *mod gerymde*' *N&Q* 214: 206-7
1969b 'An Interpretation of *Exodus* 46-53' *N&Q* 214: 364-6
1970 'The Cloud in the Interpretation of the Old English *Exodus*' *ES* 51: 297-311

1971 'Exodus 265: ægnian' N&Q 216: 283-4
1976a 'Old English Christian Poetry: The Cross in Exodus' in G. Bonner,
   ed., Famulus Christi: Essays in Commemoration of the Thirteenth
   Centenary of the Birth of the Venerable Bede (London): 193-209
1976b 'Daniel 276' N&Q 221: 390-91

Ludlum, C.D.
1954 A Critical Commentary on the Vocabulary of the Canterbury Psalter
   (Stanford diss.; DA 14: 979)

Lübke, H.
1890 'Über verwandtschaftliche Beziehungen einiger altenglischer Glossare'
   Archiv 85: 383-410

Lühr, R.
1976 'Die Wörter für oder in den germanischen Sprachen' MSzS 34: 77-94
1978 'Die germanischen Wörter für seit und Verwandtes' MSzS 37: 121-30
1980 'Althochdeutsch antlingen "Antworten"' ZfdA 109: 48-72

Lüngen, W.
1911 Das Praefix on(d)- in der altenglischen Verbalkomposition mit einem
   Anhang über das Praefix oð- (ūð-) (Kiel diss.)

Lüttgens, C.
1888 Über Bedeutung und Gebrauch der Hilfsverba im frühen Altenglischen:
   sculan und willan (Kiel diss.; Wismar)

Luick, K.
1906 'Zu ae. án' Anglia 29: 527-8
1911 'Zu den lateinischen Lehnwörtern im Altenglischen' Archiv 126: 35-9
1924 'Zu ae. ongēan' Beibl 35: 190-92

Lumiansky, R.M.
1947 'Old English onbyrð in Wærferð's Dialogues of Gregory' MLR 42: 358
1949 'The Contexts of OE ealuscerwen and meoduscerwen' JEGP 48: 116-26

Lund, J.J.
1935 The History of Words Pertaining to Certain Crafts in the Principal Indo-
   European Languages (Chicago diss.)

Luria, M.
1979-80 'Why Moses' Rod is Green' ELN 17: 161-3

m

M., A.G.
1930 'Mæsttwist' N&Q 158: 384

MacAdam, E.R.
1856 'Ancient Watermills' Ulster Journal of Archaeology 4: 6-15

MacArthur, W.
1951-2 'Malaria in England' British Medical Bulletin 8: 78

McClelland, C.B.
1966 'Horses in Beowulf: A Horse of a Different Color' TSL 11: 177-87

McCord, L.R.
1979 A Study of the Meanings of hliehhan and hleahtor in Old English
    Literature (Missouri diss.; DAI 41: 2101A)
1980 'Morris's Translation of hleahtras in Blickling Homily IV' N&Q 225:
    488-9

MacGillivray, H.S.
1902 The Influence of Christianity on the Vocabulary of Old English, Part
    I, SEP 8 (Halle)

McGovern, J.F.
1971 'The Meaning of gesette land in Anglo-Saxon Land Tenure' Speculum
    46: 589-96
1972 'The Hide and Related Land-Tenure Concepts in Anglo-Saxon England,
    A.D. 700-1100' Traditio 28: 101-18

McIntosh, A.
1947-8 'The Relative Pronouns þe and þat in Early Middle English' EGS 1:
    73-87

Mackie, W.S.
1925 'Notes on Old English Poetry' MLN 40: 91-3
1933 'Notes on the Text of the Exeter Book' MLR 28: 75-8
1938 'The Demons' Home in Beowulf' JEGP 37: 455-61
1939-41 'Notes upon the Text and Interpretation of Beowulf' MLR 34
    (1939): 515-24 / 36 (1941): 95-8

McKinnell, J.
1975 'On the Date of the Battle of Maldon' MÆ 44: 121-36

McLintock, D.R.
1959 'OE *wīs* and *(ge)wiss*' *ArL* 11: 18-20
1973 '*To forget* in Germanic' *TPS* (1972): 79-93

Maejima, G.
− 1932 'Kodai eishi no goi ni tsuite' *Eigo Eibungaku Ronbunshū* 2, 1: 64-9
  [On the vocabulary of OE poetry]

Mäkeläinen, O.
1979 'The Progeny of Germanic **skelƀ-*' *NM* 80: 352-7

Magoun, F.P., Jr.
1925 'Two Lexicographical Notes' *MLN* 40: 408-12
* 1929 'Recurring First Elements in Different Nominal Compounds in *Beowulf*
  and in the *Elder Edda*' in *Klaeber Festschrift:* 73-8
1930 'Word Formation' in M.H. Turk, ed., *An Anglo-Saxon Reader* rev. ed.
  (New York): 48a-m
1937 'Zu den ae. Zaubersprüchen' *Archiv* 171: 17-35
1942 'King Alfred's Naval and Beach Battle with the Danes in 896' *MLR* 37:
  409-14
1945a '*Noþ ð æs sweoster:* "Need's Sisters," an Old-English Counting-Down
  Charm' *AfNF* 60: 98-106
1945b 'The Domitian Bilingual of the *Old-English Annals:* Notes on the *F*-
  Text' *MLQ* 6: 371-80
1947 'On Some Survivals of Pagan Belief in Anglo-Saxon England' *Harvard
  Theological Review* 40: 33-46
1948a 'OE *ealle þráge*' *MLN* 63: 127-8
1948b 'Some Notes on King Alfred's Circular Letter on Educational Policy
  Addressed to His Bishops' *MS* 10: 93-107
1953 '*Inwlatide < onfunde?*' *MLN* 68: 540-41
1955 'The Theme of the Beasts of Battle in Anglo-Saxon Poetry' *NM* 56:
  81-90

Mahler, A.E.
1978 '*Lignum Domini* and the Opening Vision of the *Dream of the Rood:* A
  Viable Hypothesis?' *Speculum* 53: 441-59

Maisenhelder, K.
1935 *Die altenglische Partikel* and *(mit Berücksichtigung anderer germanischer Sprachen)* (Heidelberg diss.)

Maitland, F.W.
1896 'The Origin of the Borough' *EHR* 11: 13-19
1897 *Domesday Book and Beyond: Three Essays in the Early History of England* (Cambridge)

Makino, T.
− 1972 '*Beowulf* ni okeru zenchishi *in* to *on* ni kansuru ichi kosatsu' *Chūō Eibei Bungaku* 6, 12: 24-34 [An observation about the prepositions *in* and *on* which express the locative meaning "in" in *Beowulf*]
− 1974 'King Alfred's West Saxon Version of Gregory's *Pastoral Care* no Hatton MS ni okeru zenchishi *on* ni tsuite no ichi kosatsu' *Komazawa Daigaku Gaikokugo Gakubu Kenkyū Kiyō* 3, 3: 113-25 [An observation about the preposition *on* in the Hatton MS of King Alfred's West-Saxon version of Gregory's *Pastoral Care*]

Makovskii, M.M.
− 1957 'K istorii konstruktsii glagolov *byt* + prichastie I v nortumbriiskikh glossakh' Moscow, Ped. Institut inostrannykh iazykov, *Uchenye zapiski* 11: 191-9 [On the history of the formation of the verb *to be* plus participle I in the Northumbrian glosses]
1962 'Problema "geografii slov" v drevneangliiskikh dialektakh' *Voprosy iazykoznania* 2: 63-71 [The problem of "word geography" in OE dialects]
1963 'Variantnost' leksem v drevneangliiskikh glossakh kak priznak dialektnoi prinadlezhnosti slovaria' *Etimologiia:* 161-79 [Lexical variation in OE glosses as a sign of dialectal distribution of vocabulary]
* 1964 'Sravnitel'no-istoricheskaia dialektografia angliiskoi leksiki v predelakh germanskoi iazykovoi oblasti (Leksiko-etimologicheskoe i areal'no-lingvisticheskoe issledovanie)' *Etimologiia:* 236-54 [Comparative and historical dialectography of the Anglian vocabulary (an etymological and a real investigation of the Germanic word stock)]
1965 'Germanskie areal'nye paralleli v svete etimologii' *Etimologiia:* 248-63 [Germanic real parallels in the light of etymology]

Malmberg, L.
1970 '*The Wanderer: waþema gebind*' *NM* 71: 96-9
1973 'Poetic Originality in the *Wanderer* and the *Seafarer*' *NM* 74: 220-23
1977 'Grendel and the Devil' *NM* 78: 241-3

Malone, K.
1928 'The Kenning in *Beowulf* 2220' *JEGP* 27: 318-24
1929 'The Daughter of Healfdene' in *Klaeber Festschrift:* 135-58
1929-30 '*Ingeld*' *MP* 27: 257-76

1930a 'Old English *(ge)hȳdan* "heed"' in N. Bøgholm, A. Brusendorff, and
   C.A. Bodelsen, eds., *A Grammatical Miscellany Offered to Otto Jespersen
   on his Seventieth Birthday* (London and Copenhagen): 45-54
1930b 'Three Notes on *Beowulf*' *JEGP* 29: 233-6
1936 'The Inflexion of OE *gar* "spear"' *Beibl* 47: 219-20
1937a 'Old-English *cáre, cáser, cásere*' *Beibl* 48: 221-2
1937b 'The Tale of Geat and Mæðhild' *ES* 19: 193-9
1938a 'A Note on *Widsith* 9a' *Beibl* 49: 375-6
1938b 'Some Linguistic Studies of 1935 and 1936' *MLN* 53: 24-46
1939a 'Notes on *Beowulf:* XI' *Anglia* 63: 103-12
1939b *'Swerting'* *Germanic Review* 14: 235-57
1940 *'Freawaru'* *ELH* 7: 39-44; repr. in S. Einarsson and N.E. Eliason, eds.,
   Kemp Malone: Studies in Heroic Legend and in Current Speech (Copenhagen 1959): 197-201
1941 'Old English *beagas*' *Beibl* 52: 179-80
1942-3 'On *Deor* 14-17' *MP* 40: 1-18; repr. in *Kemp Malone: Studies in
   Heroic Legend and in Current Speech* (Copenhagen 1959): 142-57
1943 'Notes on *Gnomic Poem B* of the Exeter Book' *MÆ* 12: 65-7
1945 'On *Finnsburg* 39' *RES* o.s. 21: 126-7
1945-6 'Finn's Stronghold' *MP* 43: 83-5
1946 'Variation in *Widsith*' *JEGP* 45: 147-52
1947 'Old English *gār* "storm"' *ES* 28: 42-5
1951 'A Note on *Beowulf* 2466' *JEGP* 50: 19-21
1958 'Grendel and His Abode' in A.G. Hatcher and K.L. Selig, eds., *Studia
   philologica et litteraria in honorem L. Spitzer* (Bern): 297-308
1959 'The Tale of Ingeld' in S. Einarsson and N.E. Eliason, eds., *Kemp
   Malone: Studies in Heroic Legend and in Current Speech* (Copenhagen):
   1-62
1961 'A Note on *Beowulf* 489-90' *MLR* 56: 212
1962 'Two English *Frauenlieder*' *CL* 14: 106-17; repr. in *Brodeur Festschrift*
   (1963): 106-17
1965 'Some *Beowulf* Readings' in *Magoun Festschrift:* 120-23
1974 'Some English Etymologies' *Word* 26: 305-8

Mandel, J.
1976 *'The Seafarer'* *NM* 77: 538-51

Manganella, G.
1964 'Cristo e Satana' *AION-SG* 7: 273-82

Mansion, J.
1907 'Die Etymologie von *holen*' *BGdSL* 33: 547-70

Marckwardt, A.H.

1942 'The Verbal Suffix *-ettan* in Old English' *Language* 18: 275-81
1970 '*Much* and *many:* The Historical Development of a Modern English Distributional Pattern' in *Meritt Festschrift:* 50-54

Marcq, P.

1973 'Structure du système des prépositions spatiales dans le *Beowulf*' *EG* 28: 1-19

Markey, T.L.

1972a 'Germanic Terms for Temple and Cult' in E.S. Firchow et al., eds., *Studies for Einar Haugen Presented by Friends and Colleagues,* Janua linguarum, series maior 59 (The Hague and Paris): 365-8
1972b 'West Germanic *he/er-hiu/siu* and English *she*' *JEGP* 71: 390-405
1974 'Germanic **līþ-/laiþ* and Funerary Ritual' *Frühmittelalterliche Studien* 8: 179-94
1979 'Nfr. *kūch*, Engl. *key,* and the Unshifted Consonant Question' *ZdL* 46: 41-55

Marquardsen, H.

1852 *Ueber Haft und Bürgschaft bei den Angelsachsen: Vorstudie zu einer Geschichte des Habeas corpus Rechts* (Erlangen)

Marquardt, H.

1936 'Fürsten- und Kriegerkenning im *Beowulf*' *Anglia* 60: 390-95
1938 *Die altenglischen Kenningar: Ein Beitrag zur Stilkunde altgermanischer Dichtung,* Schriften der Königsberger gelehrten Gesellschaft, 14. Jahr, Geisteswissenschaftliche Klasse, Heft 3 (Halle)

Martin-Clarke, D.E.

1950 'Significant Objects at Sutton Hoo' in *Chadwick Memorial Volume:* 109-19

Martz, O.

1939 *Die Wiedergabe biblischer Personenbezeichnungen in der altenglischen Missionssprache: Wortstudien im Anschluss an die westsächsischen Evangelienübersetzungen und anglischen Evangelienglossen,* Beiträge zur englischen Philologie 33 (Bochum-Langendreer)

Mather, F.J., Jr.

1894 'Anglo-Saxon *nemne (nymðe)* and the "Northumbrian Theory"' *MLN* 9: 76-8

Matthes, H.C.
1961 'Hygd' in H. Viebrock and W. Erzgräber, eds., *Festschrift zum 75. Geburtstag von Theodor Spira* (Heidelberg): 14-31

Mattox, W.S.
1975 'Encirclement and Sacrifice in *Wulf and Eadwacer*' *An Med* 16: 33-40

Matzerath, J.
1912 *Die altenglischen Namen der Geldwerte, Masse, und Gewichte, sachlich und sprachlich erläutert* (Heidelberg)

Mayer, E.
1911 'Der germanische Uradel' *Zeitschrift der Savigny-Stiftung für Rechtsgeschichte, Germanistische Abteilung* 32: 41-228

Mayhew, A.L.
1886a '*Catchpoll* in an Anglo-Saxon Gloss' *Academy* 29: 61
1886b '*Curse* and *cross*' *Academy* 30: 107-8
1887 'The Word *blight*' *Academy* 31: 276
1888 'Does Old English *neowel* mean "dark"?' *Academy* 34: 291
1889 'The Etymology of the Word *God*' *Academy* 35: 397

Mayrhofer, M.
1970 'Germano-Iranica' *ZvS* 84: 224-30

Mazzuoli Porru, G.
1975 'Italiano *-ino*, germanico **-ina-*' *Archivio glottologico italiano* 60: 104-27

Mead, W.E.
1899 'Color in Old English Poetry' *PMLA* 14: 169-206

Meaney, A.L.
1979 'The *Ides* of the Cotton Gnomic Poem' *MÆ* 48: 23-39

Meid, W.
1965 'Spuren eines Parallelismus von *-to-* und *-st-* Suffix im Germanischen' *ZvS* 79: 291-3
1966 'Die Königsbezeichnung in den germanischen Sprachen' *Sprache* 12: 182-9

Meier, J.

1950 *Ahnengrab und Rechtsstein: Untersuchungen zur deutschen Volkskunde und Rechtsgeschichte,* Deutsche Akademie der Wissenschaften zu Berlin, Veröffentlichungen der Kommission für Volkskunde 1 (Berlin)

Meissner, P.

1934-5 'Studien zum Wortschatz Aelfrics' *Archiv* 165 (1934): 11-19 / 166 (1935): 30-9, 205-15

Meller, H.

– 1959 Ruhm *und* Herrlichkeit *in der Werken König Alfreds und Ælfrics: Eine wortgeschichtliche Untersuchung* (Berlin diss.)

Mellinkoff, D.

1963 *The Language of the Law* (Boston and Toronto)

Mellinkoff, R.

1970 *The Horned Moses in Medieval Art and Thought* (Berkeley)

Menner, R.J.

1934 'Farman vindicatus: The Linguistic Value of *Rushworth I' Anglia* 58: 1-27

1936 'The Conflict of Homonyms in English' *Language* 12: 229-44

1944 'Two Old English Words' *MLN* 59: 106-12

1947 'The Vocabulary of the Old English Poems on Judgment Day' *PMLA* 62: 583-97

1948 'Anglian and Saxon Elements in Wulfstan's Vocabulary' *MLN* 63: 1-9

1949 'The Anglian Vocabulary of the *Blickling Homilies*' in T.A. Kirby and H.B. Woolf, eds., *Philologica: The Malone Anniversary Studies* (Baltimore): 56-64

1951 'The Date and Dialect of *Genesis A* 852-2936 (Part III)' *Anglia* 70: 285-94

Merbach, H.

1884 *Das Meer in der Dichtung der Angelsachsen* (Breslau diss.)

Meringer, R.

1905-6 'Wörter und Sachen, III' *IF* 18: 204-96

Meritt, H.D.

1935 'An OE Gloss: *ober eliman . innannorum*' *MLN* 50: 77-82

* 1938a *The Construction* apo koinu *in the Germanic Languages,* Stanford

University Publications, Language and Literature 6, no. 2 (Stanford): 157-268

1938b 'Possible Elliptical Compounds in Old English Glosses' *AJP* 59: 209-17

1941a 'Some Minor Ways of Word Formation in Old English' in H. Craig, ed., *Stanford Studies in Language and Literature for the 50th Anniversary of Stanford University* (Stanford): 74-80

1941b 'Three Studies in Old English' *AJP* 62: 331-9

1944 'The Old English Glosses *deðæ* and *minnæn:* A Study in Ways of Interpretation' *JEGP* 43: 434-46

1945 'Beating the Oaks: An Interpretation of *Christ* 678-9' *AJP* 66: 1-12

1947 'Studies in Old English Vocabulary' *JEGP* 46: 413-27

1950 'Twenty Hard Old English Words' *JEGP* 49: 231-41

1954 *Fact and Lore about Old English Words,* Stanford University Publications, Language and Literature 13 (Stanford; repr. 1967)

1962 'The Leiden Gloss to *histrionibus*' *Anglia* 80: 379-83

1963 'Strange Sauce from Worcester' in *Brodeur Festschrift:* 152-4

1968a *Some of the Hardest Glosses in Old English* (Stanford)

1968b '*Thestisuir* in the *Leiden Glossary*' *Anglia* 86: 155-7

1968c 'The Old English Ghost Word *drisne*' *NM* 69: 47-53

1969 'Old English *hūnsporan*' in Atwood and Hill *Studies:* 70-72

1972 'Conceivable Clues to Twelve Old English Words' *ASE* 1: 193-205

Meroney, H.

1942 'Old English *ðær* "if"' *JEGP* 41: 201-9

1943 *Old English* upp, uppe, uppan, *and* upon (Chicago diss.)

1944a 'Two Old English Textual Errors' *MLN* 59: 40-42

1944b 'The Nine Herbs' *MLN* 59: 157-60

1945 'The Early History of *down* as an Adverb' *JEGP* 44: 378-86

Mertens-Fonck, P.

1959 'Some Problems of the *Vespasian Psalter*' *ES* 40: 170-73

Merwe Scholtz, H. van der

1928 *The Kenning in Anglo-Saxon and Old Norse Poetry* (Utrecht and Nijmegen)

Metcalf, A.A.

1963 'Ten Natural Animals in *Beowulf*' *NM* 64: 378-89

1970 '*West* in *Maldon*' *PLL* 6: 314-16

*1973 *Poetic Diction in the Old English Meters of Boethius,* De proprietatibus litterarum, series practica 50 (The Hague and Paris)

Mettig, R.

1910 *Die französischen Elemente im Alt- und Mittelenglischen (800-1258): Ein Beitrag zur Geschichte des englischen Wortschatzes* (Marburg diss.; *EStn* 41: 177-91)

Meyer, E.M.

1926 *Die Bedeutungsentwicklung von germanischen* *mōða- (Leipzig diss.; Halle)

Meyer, W.

1921 '*Wealhþeo(w)*' *Beibl* 32: 94-101
1942 'Die Bedeutung des altenglischen Wortes *hūru*' *Beibl* 53: 87-90

Mezger, F.

*1921 *Angelsächsische Völker- und Ländernamen* (Berlin diss.)
1931a 'Ae. *fæsl*, n. "Nachkommenschaft" und ae. *cnósl* "Nachkommenschaft, Geschlecht, Familie, Vaterland"' *Archiv* 160: 91-2
1931b 'Old English *ersc* ("stubble-field")' *PMLA* 46: 90-92
1932 'Ae. *forecynren*, n. "Nachkommenschaft"- *mǽgcynren*, n. "Familie, Linie"-*cynren*, n. "Art, Gattung, Familie, Verwandtschaft, Generation, Nachkommenschaft"' *Archiv* 161: 228-9
1933a 'Ae. *cræftiga* "artifex"-ae. *byrdicga* "plumaria"' *Archiv* 163: 42-6
1933b 'Middle English *run*' *PMLA* 48: 1036-40
1934 'Ahd. *galstar*-ae. *gealdor;* ahd. *lastar*-ae. *leahtor*' *ZvS* 61: 289-91
1935a 'Ae. *fleard* n. = aisl. *flárád* n.- ae. *reord* < **rereð?*' *Archiv* 167: 66-7
1935b 'Ae. *trintreg(a)* < **tind-treg(a)?*' *Archiv* 167: 252-3
1935c 'Der germanische Kult and die ae. Feminina auf -*icge* und -*estre*' *Archiv* 168: 177-84
1937 'Ae. *eart, earð, arð* "du bist" und got. *sijum* "wir sind"' *ZvS* 64: 137-41
1938a 'Gehört ae. *earwunga* "gratis," got. *arwjo*, ahd. *arw(ing)ūn* zu got. *arjan* ... "pflügen"?' *Archiv* 173: 209-10
1938b 'Got. *niuklahs* "wie ein Kind, unmündig," *niuklahei* "Kleinmut, Unverstand": ae. *cild;* got. *kalkjom*' *Archiv* 174: 78-9
1939a 'Ae. *genǽstan* "streiten": ae. *hǽst* "Heftigkeit, Streit"' *Archiv* 175: 97-8
1939b 'OE *gehygd, hyht, hlyst, geþyld*' *AfNF* 54: 229-34
1941 'OE *tán:* Idg. *dῠōu, *dῠoi –?' *JEGP* 40: 348
1942 'The Formation of OHG *diorna*, OS *thiorna*, Goth *widwauna*, and OE *níwerne*' *MLN* 57: 432-3
1943a 'Two Etymologies' *Language* 19: 261-3
1943b 'Did the Institution of Marriage by Purchase Exist in Old Germanic Law?' *Speculum* 18: 369-71

1944 *'On fæder feorme, Beowulf* line 21' *MLN* 59: 113-14
1946 'Goth. *aglaiti* "unchastity," OE *aglæc* "distress"' *Word* 2: 66-71
1948-9 'Got. *fraujinassus,* ae. *fréot,* aks. *svobodĭ*' *ZvS* 69: 204-6
1951a 'OE *hāmweorðung, Beowulf* 2998' *JEGP* 50: 243-5
1951b 'Two Notes on *Beowulf*' *MLN* 66: 36-8
1952 'Self-Judgment in OE Documents' *MLN* 67: 106-9
1955 'Zu einigen idg. *g-* und *l*-Bildungen' *ZvS* 72: 97-118
1958 'Ae. *intinga,* got. *inilō*' *ZvS* 75: 210
1960a 'German. *aiþa-* "Eid, Eideshelfereid": got. *aiþei* "Mutter"' *ZvS* 76: 85-6
1960b 'Ahd. *ēohaft:* got. *liugom hafts*' *ZvS* 76: 87-8
1960c 'Germ. *armaz* "vereinsamt, verlassen, friedlos": heth. *araḫza* "ausserhalb, ringsum"' *ZvS* 76: 178-80
1960d 'Got. *hunsl* n. "Opfer"' *ZvS* 76: 303-4
1960e 'Got. *jains* "jener"' *ZvS* 76: 305
1961 'Heth. *kiššan:* ae. *hislīc*' *ZvS* 77: 85-6
1965a 'Germ. *frijōnd-* "Verwandte"' *ZvS* 79: 32-8
1965b 'Germ. Adjektiva auf *-iska-*' *ZvS* 79: 38-41
1965c 'Ae. *ǽnett:* ahd. *einōti:* mnd. *einihte*' *ZvS* 79: 41-6
1968 '**au-* in **au-dh* "eigen; Besitz" gr. *autos;* germ. **au-þj-a-* "abgelegen"' *ZvS* 82: 288-97
1969a 'An. *vesall* "arm, elend": an. *sal* m. "Zahlung," germ. **saljan* "übergeben" und **sēl(i)a-* "gut, glücklich"' *ZvS* 83: 124-49
1969b 'Germanisch **hulþa-* Adjektiv' *ZvS* 83: 150-52
1970 'Ahd. *fratāt*' *ZvS* 84: 137-9

Michel, K.
* 1912 *Die mit* -i- *abgeleiteten denominativen Verba im Altgermanischen* (Giessen diss.; Darmstadt)

Michiels, H.
* 1912 *Über englische Bestandteile altdeutscher Glossenhandschriften,* BBzA 15 (Bonn)

Midgley, G.
1959 *'The Wanderer,* lines 49-55' *RES* n.s. 10: 53-4

Miedema, H.T.J.
— 1970 'Het friese toponiem *Kie,* oudfrees *Kee,* oudeng. *cyth,* "kith, homeland, native place"' *Nku* 2: 221-4
— 1972a 'Nederlands *keen,* engels *chine,* fries *sein*' *Nku* 4: 40-45
— 1972b 'De oudengelse muntnamn *sceat* en het oudfriese diminutivum

skeisen "duit"' *Nku* 4: 320-22

1972-3 'Ist die altfriesische Präposition *til* "bis" ein altnordisches Lehnwort der Wikingerzeit?' *Us Wurk* 21-2: 173-80

Mikami, T.

— 1966 '*Beowulf* ni okeru hiteigo ni tsuite' *Meiji Gakuin Daigaku Daigakuin IO Shūnen Kinen Ronbunshū* 12 (Tokyo): 339-54 [On negative words in *Beowulf*]

1968 'OE shi ni okeru "Sea" no dōigo ni tsuite — *Beowulf* o chūshin ni' *Tōkai Daigaku Bungakubu Kiyō* 9: 57-67 [On the OE synonyms for sea, especially in *Beowulf*]

1969 'OE shi ni okeru "Warrior" no dōigo ni tsuite — *Beowulf* o chūshin ni' *Tōkai Daigaku Bungakubu Kiyo* 11, 2: 71-86 [On the OE synonyms for warrior, especially in *Beowulf*]

*1974-6 'Studies in the Language of *Beowulf*' *Tōkai Daigaku Bungakubu Kiyō* 20, 2 (1974): 89-120 / 23, 7 (1975):42-52 / 24, 2 (1976): 55-66 / 25, 7 (1976): 146-56 / 26, 1 (1976): 77-88

Mikkola, J.J.

1898 'Etymologische Beiträge' *Beiträge zur Kunde der indogermanischen Sprachen* 21: 218-25

1899 'Baltische Etymologien' *Beiträge zur Kunde der indogermanischen Sprachen* 22: 241

Milani, C.

1978 'Anglico-Celtica' *Istituto Lombardo, Classe di lettere e scienze morali e storiche, Rendiconti* 112: 286-96

Miller, M.Y.

1975 *The Concept of Deprivation in Old English Poetry* (Pennsylvania diss.; *DAI* 36: 2851A)

Miller, T.

1889 'The Position of Grendel's Arm in Heorot' *Anglia* 12: 396-400

1894 'Grendel' *Academy* 45: 396

Millns, T.

1977 '*The Wanderer* 98: *weal wundrum heah wyrmlicum fah*' *RES* n.s. 28: 431-8

Mills, C.R.
1976 'Stylistic Applications of Ethnosemantics: Basic Color Terms in *Brunan-burh* and *Maldon' Language and Style* 9: 164-70

Millward, C.M.
1971 *Imperative Constructions in Old English,* Janua linguarum, series practica 124 (The Hague and Paris)

Mincoff, M.K.
1933 *Die Bedeutungsentwicklung der ags. Ausdrücke für* Kraft *und* Macht, Palaestra 188 (Leipzig)
1943 *Zur angelsächsischen Dichtersprache,* Godisnik na universiteta Sv. Climenti Ochridski 39 (Sofia)

Minkoff, H.
1976 'Some Stylistic Consequences of Ælfric's Theory of Translation' *SP* 73: 29-41

Mirarchi, G.
1980 'Il duale ellittico nella poesia anglosassone: I, *Widsith* 103; II, *Cristo e Satana* 409; III, *Genesi* 387; IV, *Beowulf* 2002; V, *La Discesa all'Inferno* 135' *AION Filologia Germanica* 23: 197-257

Mirow, C.
− 1975 *Aspects of Fame in Beowulf* (London M.A. thesis)

Mitchell, B.
1963a '"Until the Dragon comes ..." Some Thoughts on *Beowulf' Neophil* 47: 126-38
1963b 'Old English Syntactical Notes' *N&Q* 208: 326-8
1964 'Pronouns in Old English Poetry − Some Syntactical Notes' *RES* n.s. 15: 129-41
1965a 'Some Problems of Mood and Tense in Old English' *Neophil* 49: 44-57
1965b 'The Status of *hwonne* in Old English' *Neophil* 49: 157-60
1965c 'Bede's *habere* = Old English *magan?' NM* 66: 107-11
1967 '*Swa* in *Cædmon's Hymn,* line 3' *N&Q* 212: 203-4
1968a 'Two Syntactical Notes on *Beowulf' Neophil* 52: 292-8
1968b 'More Musings on Old English Syntax' *NM* 69: 53-63
1968c 'Some Syntactical Problems in the *Wanderer' NM* 69: 172-98
1969a 'Five Notes on Old English Syntax' *NM* 70: 70-84
1969b 'Postscript on Bede's *mihi cantare habes' NM* 70: 369-80
1974 'Bede's Account of the Poet Cædmon: Two Notes' in G. Turville-Petre

and J.M. Martin, eds., *Iceland and the Mediaeval World: Studies in Honour of Ian Maxwell* (Melbourne): 126-31

1975 'Linguistic Facts and the Interpretation of Old English Poetry' *ASE* 4: 11-28

1976 'Some Problems Involving Old English Periphrases with *beon/wesan* and the Present Participle' *NM* 77: 478-91

1977 'Old English *ac* as an Interrogative Particle' *NM* 78: 98-100

1978 'Old English *oð þæt* Adverb?' *N&Q* 223: 390-94

*1978-80 'Prepositions, Adverbs, Prepositional Adverbs, Postpositions, Separable Prefixes, or Inseparable Prefixes, in Old English?' *NM* 79 (1978): 240-57; with A.B. Kingsmill, *NM* 81 (1980): 313-17

1979a 'F. Th. Visser, *An Historical Syntax of the English Language:* Some Caveats Concerning Old English' *ES* 60: 537-42

1979b 'Old English *self:* Four Syntactical Notes' *NM* 80: 39-45

Mittner, L.

1939 'Schicksal und Werden im Altgermanischen' *Wörter und Sachen* N.F. 2: 253-80

1955 *Wurd: Das Sakrale in der altgermanischen Epik,* Bibliotheca Germanica 6 (Bern)

Miyazaki, T.

1966 'Conjunction *þæt* in an Anglo-Saxon Chronicle' *Kagoshima Daigaku Bunka Hōkoku* 1: 127-54

– 1977 'Ko eishi ni okeru tōin kōsei ni tsuiteno ichi kōsatsu' *Yokohama Ichiritsu Daigaku Ronsō Jinbun Kagaku Keiretsu* 29, 1, 12: 93-120 [An observation on the structure of suffixes in OE poetry]

Mogami, T.

– 1972 '*Mid, ac* nado – haigo tenbyō' *Kanazawa Daigaku Kyōyōbu Ronshū (Jinbun Kagaku hen)* 9, 2: 21-31 [Comments on discarded words – *mid, ac,* etc.]

– 1973 '*Āncra, gǣstan* nado – haigo tenbyō' *Aoyama Gakuin Joshi tanki Daigaku Kiyō* 27, 11: 65-92 [Comments on discarded words – *ancra, gæstan,* etc.]

– 1975 '*Āblendan, æht* nado – haigo tenbyō' *Nihon Daigaku Eibungakkai Kaihō* 23, 3: 377-93 [Comments on discarded words – *ablendan, æht,* etc.]

– 1977 '*Gospels* to Anglo-Saxon haigo' *Kiyō (shakai Jinbun kagaku hen)* 25, 1: 31-46 [The Gospels and Anglo-Saxon discarded words]

Mohr, W.
1933 *Kenningstudien: Beiträge zur Stilgeschichte der altgermanischen Dichtung*, Tübinger germanistische Arbeiten 19 (Stuttgart)

Moisl, H.
1980 'Celto-Germanic *wātu- / wōtu- and Early Germanic Poetry' *N&Q* 225: 98-9

Monroe, B.S.
1916 'Notes on the Anglo-Saxon *Andreas' MLN* 31: 374-7

Moore, B.
1975-6 '*Eacen* in *Beowulf* and Other Old English Poetry' *ELN* 13: 161-5
1980 'The Thryth-Offa Digression in *Beowulf*' *Neophil* 64: 127-33

Moore, S.
1911 'The Old English *Genesis*, ll. 1145 and 1146-8' *MLR* 6: 199-202
1913 'Notes on the Old English *Christ*' *Archiv* 131: 311-14
1919 '*Beowulf* Notes' *JEGP* 18: 205-16
1929 'Notes on *Beowulf*' in *Klaeber Festschrift*: 208-12

Morris, C.
1967 'William I and the Church Courts' *EHR* 82: 449-63

Morris, R.
1889 'The Etymology of the Word *God*' *Academy* 35: 413

Morris, W.A.
1916 'The Office of Sheriff in the Anglo-Saxon Period' *EHR* 31: 20-40

Morris, W.S.
1968 *Possible Solutions to Some Old English Words of Uncertain Etymology* (Stanford diss.; *DA* 29: 587A)

Morrison, S.
1979-80 'OE *cempa* in Cynewulf's *Juliana* and the Figure of the *Miles Christi*' *ELN* 17: 81-5
1980 '*Beowulf* 698a, 1273a: *frōfor ond fultum*' *N&Q* 225: 193-6

Mossé, F.
1938 *Histoire de la forme périphrastique* être + participe présent *en germanique. Première partie: Introduction, ancien germanique. Deuxième partie:*

Vieil-anglais, moyen-anglais et anglais moderne, Collection linguistique 42, 43 (Paris)
1948 'Poésie saxonne et poésie anglaise à l'époque carolingienne (A propos de *Christ III*)' *EG* 3: 157-65

Most, S.M. (see also Ingersoll)
1969 *Intensive and Restrictive Modification in a Select Corpus of Old English Poetry and Prose* (Northwestern diss.; *DAI* 30: 2992A)

Mottausch, K.-H.
1961 'Germanisch *hlaupan' ZvS* 77: 129-39

Motz, L.
1977 *'Burg-berg, burrow-barrow' IF* 81 (1976): 204-20

Muir, A.L.
1948 'Some Observations on the Early English Psalters and the English Vocabulary' *MLQ* 9: 273-6

Mukhin, A.M.
– 1956 'K voprosu o znachenii i upotreblenii soslagatel'nogo nakloneniia v kosvennoi rechi v drevneangliiskom iazyke' Leningrad, Ped. Institut, *Uchenye zapiski* 3 [On the question of the meaning and use of conjunctions in indirect speech in OE]
* 1957 'Slovoslozhenie i slovosochetanie (Na materiale drevneangliiskogo iazyka)' *Problemy sravreniia:* 35-44 [Word formation and word combination (based on OE material)]

Muller, J.W.
1886 'Ags. *Genesis* 431' *BGdSL* 11: 363-4

Munske, H.H.
1964 *Das Suffix* *-inga/-unga *in den germanischen Sprachen* (Marburg diss.)
1970 'Angelsächsisch-altfriesische Beziehungen in der Rechtsterminologie für Missetaten' in T. Hoekema et al., eds., *Flecht op 'e koai: Studzjes oanbean oan Prof. Dr. W.J. Buma* (Groningen): 40-52
1973 *Der germanische Rechtwortschatz im Bereich der Missetaten: Philologische und sprachgeographische Untersuchungen, I: Die Terminologie der älteren westgermanischen Rechtsquellen,* Studia linguistica Germanica 8 (Berlin and New York)

Murphy, J.J.
1970 'The Rhetorical Lore of the *boceras* in Byrhtferth's *Manual*' in *Meritt Festschrift:* 111-24

Murray, J.A.H.
1896 'An Unrecorded English Verb' *Academy* 49: 138-9

Must, G.
1957 'The Etymology of German *hengst* "stallion," Swedish *häst* "horse"' *JEGP* 56: 60-64
1960 'English *holy*, German *heilig*' *JEGP* 59: 184-9
1961 'The Origin of the German Word *ehre* "honor"' *PMLA* 76: 326-9

Mustanoja, T.F.
1950 'Notes on Some Old English Glosses in Aldhelm's *De laudibus virginitatis*' *NM* 51: 49-61

Mutt, O.
− 1955 *A Contribution to the Historical Study of the Attributive Use of Substantives in English* (Tartu Universitet diss.)
1962 'On the Preconditions in Old English that facilitated the Subsequent Development of the Use of Substantives in the Common Case as Prepositive Attributes' Tartu, Gosudarstvennyi Universitet, *Uchenye zapiski* 117, Trudy po filologii no. 1: 229-45
1968 'The Use of Substantives as Premodifiers in Early English' *NM* 69: 578-96

Nagano, Y.
— 1956 'On Some Peculiarities of Word Formation in Anglo-Saxon Poetry'
Studies in English Literature and Language 6, 7: 23-46
1965 'The Use of *habban* + Past Participle in *Beowulf*' *Essays and Studies in English Literature and Language* (Kyushu University) 15, 1: 93-109

Nagashima, D.
1972 'A Historical Study of the Introductory *there,* Part I: The Old English Period' *Osaka Daigaku Kyōyōbu Kenkyū Shuroku* 20 (*Gaikokugo Gaikoku Bungaku* 8) 3: 135-68

Nagucka, R.
1979 'Syntax and Semantics of *hatan* Compounds' *Kwartalnik Neofilologiczny* 26: 19-28

Napier, A.S.
1881 'Zu *Andreas* 1182' *Anglia* 4: 411
1889a 'Old Northumbrian Glosses in the Vatican' *Academy* 35: 342, 449
1889b 'Old Northumbrian Glosses in MS. Palatine 68' *Academy* 36: 119-20
1889c 'Odds and Ends' *MLN* 4: 137-40
1891 'A Passage in the Old English Chronicle' *Academy* 40: 589
1892 'Some English Etymologies' *Academy* 41: 447
1894a 'Some English Etymologies' *Academy* 45: 457
1894b 'Old English *nemne (nymðe)*' *MLN* 9: 159
1896 'An Unrecorded English Verb' *Academy* 49: 158
1897 'Old and Middle English Notes' *Modern Quarterly of Language and Literature* 1: 51-3
1898a 'Werwolf' *BGdSL* 23: 571-3
1898b 'Old English Notes' *Modern Quarterly of Language and Literature* 2: 130-31
1899a 'Zum altenglischen Boetius' *BGdSL* 24: 245-6
1899b 'Aengl. *getæl, getel* "Zahl"' *BGdSL* 24: 246-8
1899c 'On Some Old English Ghost-Words' *JGP* 2: 359-62
1903-4 'Old English Notes' *MP* 1: 393-5
1906 'Contributions to Old English Lexicography' *TPS* (1903-6): 265-358

Nazareth, L.A.C.
1979 *Language as Theme in the Old English Exodus* (State University of New York, Stony Brook diss.; *DAI* 40: 2656A)

Neckel, G.
1916 'Under Edoras' *BGdSL* 41: 163-70

Neniukova, A.S.
− 1951 *Predlogi i obstoiatel'stvennye narechiia v drevneangliiskom iazyke (Po materialu Anglo-Saksonskoi khroniki)* (Moscow, Universitet diss.) [Prepositions and adverbs in OE (based on the *Anglo-Saxon Chronicle*)]
*1955 'Predlogi i obstoiatel'stvennye narechiia v drevneangliiskom iazyke (Ikh znachenie i upotreblenie po materialam *Anglo-Saksonskoi khroniki*)' Gorkii, Gos. ped. Institut inostrannykh iazykov, *Uchenye zapiski* 1: 59-87 [Adverbs and adverbial modifiers of time, place, manner in OE (meaning and usage in the *Anglo-Saxon Chronicle*)]
1958 'Nekotorye cherty sistemy predlogov i obstoiatel'stvennykh narechii v drevneangliiskom iazyke (Ikh morfologiia i sintaksicheskaia kharakteristika po materialy *Anglo-Saksonskoi khroniki*)' Gorkii, Gos. ped. Institut inostrannykh iazykov, *Uchenye zapiski* 9: 3-52 [A study of the systems of prepositions and non-qualifying adverbs in OE (their morphological and syntactic characteristics, using the *Anglo-Saxon Chronicle*)]

Neuman, E.
1924 'Ist das Wort *humle* in den germanischen Sprachen ein Lehnwort?' in *Festschrift für Eugen Mogk zum 70. Geburtstag* (Halle): 424-32

Nichols, A.E.
1964 '*Awendan:* A Note on Ælfric's Vocabulary' *JEGP* 63: 7-13

Nicholson, L.E.
1964 'The Literal Meaning and Symbolic Structure of *Beowulf*' *Classica et mediaevalia* 25: 151-201

Nickel, G.
1966a *Die 'Expanded Form' im Altenglischen: Vorkommen, Funktion, und Herkunft der Umschreibung* beon/wesan + *Partizip präsens*, Kieler Beiträge zur Anglistik und Amerikanistik 3 (Neumünster)
1966b 'Operational Procedures in Semantics, with Special Reference to Medieval English' *Monograph Series on Language and Linguistics: Report of the 17th Annual Round Table Meeting on Linguistic and Language Studies* (Washington): 35-43
1967 'An Example of a Syntactic Blend in Old English' *IF* 72 (1967-8): 261-74
1972 'Problems of *Beowulf*-Research with Special Reference to Editorial Questions' *NM* 73: 261-8

Nicolai, O.
1907 *Die Bildung des Adverbs im Altenglischen* (Kiel diss.)

Niwa, Y.

−1958 'Concerning *ge-* in Old English *gebringan* and *gelædan*' *Eigo Eibungaku Kenkyū* 5, 2, 11: 194-210

−1959 '*Saxon Chronicle* ni arawareru Verb-Prefix *ge-* no tadōshika ni tsuite' *Eibungaku Kenkyū* 35, 2, 3: 245-65 [The change into a transitive verb of the verb-prefix *ge-* in the *Saxon Chronicle*]

−1962 '*Saxon Chronicle A* ni arawareru dōshi fukushi ketsugō no kyōjiteki kenkyū' *Nagoya Daigaku Kyōyōbu Kiyō* 6, 7: 10-33 [Simultaneous research on the union of verb and adverb in *Saxon Chronicle A*]

1966 'The preverb *ge-* added to *niman* in the OE Gloss to the *Lindisfarne Gospels*' *SEL* (Tokyo) *English Number:* 65-79

−1968 'Preverb *ge-* no imi kōzō − Igisoteki kōsatsu −' *IVY (Nagoya Daigaku)* 7, 3: 157-70 [Semantic structure and discussion of preverb *ge-*]

1973 *Kodai Eigo Dōshi Settōji* Ge- *no kenkyū* (Tokyo) [OE preverbal *ge-*]

1974 'On the Collective Meaning of OE Preverb *ge-*' *SEL* (Tokyo) *English Number:* 155-67

−1976 'OE *Vespasian Psalter* ni arawareru dōshi fukushi ketsugo ni tsuite' *Nagoya Daigaku Kyōyōbu Kiyō C* 20, 2: 25-48 [On verb-adverb bondings in the OE *Vespasian Psalter*]

−1977 'OE *Vespasian Psalter* ni arawareru dōshi fukushi ketsugo no kyōki kankei ni tsuite − *A* to *IN* −' *Nagoya Daigaku Kyōyōbu Gogaku Center Kiyō C* 21, 3: 55-71 [On semantic relationships of verb-adverb bondings that appear in the OE *Vespasian Psalter* − *A* and *IN* −]

1980 'OE *Vespasian Psalter* ni arawareru dōshi fukugōkei no kyōki kankei ni tsuite (IV) −*Geond-, forþ-, ut-, up-, onweg-*' *Nagoya Daigaku Sōgō Gengo Center Gengo Bunka Ronshū* 1: 33-52 [Syntactic relationships of compound verbs that appear in the OE *Vespasian Psalter*]

Nolan, B. and Bloomfield, M.W.

1980 '*Bēotword, gilpcwidas,* and the *gilphlæden* Scop of *Beowulf*' *JEGP* 79: 499-516

Nordgård, O.

1921 'Forklaringer til de viktigste av kongespeilets dyrenavne' in *Konungs Skuggsjá Speculum Regale,* Udgivet efter Håndskrifterne af det Kongelige Nordiske Oldskriftselskab 2 (Copenhagen): 107-17

Norman, F.

1937 '*Deor:* A Criticism and an Interpretation' *MLR* 32: 374-81

Nowakowski, M.

1978 *A Study in Generative Historical Linguistics. On Language Change:*

Some Aspects of Old English Nominalizations, Seria filologia angielska
9 (Poznan)

Nowicki, H.
1977 'Ahd. As. *thiorna' ZdA* 106: 83-7

O

Oberdörffer, W.

1908 *Das Aussterben altenglischer Adjektive und ihr Ersatz im Verlaufe der englischen Sprachgeschichte* (Kiel diss.)

O'Dwyer, P.F.

1967-8 'Old English *unwitweorc:* A Ghost Word' *ELN* 5: 79-80

Oehl, W.

1940 'Ags. *mamor* "Schlaf" und Elementar-Paralleles' *IF* 57: 2-24

Offe, J.

1908 *Das Aussterben alter Verba und ihr Ersatz im Verlaufe der englischen Sprachgeschichte* (Kiel diss.)

Ogawa, H.

1968 '*Magan, motan, sculan,* and *willan* in OE Poetry: Their Uses in Object Clauses' *Maekawa Shun-ichi Kyōju Kanreki Kinen Ronbunshū* 12: 255-66

Ogawa, K.

– 1968 '*Beowulf* ni okeru *wyrd* ni tsuite no ichi kōsatsu' *Eigo Eibungaku Kenkyū (Ichikawa)* 2, 12: 10-14 [An observation on the word *wyrd* in *Beowulf*]

Ogilvy, J.D.A.

1964 'Unferth: Foil to Beowulf?' *PMLA* 79: 370-75

1979 'Beowulf, Alfred, and Christianity' in M.H. King and W.M. Stevens, eds., *Saints, Scholars, and Heroes: Studies in Medieval Culture in Honour of Charles W. Jones* (Collegeville, Minn.): I, 59-66

Ogura, M.

1979 '*Cweðan* and *secgan* in Old English Prose' *Senshu Daigaku Bunken Ronshu* 4: 1-30

1981 *The Syntactic and Semantic Rivalry of* quoth, say, *and* tell *in Medieval English,* Kansai University of Foreign Studies Intercultural Research Institute Monograph 12 (Tokyo)

Oka, F.

– 1967-8 '*Anglo-Saxon Chronicles* ni okeru genitive to zenchishi *of* no kinō ni tsuite (1)-(4)' *Eibungaku Shichō* 40, 12 (1967): 55-108; *Kiyō* 10, 1 (1967) 89-111 / 11, 3 (1968): 85-128; *Ronshu* 8 (1968): 103-39 [On the functions of the preposition *of* in the *Anglo-Saxon Chronicles*]

– 1969 'Parker MS. ni okeru zenchishi *oþ* to *for* no kinō ni tsuite' *Eibungaku*

Shichō 42, 12: 151-64 [On the function of the prepositions *oþ* and *for* in the Parker MS.]

1970-74 '*Anglo-Saxon Chronicles* ni okeru dative oyobi zenchishi *to* no kinō ni tsuite (1)-(4)' *Eibungaku Shichō* 43, 12 (1970): 71-102; *Ronshu* 11, 1 (1971): 39-56 / 13, 2 (1973): 85-106 / 14, 3 (1974): 119-45 [On the function of the dative and the preposition *to* in the *Anglo-Saxon Chronicles*]

— 1973 '*Anglo-Saxon Chronicle* MS. C (Cotton Tiberius B. i) ni okeru zenchishi *on* oyobi *æt, in, into* no kinō ni tsuite' *Kiyō* 14, 3: 149-84 [On the function of the prepositions *on, æt, in,* and *into* in the *Anglo-Saxon Chronicle* MS. C]

— 1974 '*Anglo-Saxon Chronicle* MS. D (Cotton Tiberius B. iv) ni okeru zenchishi *on* oyobi *æt, in, into* no kinō ni tsuite' *Kiyō* 15, 3: 101-40 [On the function of the prepositions *on, æt, in,* and *into* in the *Anglo-Saxon Chronicle* MS. D]

Okasha, E.
1976 '*Beacen* in Old English Poetry' *N&Q* 221: 200-7

Oleson, T.J.
1955 *The* Witenagemot *in the Reign of Edward the Confessor: A Study in the Constitutional History of Eleventh-Century England* (Toronto)

Oliphant, R.
1963 '*Ætnes* and *ytend:* Two Rare Old English Glossary Words' *PQ* 42: 249-50
1964 'Two Questionable Old English Compounds: *dungrǽg* and *tīdscriptor*' *PQ* 43: 123-5
1965 'Dark Lemmata Documented for Common Old English Words' *JEGP* 64: 489-95

Olsen, M.
1930 'Angelsächsisch *dyde*' *Norsk Tidsskrift for Sprogvidenskap* 4: 279-81

Olszewska, E.S.
1935 'Legal Borrowings from Norse in Old and Middle English' *Saga-Book* 11: 233-8

O'Neill, P.
1981 'Old English *brondeguī*' *ES* 62: 2-4

Onions, C.T.

1933 'Old English *hrohian* (see *M.Æ.* I 208)' *MÆ* 2: 73

Ono, S.

—1955 '*The Peterborough Chronicle* ni okeru jodŏshi' *Gakushūin Daigaku Bungakubu Kenkyū Nenpō* 2, 11: 157-90 [Auxiliary verbs in the *Peterborough Chronicle*]

—1956 '*Motan* no imi sono hensen' *Gakushūin Daigaku Bungakubu Kenkyū Nenpō* 3, 3: 117-92 [The Meaning of *motan* and its change]

1958 'Some Notes on the Auxiliary **motan*' *Anglica* 3, 3, 6: 64-80

—1959 '*Cunnan* "can" to *magan* "may"' *Gakushūin Daigaku Bungakubu Kenkyū Nenpō* 5, 3: 289-323 [*Cunnan* "can" and *magan* "may"]

1975 'The Old English Verbs of Knowing' *SEL* (Tokyo) *English Number:* 33-60

Opland, J.

1971 '*Scop* and *imbongi* — Anglo-Saxon and Bantu Oral Poets' *ESA* 14: 161-78

1976 '*Beowulf* on the Poet' *MS* 38: 442-67

1980 *Anglo-Saxon Oral Poetry: A Study of the Traditions* (New Haven and London)

Orrick, A.H.

1956 '*Reðes ond hattres, Beowulf* 2523' *MLN* 71: 551-6

Ortoleva, G.

1979 '*Waldere* II, 21b: *þonne ha[n]d wereð*' *AION, Filologia Germanica* 22: 117-79

Osborn, M.L.

1969a 'Laying the Roman Ghost of *Beowulf* 320 and 725' *NM* 70: 246-55

1969b 'Some Uses of Ambiguity in *Beowulf*' *Thoth* 10: 18-35

1970 'The Finnsburh Raven and *guðrinc astah*' *Folklore* 81: 185-94

1978a '*Reote* and *ridend* as Musical Terms in *Beowulf:* Another Kind of Harp?' *Neophil* 62: 442-6

1978b 'Venturing upon Deep Waters in the *Seafarer*' *NM* 79: 1-6

Oshitari, K.

1973 'The Sea in *Beowulf*' *SEL* (Tokyo) *English Number:* 3-18

Ostheeren, K.
1964 *Studien zum Begriff der Freude und seinen Ausdrucksmitteln in altenglischen Texten (Poesie, Alfred, Aelfric)* (Berlin diss.; Heidelberg)

Osthoff, H.
1895 'Air. *uan;* ags. *éanian:* griech. *αυνóc' IF* 5: 324-7
1903 'Ags. *blǣce, blǣcðrüstfel' EStn* 32: 181-5

Otten, K.
1964 *König Alfreds Boethius,* SEP N.F. 3 (Tübingen)

Overholser, L.C.
1971 *A Comparative Study of the Compound Use in Andreas and Beowulf* (Michigan diss.; *DAI* 32: 1498A)

Owen, G.R.
1979 'Wynflæd's Wardrobe' *ASE* 8: 195-222

Owen, W.J.B.
1950 '*Wanderer,* lines 50-57' *MLN* 65: 161-5

ҏ

P., J.
1859 'Names of Numbers, and the Hand' *N&Q* ser. 2, 8: 529-30

Padel, O.J.
1973 'Cornish Language Notes' *Cornish Studies* 1: 57-9

Padelford, F.M.
1899 *Old English Musical Terms*, BBzA 4 (Bonn)

Page, R.I.
1958 'Northumbrian *æfter* (= in memory of) + Accusative' *SN* 30: 145-52
1969 'Old English *cyningstan*' *Leeds Studies* n.s. 3: 1-5
1970 *Life in Anglo-Saxon England* (London and New York)
1971 'How Long did the Scandinavian Language Survive in England? The Epigraphical Evidence' in *Whitelock Festschrift*: 165-82
1973 *An Introduction to English Runes* (London)
1979 'OE *fealh*, "harrow"' *N&Q* 224: 389-93

Palmer, A.H.
1893 '*Scūrheard*' *MLN* 8: 61

Parker, R.E.
1956 '*Gyd, leoð*, and *sang* in Old English Poetry' *TSL* 1: 59-63

Paroli, T.
1976 '*Lupi* e *malfattori* tra filologia e semantica' *AION-SG*, Studi nederlandesi / Studi nordici 19: 155-66

Patrick, M.D.
1969-70 '*The Wife's Lament*, 27-41' *Expl* 28: item 50

Paues, A.C.
1931 '*Cincdaðenan* in the Will of Wynflæd' *MLR* 26: 168-9

Payne, F.A.
1974 'Three Aspects of *wyrd* in *Beowulf*' in *Pope Festschrift*: 15-35

Payne, J.F.
1904 *English Medicine in the Anglo-Saxon Times*, Fitz-Patrick Lectures for 1903 (Oxford)

Pearce, J.W.
1891 'The Regimen of *wyrðe* in the *Historia ecclesiastica*' *MLN* 6: 1-2
1892a 'Anglo-Saxon *scur-heard*' *MLN* 7: 193-4
1892b 'Old English *scurheard*' *MLN* 7: 253-4

Pearce, T.M.
1966 'Beowulf's Moment of Decision in Heorot' *TSL* 11: 169-76

Pedersen, H.
1930 'Oldengelsk *fæmne*' in N. Bøgholm, A. Brusendorff, and C.A. Bodelsen, eds., *A Grammatical Miscellany Offered to Otto Jespersen on his Seventieth Birthday:* 55-68
1941-2 'Angl. *wife* et *woman*' *SN* 14: 252-4

Peeters, C.
1970 'Ahd. *sān(o)*, ae. *sōna*, got. *suns*' *ZvS* 84: 231-2
1972 'On *how* in Germanic' *Studia linguistica* 26: 116-19
1973 'On English *lie*, Old English *lēogan* "mentiri"' *ES* 54: 58-9
1974a 'The Word for *tree* in the Germanic Languages and the Reconstruction of Proto-Germanic' *ZvS* 88: 129-33
1974b 'Germanic **kwō(z)* "cow"' *ZvS* 88: 134-6
1977 'Notes on Germanic Etymologies' *ZvS* 91: 166-9

Pelevina, N.F. –
– 1957-8 'O sovmeshchenii znachenii *zvuka* i *sveta* (Na materiale drevne-angliiskogo iazyka)' Chernovtsy, Universytet, *Nauchnyi ezhegodnik:* 280-81 [On the association of meanings of *light* and *sound* (based on OE material)]
* 1959-60 'Slova so znacheniem *belyi, svetlyi* i *chernyi, temnyi* v drevne-angliiskom iazyke' Chernovtsy, Universytet, *Nauchnyi ezhegodnik:* 315-17 [Words meaning *white, bright* and *black, dark* in OE]

Pelteret, D.A.E.
1978 'Expanding the Word Hoard: Opportunities for Fresh Discoveries in Early English Vocabulary' *Indiana Social Studies Quarterly* 31: 56-65
1981 'Slave Raiding and Slave Trading in Early England' *ASE* 9: 99-114

Peltola, N.
1959 'On the "identifying" *swa (swa)* Phrase in Old English' *NM* 60: 156-73
1971 'Observations on Intensification in Old English Poetry' *NM* 72: 649-90
1972 'Grendel's Descent from Cain Reconsidered' *NM* 73: 284-91

Penttilä, E.
1956 *The Old English Verbs of Vision: A Semantic Study,* Mémoires de la
Société néophilologique de Helsinki 18 (Helsinki)
1958 'A Sense-Development of Verbs Denoting Emission of Light' *NM* 59:
161-72

Pepperdene, M.W.
1966 'Beowulf and the Coast-Guard' *ES* 47: 409-19

Persson, P.
*1912 *Beiträge zur indogermanischen Wortforschung,* Skrifter utgifna af
K. Humanistiska Vetenskapssamfundet i Uppsala 10, nos. 1 and 2 (Uppsala)

Peters, R.A.
1960 'OE *ceargest' N&Q* 205: 167
1961 *A Study of the Old English Words for Demon and Monster and their
Relation to English Place-Names* (Pennsylvania diss.; *DA* 22: 253)
1963 'OE *ælf, -ælf, ælfen, -ælfen' PQ* 42: 250-57

Petersen, W.
1935 'The Dual Personal Pronouns in Germanic' *JEGP* 34: 64-7

Peterson, P.W.
*1953 'Dialect Grouping in the Unpublished Vercelli Homilies' *SP* 50: 559-65

Pettitt, T.
1976 *'Beowulf:* The Mark of the Beast and the Balance of Frenzy' *NM* 77:
526-35

Pfannkuche, K.
1908 *Der Schild bei den Angelsachsen* (Halle-Wittenberg diss.; Halle)

Pfeilstücker, S.
1936 *Spätantikes und germanisches Kunstgut in der frühangelsächsischen
Kunst. Nach lateinischen und altenglischen Schriftquellen* (Bonn diss.;
Berlin)

Pheifer, J.D.
1960 *'Waldere* I, 29-31' *RES* n.s. 11: 183-6
1965 *'The Seafarer* 53-55' *RES* n.s. 16: 282-4

Phelps, W.H.
1962 '*Deor dædscua:* A Note on the Old English *Christ*' *N&Q* 207: 131-2

Philippson, E.A.
1929 *Germanisches Heidentum bei den Angelsachsen,* Kölner anglistische Arbeiten 4 (Leipzig)

Philipsen, H.
1887 *Über Wesen und Gebrauch des bestimmten Artikels in der Prosa König Alfreds auf Grund des Orosius (Hs. L.) und der Cura Pastoralis* (Greifswald diss.)

Phillpotts, B.S.
1929 '*The Battle of Maldon:* Some Danish Affinities' *MLR* 24: 172-90

Phoenix, W.
*1918 *Die Substantivierung des Adjektivs, Partizips, und Zahlwortes in Angelsächsischen* (Berlin diss.)

Piatigorskaia, V.A.
– 1949 *Istorii predloga* from (*K voprosu o razvitii znacheniia predlogov v angliiskom iazyke*) (Moscow, Universitet diss.) [The history of the preposition *from* (the question of the development of the meaning of the preposition in English)]

Piccolini, A.
1980 'Sui presunti influssi nordici nel *Waldere*' *AION Filologia Germanica* 23: 159-80

Pickford, T.E.
1976 '*Holmwudu* in the *Dream of the Rood*' *NM* 77: 561-4

Picton, J.A.
1883 '*Seal = sigillum: sign = signum*' *N&Q* ser. 6, 7: 402-4

Piirainen, E.
1971 *Germ.* *froð- *und germ.* *klōk-: *Eine bedeutungsgeschichtliche Untersuchung zu Wörtern für Klugheit und pflanzliches Wachstum,* Mémoires de la Société néophilologique de Helsinki 37 (Helsinki)

Pilch, H.
1951 *Der Untergang des Präverbs ge- im Englischen* (Kiel diss.)

1952-3 'Das ae. Präverb *ge-*' *Anglia* 71: 129-39
1955 'Der Untergang des Präverbs *ge-* im Englischen' *Anglia* 73: 37-64

Pilloni, M.V.
* 1979 *Le preposizioni nella* Cronaca Anglosassone: *Analisi sincronica et diacronica* (Cagliari diss.)

Piltz, O.
1849-53 'Zur englischen Wortbildungslehre vom Standpunkte der geschicht-
lichen Sprachforschung' *Archiv* 6 (1849): 371-89 / 8 (1851): 36-58 / 10
(1852): 361-80 / 11 (1852): 192-208, 365-82 / 12 (1853): 295-312 / 13
(1853): 293-309 / 14 (1853): 342-78

Platt, J.
1883 'Angelsaechsisches' *Anglia* 6: 171-8

Plummer, C.
1891 'Two Passages in the Saxon Chronicle' *Academy* 40: 14

Pogatscher, A.
1888 *Zur Lautlehre der griechischen, lateinischen, und romanischen Lehn-
worte im Altenglischen,* Q&F 64 (Strassburg)
1894 'Zu *Beowulf* 168' *BGdSL* 19: 544-5
1895 'Altengl. *bredweall*' *EStn* 20: 148
1900 'Englische Etymologien' *EStn* 27: 217-27
1901 'Das westgermanische Deminutivsuffix *-inkil*' *Anglia* 23: 310-15
1902-3 'Etymologisches' *Beibl* 13 (1902): 13-16, 233-6 / 14 (1903): 181-5
1904 'Ueber den Ursprung des westgermanischen Deminutivsuffixes *-inkil*'
Beibl 15: 238-47
1908a 'Zur Behandlung von lat. *u̯* in altenglischen Lehnwörtern' in C. von
Kraus and A. Sauer, eds., *Untersuchungen und Quellen zur germanischen
und romanischen Philologie, Johann von Kelle dargebracht von seinem
Kollegen und Schülern,* Prager deutsche Studien 8-9: 81-95
1908b 'Etymologisches und Grammatisches' *Anglia* 31: 257-75
1925 'Altenglisch *Grendel*' in F. Wild, ed., *Neusprachliche Studien: Festgabe
Karl Luick zu seinem sechzigsten Geburtstage* (Marburg): 151

Pokorny, J.
1929 'Ags. *mattoc* "Hacke" ein slavisches Lehnwort?' *Zeitschrift für slavische
Philologie* 5: 393-4

Polanyi, L.
1977 'Lexical Coherence Phenomena in Beowulf's Debate with Unferth' *Rackham Literary Studies* 8: 25-37

Poli, D.
1976 'Protostoria, lingua, e cultura nell' area del Mare del Nord, II' *AION-SG*, Studi nederlandesi / Studi nordici 19: 103-41

Pollock, F.
1893 'Anglo-Saxon Law' *EHR* 8: 103-41

Poltavtseva, E.A.
− 1958 'Predposylki voznikoveniia konstruktsii *there is* v drevneangliiskom iazyke' Leningrad, Ped. Institut im. Gertsena, *Uchenye zapiski* 157: 15-30 [The prerequisites for the appearance of the construction *there is* in OE]

Pontán, R.
1917 'Three OE Textual Notes' *MLR* 12: 69-72

Pope, J.C.
1971 'Ælfric and the Old English Version of the Ely Privilege' in *Whitelock Festschrift:* 85-113
1974a 'Second Thoughts on the Interpretation of the *Seafarer' ASE* 3: 75-86
1974b 'An Unsuspected Lacuna in the Exeter Book: Divorce Proceedings for an Ill-matched Couple in the Old English *Riddles' Speculum* 49: 615-22
1981 'The Text of a Damaged Passage in the Exeter Book: *Advent (Christ I)* 18-32' *ASE* 9: 137-56

Potter, S.
1931 'On the Relation of the Old English Bede to Werferth's Gregory and to Alfred's Translations' *Věstnik Královské Čéské Společnosti Nauk Třída Filosoficko-Historicko-Jazykozpynta Ročnik 1930* 33: 1-76
1948 'The Old English *Pastoral Care' TPS* (1947): 114-25
1952 'On the Etymology of *dream' ArL* o.s. 4: 148-54
1952-3 'Commentary on King Alfred's *Orosius' Anglia* 71: 385-437
1964 'On the Etymology of *plough' Prace Filologiczne* 18, 2: 103-8

Pottle, F.A.
1931 '*Næs gĭt yfel wĭf* in the Old English *Apollonius' JEGP* 30: 21-5

Preuninger, R.M.

1941 *The Words for* will, desire, seek, like, choose, *and* demand *in the Old Germanic Dialects* (Brown diss.)

Price, M.B.

1896 *Teutonic Antiquities in the Generally Acknowledged Cynewulfian Poetry* (Leipzig)

Prideaux, W.F.

1898 'The Gates of London' *N&Q* ser. 9, 1: 1-3

Prokof'eva, E.V.

1961 'Prefiksal'noe slovoobrazovanie sushchestvitel'nykh v angliiskom iazyke (Drevneangliiskii period)' Leningrad, Universitet, *Uchenye zapiski* 283, Ser. filol. nauk 56: 121-8 [Word-formation of substantives with prefixes in English (OE period)]

Prokosch, E.

1929 'Two Types of Scribal Errors in the *Beowulf* MS.' in *Klaeber Festschrift:* 196-207

Prollius, M.

1888 *Ueber den syntactischen Gebrauch des Conjunctivs in den Cynewulfschen Dichtungen Elene, Juliana, und Christ* (Marburg diss.)

Puhvel, M.

1963-4 '*Lices feorm,* l. 451, *Beowulf*' *ELN* 1: 159-63

Pupchenko, B.

1960 'Iz istorii razvitiia konstruktsii s predlogom *of* v angliiskom iazyke (Na materiale drevneangliiskogo perioda)' Dnepropetrovsk, Gos. Universitet im 300- letiia vossoedineniia Ukrainy s Rossiei, *Nauchnye zapiski* 70: 71-83 [History of the development of constructions with the preposition *of* in English (based on material from the OE period)]

q

Quinn, J.J.
1961 'Ghost Words, Obscure Lemmata, and Doubtful Glosses in a Latin-Old
English Glossary' *PQ* 40: 313-18
1966 'Some Puzzling Lemmata and Glosses in MS. Cotton Cleopatra A III'
PQ 45: 434-7

Quirk, R.
1954 *The Concessive Relation in Old English Poetry*, YSE-124 (New Haven)
*1963 'Poetic Language and Old English Metre' in A. Brown and P. Foote,
eds., *Early English and Norse Studies presented to Hugh Smith in Honour
of his Sixtieth Birthday* (London): 150-71; repr. in R. Quirk, *Essays on
the English Language* (London 1968): 1-19

Quirk, R. and Wrenn, C.L.
1955 *An Old English Grammar* (London): 104-19

r

R, C.I.
1850 *'Lærig'* *N&Q* ser. 1, 1: 387

Raevskii, M.V.
1965 'K etimologii nemetskogo prilagatel'nogo *gesund'* *Etimologiia:* 264-6
[On the etymology of the Germanic adjective *gesund*]

Rahtz, P. and Bullough, D.
1977 'The Parts of an Anglo-Saxon Mill' *ASE* 6: 15-37

Rankin, J.W.
1909-10 'A Study of the Kennings in Anglo-Saxon Poetry' *JEGP* 8 (1909): 357-422 / 9 (1910): 49-84

Rauch, I.
1964 'A Problem in Historical Synonymy' *Linguistics* 6: 92-8

Rauh, H.
*1936 *Der Wortschatz der altenglischen Uebersetzungen des Matthaeus-Evangeliums untersucht auf seine dialektische und zeitliche Gebundenheit* (Berlin diss.)

Raw, B.C.
1961 'A Latin-English Word-List in MS. Arundel 60' *EGS* 7: 37-42
1978 *The Art and Background of Old English Poetry* (London)

Redbond, W.J.
1932 'Notes on the Word *gar-secg'* *MLR* 27: 204-6
1935 'The Old English Word *sætilcas'* *MLR* 30: 310-11
1936 'Notes on the Word *eolhx'* *MLR* 31: 55-7

Regel, K.
1865 'Anzeige von Grein's *Sprachschatz der angelsächsischen Dichter'* *ZvS* 14: 232-40, 287-316

Reibel, D.A.
*1963 *A Grammatical Index to the Compound Nouns of Old English Verse* (Indiana diss.; *DA* 25: 465)

Reichardt, P.F.
1974 *'Guthlac A* and the Landscape of Spiritual Perfection' *Neophil* 58: 331-8

Reid, R.R.
1920 'Barony and Thanage' *EHR* 35: 161-99

Rein, W.
1911 *Die Mass- und Gewichtsbezeichnungen des Englischen: Ein Beitrag zur Bedeutungsgeschichte* (Giessen)

Reinhard, M.
1976 *On the Semantic Relevance of the Alliterative Collocations in Beowulf,* SAA 92 (Bern)

Reinius, J.
1897 'Ags. *neorxnawang' Anglia* 19: 554-6
1903 *On Transferred Appellations of Human Beings Chiefly in English and German: Studies in Historical Sematology* (Uppsala diss.; Göteborg)

Reisgof, M.V.
− 1940 'K istorii mestnykh predlogov v angliiskom iazyke' Moscow, Gos. ped. Institut inostrannykh iazykov, *Uchenye zapiski* 2 [On the history of prepositions of place in English]

Rendall, T.
1974 'Bondage and Freeing from Bondage in Old English Religious Poetry' *JEGP* 73: 497-512

Renoir, A.
1957 '*Romigan ures rices:* A Reconsideration' *MLN* 72: 1-4

Rice, R.C.
1974-5 '*Hreowcearig* "penitent, contrite"' *ELN* 12: 243-50
1977 'The Penitential Motif in Cynewulf's *Fates of the Apostles* and in his Epilogues' *ASE* 6: 105-19

Rigby, M.
1962 '*The Seafarer, Beowulf* l. 769, and a Germanic Conceit' *N&Q* 207: 246

Riggers, B.
1958 *Das Volk der Angeln oder Sachsen: Ein Beitrag zur Lösung der Angelsachsenfrage* (Hamburg diss.)

Rissanen, M.
1967a *The Uses of* one *in Old and Early Middle English,* Mémoires de la

Société néophilologique de Helsinki 31 (Helsinki)
1967b 'Two Notes on Old English Poetic Texts' *NM* 68: 276-88
1967c 'Old English *þæt an* "only"' *NM* 68: 409-28
1969 'The Theme of "exile" in the *Wife's Lament*' *NM* 70: 90-104

Ritter, O.
1904 'Zur Herkunft von ne. *elk*' *Beibl* 15: 301-3
1905 'Zum ae. *gerefa*' *Archiv* 115: 163-5
1907 'Englische Etymologien' *Archiv* 119: 177-83
1909a 'Zum Vokalismus von altengl. *frio, freo* "frei"' *Archiv* 122: 98-9
1909b 'Zur Etymologie von altengl. *simbles* (*Archiv* CXIX, 180)' *Archiv* 122: 99
1910a *'Neorxnawang'* *Anglia* 33: 467-70
1910b 'Etymologieen' *Anglia* 33: 471-9
1910c 'Englische Etymologien' *Archiv* 125: 159-62
1911 'Noch einmal ae. *neorxnawang*' *Anglia* 34: 528
1920 'Beiträge zur englischen Wortkunde' *EStn* 54: 92-101
1922 *Vermischte Beiträge zur englischen Sprachgeschichte: Etymologie, Ortsnamenkunde, Lautlehre* (Halle)
1925 'Zum Vokalismus von ae. *tien, ten* "zehn"' *EStn* 59: 155-7
1927-8 'Beiträge zur altenglischen Wort- und Namenkunde' *EStn* 62: 106-12

Rittershaus, A.
1899 *Die Ausdrücke für Gesichtsempfindungen in den altgermanischen Dialekten: Ein Beitrag zur Bedeutungsgeschichte: Erster Teil*, Abhandlungen herausgegeben von der Gesellschaft für deutsche Sprache in Zürich (Zurich)

Robbins, S.W.
*1976 *Relative Clauses in Old English* (State University of New York, Stony Brook diss.; *DAI* 37: 4330A)

Roberts, J.
1970 'Traces of Unhistorical Gender Congruence in a Late Old English Manuscript' *ES* 51: 30-37
1978 'Towards an Old English Thesaurus' *Poetica* (Tokyo) 9: 56-72
1980 'Old English *un-* "very" and Unferth' *ES* 61: 289-92

Robins, J.D.
1927 *Color Words in English* (Chicago diss.)

Robinson, F.C.

1961 *Variation: A Study in the Diction of Beowulf* (North Carolina, Chapel Hill diss.; *DA* 22: 2798)

1962 'Notes on the Old English *Exodus' Anglia* 80: 363-78

1965a 'Old English Lexicographical Notes' *Philologica Pragensia* 8: 303-7

1965b 'Beowulf's Retreat from Frisia: Some Textual Problems in ll. 2361-62' *SP* 62: 1-16

1966a 'Notes and Emendations to Old English Poetic Texts' *NM* 67: 356-64

1966b '*Beowulf* 1917-19' *N&Q* 211: 407-8

1966c 'Two Non-Cruces in *Beowulf*' *TSL* 11: 151-60

1967 'European Clothing Names and the Etymology of *girl*' in W.W. Arndt, F.E. Coenen, P.W. Brosman, and W.P. Friederich, eds., *Studies in Historical Linguistics in Honor of George Sherman Lane,* University of North Carolina Studies in Germanic Languages and Literature 58 (Chapel Hill): 233-40

1968a 'The Significance of Names in Old English Literature' *Anglia* 86: 14-58

1968b 'The Royal Epithet *Engle leo* in the Old English *Durham* Poem' *MÆ* 37: 249-52

1968c 'Some Uses of Name-Meanings in Old English Poetry' *NM* 69: 161-71

1970a 'Personal Names in Medieval Narrative and the Name of Unferth in *Beowulf*' in H.H. Creed, ed., *Essays in Honor of Richeborg Galliard McWilliams* (Birmingham, Ala.) 43-8

1970b 'Lexicography and Literary Criticism: A Caveat' in *Meritt Festschrift:* 99-110

1973a 'Old English *awindan, of,* and *sinhere*' in *Koziol Festschrift:* 266-71

1973b 'Anglo-Saxon Onomastics in the Old English *Andreas' Names* 21: 133-6

1974 'Elements of the Marvelous in the Characterization of Beowulf: A Reconsideration of the Textual Evidence' in *Pope Festschrift:* 119-37

1975 'Artful Ambiguities in the Old English "Book-Moth" Riddle' in *McGalliard Festschrift:* 355-62

1976 'Some Aspects of the *Maldon* Poet's Artistry' *JEGP* 75: 25-40

1979 'Two Aspects of Variation in Old English Poetry' in D.G. Calder, ed., *Old English Poetry: Essays on Style* (Berkeley, Los Angeles, and London) 127-45

Roeder, F.

1899 *Die Familie bei den Angelsachsen: Eine kultur- und litterarhistorische Studie auf Grund gleichzeitiger Quellen,* SEP 4 (Halle)

1907a 'Die "Schoss-" oder "Kniesetzung": Eine angelsächsische Verlobungszeremonie' in *Nachrichten von der königlichen Gesellschaft der Wissen-*

schaften zu Göttingen, phil-hist. Klasse (Berlin): 300-14

1907b 'Der "Schatzwurf", ein Formalakt bei der angelsächsischen Verlobung' in *Nachrichten von der königlichen Gesellschaft der Wissenschaften zu Göttingen, phil-hist. Klasse* (Berlin): 373-83

1909 'Zur Deutung der angelsächsischen Glossierungen von *paranymphus* und *paranympha* (*pronuba*): Ein Beitrag zur Kenntnis des ags. Hochzeitsrituells' in *Nachrichten von der königlichen Gesellschaft der Wissenschaften zu Göttingen, phil-hist. Klasse* (Berlin): 14-41

Röhling, M.

1914 *Das Präfix* ofer- *in der altenglischen Verbal- und Nominal-Komposition mit Berücksichtigung der übrigen germanischen Dialekte* (Kiel diss.; Heidelberg)

Rogers, H.L.

1955 'Beowulf's Three Great Fights' *RES* n.s. 6: 339-55

Roper, A.H.

1962 'Boethius and the Three Fates of *Beowulf*' *PQ* 41: 386-400

Rosenberg, B.A.

1966 'The Meaning of *Æcerbot*' *Journal of American Folklore* 79: 428-36

Rosenthal, D.

1974 *Tod: Semantische, stilistische, und wortgeographische Untersuchungen auf Grund germanischer Evangelien- und Rechtstexte*, Göteborger germanistische Forschungen 12 (Göteborg)

Rosier, J.L.

1962 'Design for Treachery: The Unferth Intrigue' *PMLA* 77: 1-7
1963 'The Uses of Association: Hands and Feasts in *Beowulf*' *PMLA* 78: 8-14
1964a 'Ten Old English Psalter Glosses' *JEPG* 63: 1-6
1964b 'The Literal-Figurative Identity of the *Wanderer*' *PMLA* 79: 366-9
1965 'A Textual Ambiguity in *Beowulf: stod on stapole*' *MÆ* 34: 223-5
1966a 'God on the Warpath: *Genesis A* 2112' *Archiv* 202: 269-71
1966b 'Lexicographical Genealogy in Old English' *JEGP* 65: 295-302
1966c '*Icge gold* and *incge lafe* in *Beowulf*' *PMLA* 81: 342-6
1966d 'The *unhlitm* of Finn and Hengest' *RES* n.s. 17: 171-4
1968 '*Heafod* and *helm:* Contextual Composition in *Beowulf*' *MÆ* 37: 137-41
1970a 'Death and Transfiguration: *Guthlac B*' in *Meritt Festschrift:* 82-92
1970b '*Hrincg* in *Genesis A*' *Anglia* 88: 334-6

1974 'What Grendel Found: *heardran hæle*' *NM* 75: 40-49
*1977 'Generative Composition in *Beowulf*' *ES* 58: 193-203
1978a 'Four Old English Psalter Glosses' *Philologica Pragensia* 21: 44-5
1978b 'A Different Hyssop: Old English *hlenortear*' *Word* 29: 110-13

Ross, A.S.C.
1932a 'Old English *gebidæþ*' *MLN* 47: 377
1932b 'Notes on Some Words in the *Lindisfarne Gospels*' *MLR* 27: 451-3
*1932c 'The Errors in the Old English Gloss to the *Lindisfarne Gospels*'
    RES o.s. 8: 385-94
1932-3 'Notes on Some Old English Words' *EStn* 67: 344-9
1933a 'The Accusative and Dative of the Pronouns of the First and Second
    Persons in Germanic' *JEGP* 32: 481-2
1933b 'Notes on the Method of Glossing employed in the *Lindisfarne
    Gospels*' *TPS* (1931-2): 108-19
1934 'OE *weofod, wibed, wigbed*' *Leeds Studies* o.s. 3: 2-6
1936 'Sex and Gender in the *Lindisfarne Gospels*' *JEGP* 35: 321-30
1937 *Studies in the Accidence of the Lindisfarne Gospels*, Leeds School of
    English Language: Texts and Monographs 2 (Leeds)
1942 'Four Examples of Norse Influence in the Old English Gloss to the
    Lindisfarne Gospels' *TPS* (1940): 39-52
*1943 'Prolegomena to an Edition of the Old English Gloss to the *Lindisfarne
    Gospels*' *JEGP* 42: 309-21
1948-9 'Hengist's Watchword' *EGS* 2: 81-101
1949-50 'Miscellaneous Notes on *Cædmon's Hymn* and *Bede's Death Song*'
    EGS 3: 88-96
1957 'Aldrediana III: *sniueð*' *NM* 58: 144-7
1958 'On the "text" of the Anglo-Saxon Gloss to the *Lindisfarne Gospels*:
    Aldrediana VI' *Journal of Theological Studies* n.s. 9: 38-52
1959 *Aldrediana I: Three Suffixes*, Moderna Språk, Language Monographs
    3 (Stockholm): 1-28
1960a 'A Hitherto Unnoticed Anglo-Saxon Sound-Change: Aldrediana VIII'
    in W. Iser, and H. Schabram, eds., *Britannica: Festschrift für Hermann M.
    Flasdieck* (Heidelberg): 215-20
1960b 'Aldrediana XI: The *u*-orthographies' *SGG* 1: 115-59
1961a '*Bede's Death-Song* and *Rushworth 2*' *EGS* 7: 80
1961b 'Aldrediana XIV: *felle-read*' *NM* 62: 1-10
1961c 'Aldrediana II: Observations upon Certain Words of the Lindisfarne
    Gloss' *ZvS* 77: 258-95
1963 'Three Lexicographical Notes' *EPS* 8: 30-35
1965 '*Fox*' *EPS* 9: 1-46
1967 '*This* in the *Lindisfarne Gospels* and the *Durham Ritual*: Aldrediana

XVI' *N&Q* 212: 284-8

1968a 'Aldrediana XVII: *Ritual* Supplement' *EPS* 11: 1-43

1968b 'Aldrediana XX: Notes on the Preterite-Present Verbs' *EPS* 11: 44-50

1968c 'Aldrediana XV: On the Vowel of Nominal Composition' *NM* 69: 361-74

1968d '*You* in the North' *N&Q* 213: 323-4

1968e 'Notes on Some Words in the Anglo-Saxon Gloss to the *Durham Ritual:* Aldrediana IIA' *N&Q* 213: 405-7

1968f 'The Earliest Occurrence of *riding*' *N&Q* 213: 444

1969a '*Whilom*' *N&Q* 214: 47-8

1969b 'Aldrediana XIX: On Some Forms of the Anomalous and Contracted Verbs in the Anglo-Saxon Glosses to the *Lindisfarne Gospels* and the *Durham Ritual*' *TPS* (1968): 67-105

1970a 'Aldrediana XXI: The Correspondent of West Saxon *wunian*' *NM* 71: 529-33

1970b 'Conservatism in the Anglo-Saxon Gloss to the *Durham Ritual:* Aldrediana XXII' *N&Q* 215: 363-6

1971a 'Two Vestigial Distinctions in the Late North Northumbrian Dialect of Anglo-Saxon' *ArL* n.s. 2: 117-27

1971b 'Aldrediana XXIII: Notes on the Accidence of the *Durham Ritual*' *Leeds Studies* n.s. 5: 53-67

1972 'Notes on Some Further Words in the Anglo-Saxon Gloss to the *Durham Ritual:* Aldrediana IIB' *NM* 73: 372-80

1974 'Old English *secgan*' *N&Q* 219: 284

1975 'OE *leoht* "world"' *N&Q* 220: 196

*1976-7 'Notes on the Accidence of *Rushworth 1, 2*' *NM* 77 (1976) 492-509 / 78 (1977) 300-8

1977 'OE nap. *broðro*, etc.' *IF* (1976) 81: 180

*1978 'A Point of Comparison between Aldred's Two Glosses' *N&Q* 223: 197-9

*1979 'The Rare Words of *Rushworth 1*' *N&Q* 224: 495-8

1980 'The Correspondent of West Saxon *cweðan* in Late Northumbrian and *Rushworth 1*' *NM* 81: 24-33

*1981a 'Aldredian Comments on two Articles by the late Professor Flasdieck' *Anglia* 99: 390-93

*1981b 'The Use of Other Latin Manuscripts by the Glossators of the *Lindisfarne* and *Rushworth Gospels*' *N&Q* 226: 6-11

Ross, A.S.C. and Bailey, H.W.

1934 'Old English *afigen:* Ossete *fezonag, fizonag**' *Leeds Studies* o.s. 3: 7-9

Ross, A.S.C. and Britton, G.C.
1960 'Aldrediana X: Manifesta' *Anglia* 78: 129-68

Ross, A.S.C. and Thomson, R.L.
1979 'An early occurrence of *brooch*' *N&Q* 224: 498

Round, J.H.
1887 'Molmen and Molland' *EHR* 2: 103
1890 '*Gafol*' *EHR* 5: 523-4
1892 'The words *solinum* and *solanda*' *EHR* 7: 708-12

Rowan, H. and H., A.
1868 'Derivation of *England*' *N&Q* ser. 4, 1: 27, 112-13

Royster, J.F.
1908 'On Old English *leod*' *MLN* 23: 121-2
1918 'The Causative use of *hatan*' *JEGP* 17: 82-93
1922 'Old English Causative Verbs' *SP* 19: 328-56

Rubke, H.
1953 *Die Nominalkomposita bei Aelfric: Eine Studie zum Wortschatz
Aelfrics in seiner zeitlichen und dialektischen Gebundenheit* (Göttingen
diss.)

Rudolph, R.S.
1967 *The Old English Synonyms for* brave (Wisconsin diss.; *DA* 28: 658A)

Rüden, M. von
1978 Wlanc *und Derivate im Alt- und Mittelenglischen: Eine wortgeschichtliche Studie,* Europäische Hochschulschriften, Reihe 14: Angelsächsische
Sprache und Literatur 61 (Frankfurt, Bern, and Las Vegas)

Rushford, M.S.
1942 *A Phonological and Semasiological Comparison and Commentary on a
Select Religious Vocabulary in the Latin Text and Old English Version of
Bede's Ecclesiastical History of the English Nation* (Brooklyn, St. John's
University diss.)

Russom, G.R.
1978 'A Germanic Concept of Nobility in the *Gifts of Men* and *Beowulf*'
Speculum 53: 1-15

Ryan, W.M.
1969 'Word-Play in Some Old English Homilies and a Late Middle English Poem' in Atwood and Hill *Studies:* 265-78

Rypins, S.I.
1918 'Notes on Old English Lexicography' *MLN* 33: 440-41

Sachova, N.I.
−1965 *Smyslovoe razvitie imeni sushchestvitel'nogo* work *i glagola* to work *i obrazovannych ot ich osnov proizvodnych i slozhnych slov v angliiskom iazyke* (Moscow diss.)

Safarov, Sh.
−1976 'O nekotorykh leksiko-semanticheskikh gruppakh drevneangliiskikh glagolov' Samarkand, Gos. Universitet, *Trudy* n.s. 326: 133-42; *OEN* 12, 2: 37 [On certain lexical-semantic groups of OE verbs]

Sakai, T.
−1972 'Kiristo kyō no torai to OE no goi' *Kiristo Kyō Bunka Kenkyūsho Kenkyū Nenpō* 6, 3: 16-30 [Transmission of Christianity and OE vocabulary]

Salmon, V.
1959 'Some Connotations of *cold* in Old and Middle English' *MLN* 74: 314-22
1960 '*The Wanderer* and *The Seafarer* and the Old English Conception of the Soul' *MLR* 55: 1-10

Salus, P.H.
1963 'OE *eoletes*' *Lingua* 12: 429-30
1965 'OE *eoletes* Once More' *Lingua* 13: 451

Samuels, M.L.
1950 'The *ge*-Prefix in the Old English Gloss to the *Lindisfarne Gospels*' *TPS* (1949): 62-116

Sanderlin, G.
1938 'A Note on *Beowulf* 1142' *MLN* 53: 501-3

Sandred, K.I.
1966 'On the Terminology of the Plough in England' *SN* 38: 323-38
1971 'New Light on an Old English Landmark' *NB* 59: 37-9

Sarrazin, G.
1886 'Der Schauplatz des ersten Beowulfliedes und die Heimat des Dichters' *BGdSL* 11: 159-83
1897-1910 'Neue *Beowulf*-Studien' *EStn* 23 (1897): 221-67 / 35 (1905): 19-27 / 42 (1910): 1-24
1907 'Zur Chronologie und Verfasserfrage angelsächsischer Dichtungen'

EStn 38: 145-95
1913 *Von Kädmon bis Kynewulf: Eine litterarhistorische Studie* (Berlin)

Sasabe, H.
– 1964 'Kodai eishi ni okeru shiki no gainen' *Eibungaku Hyōron* (Kyoto) 15, 3: 1-23 [The four seasons in OE poetry]
– 1969 'OE *frēond* ni tsuite-imironteki' *Eibungaku Hyōron* (Kyoto) 24, 3: 1-14 [On OE *freond* – semantic discussion]

Scaffidi-Abbate, A.
1975 '*Stōd on stapole* e *stapul ǣren*' *AION-SG Filologia Germanica* 18: 143-58

Schaar, C.
1949 *Critical Studies in the Cynewulf Group*, LSE 17 (Lund and Copenhagen)
1962 '*Brondhord* in the Old English Rhyming Poem' *ES* 43: 490-91

Schabram, H.
1954 *Die Adjektive im Sinnbezirk von* kühn, mütig, tapfer *in der angelsächsischen Poesie (unter weitgehender Berücksichtigung der Prosa): Ein Beitrag zur ags. Wortbedeutungslehre* (Cologne diss.)
1956 'Zur Bedeutung von ae. *cēne*' *Anglia* 74: 181-7
1957 'Zur Bedeutung und Etymologie von ae. *rōf*' *Anglia* 75: 259-74
1958 'Ae. *þ(r)istra* "coniuncla"' *Anglia* 76: 411-21
1960 'Die Bedeutung von *gal* und *galscipe* in der ae. *Genesis B*' *BGdSL* 82: 265-74
1965a *Superbia: Studien zum altenglischen Wortschatz. Teil I, Die dialektale und zeitliche Verbreitung des Wortguts* (Munich)
1965b '*Andreas* und *Beowulf*: Parallelstellen als Zeugnis für literarische Abhängigkeit' *Nachrichten der Giessener Hochschulgesellschaft* 31: 201-18
1968a 'Ae. *beohata, Exodus* 253' in H.E. Brekle, and L. Lipka, eds., *Wortbildung, Syntax, und Morphologie: Festschrift zum 60. Geburtstag von Hans Marchand* Janua linguarum, series maior 36 (The Hague and Paris): 203-9
1968b 'Zu einer neuen Deutung von *Beowulf* 1011f.' *IF* 73 (1968-9): 143-5
1969 'Kritische Bemerkungen zu Angaben über die Verbreitung altenglischer Wörter' in *Mertner Festschrift*: 89-102
1970a 'Bemerkungen zu den ae. Nomina agentis auf *-estre* und *-icge*' *Anglia* 88: 94-8
1970b 'Etymologie und Kontextanalyse in der altenglischen Semantik' *ZvS* 84: 233-53

1973 'Das altenglische *superbia*-Wortgut: Eine Nachlese' in *Koziol Festschrift:* 272-9

1974 'Ae. *wlanc* und Ableitungen: Vorarbeiten zu einer wortgeschichtlichen Studie' in P.G. Buchloh, I. Leimberg, and H. Rauter, eds., *Studien zur englischen und amerikanischen Sprache und Literatur: Festschrift für Helmut Papajewski* (Neumünster): 70-88

1975 'Bezeichnungen für *Bauer* im Altenglischen,' in R. Wenskus, H. Jankuhn, and K. Grinda, eds., *Wort und Begriff* Bauer, Abhandlungen der Akademie der Wissenschaften in Göttingen, phil-hist. Klasse, III. Folge, Nr. 89 (Göttingen): 73-88

1979 'Stonc, *Beowulf* 2288' in R. Acobian, ed., *Festgabe für Hans Pinsker zum 70. Geburtstag* (Vienna): 144-56

1980 'Bezeichnungen für den Pflug und seine Teile im Altenglischen' in H. Beck, D. Denecke, and H. Jankuhn, eds., *Untersuchungen zur eisenzeitlichen und frühmittelalterlichen Flur in Mitteleuropa und ihrer Nutzung,* Teil 2, Abhandlungen der Akademie der Wissenschaften in Göttingen, phil-hist. Klasse, III. Folge, Nr. 116 (Göttingen): 99-125

Schaubert, E. von

1949 *Bedeutung und Herkunft von altenglischem* feormian *und seiner Sippe,* Hesperia: Ergänzungsreihe: Schriften zur englischen Philologie 13 (Göttingen and Baltimore)

Scheberle, J.W.

1957 'The Problem of *husl*' *University of Portland Review* 10, 1: 11-16

Scheinert, M.

1905 'Die Adjectiva im Beowulfepos als Darstellungsmittel' *BGdSL* 30: 345-430

Scheler, M.

*1961 *Altenglische Lehnsyntax: Die syntaktischen Latinismen im Altenglischen* (Berlin)

1972 'Zum Bedeutungswandel des englischen *to show* ("schauen > zeigen")' *Archiv* 209: 357-60

Scheller, M.

1959 *Vedisch* priyá- *und die Wortsippe* frei, freien, Freund: *Eine Bedeutungsgeschichtliche Studie,* Ergänzungshefte zur *Zeitschrift für vergleichende Sprachforschung* auf dem Gebiet der indogermanischen Sprachen 16 (Göttingen)

Schelp, H.
1956 *Der geistige Mensch im Wortschatz Alfreds des Grossen* (Göttingen diss.)

Schemann, K.
*1882 *Die Synonyma im Beówulfsliede mit Rücksicht auf Composition und Poetik des Gedichtes* (Münster diss.; Hagen)

Scherer, G.
1928 *Zur Geographie und Chronologie des angelsächsischen Wortschatzes, im Anschluss an Bischof Waerferth's Übersetzung der Dialoge Gregors* (Berlin diss.; Leipzig)

Schik, B.
1971 *Das Problem der 'Gefolgschaft' im Beowulf* (Kiel diss.)

Schilling, H.
1886 *König Ælfred's angelsächsische Bearbeitung der Weltgeschichte des Orosius* (Halle)
1887 'The Finnsburg-Fragment and the Finn-Episode' *MLN* 2: 146-50

Schleif, M.
1962 *Studies in the Vocabulary of the Old English Benedictine Rule* (Berlin Staatsexamensarbeit)

Schlenk, K.F.
1950 *Studien zum Gebrauch von* dream *in der angelsächsischen Poesie* (Marburg diss.)

Schlepper, E.
*1936 *Die Neubildung von Substantiven in den Übersetzungen König Alfreds mit einem Ausblick auf Chaucer* (Münster diss.; Gütersloh)

Schlepper, W.E.W.H.
1971 Pity und Piety: *Eine Wortgeschichte* (Bonn diss.)

Schlutter, O.B.
1896a 'Notes: Stray Gleanings' *AJP* 17: 84-8
1896b 'Notes on Hall's *Concise Anglo-Saxon Dictionary'* *MLN* 11: 161-8, 204-10, 256.
1897-8a 'Zu Sweet's *Oldest English Texts' Anglia* 19 (1897): 101-16, 461-98 / 20 (1898): 136-8, 381-96

1897-8b 'On Old English Glosses' *JGP* 1 (1897): 59-65, 312-33 / 2 (1898): 31-2

1898 'Contributions to Old-English Lexicography' *MLN* 13: 147-52

1899 'The OE *āgniden*' *MLN* 14: 196

1899-1902 'Anglo-Saxon Glosses' *MLN* 14 (1899): 159-60 / 17 (1902): 61-2

1900 'Some Celtic Traces in the Glosses' *AJP* 21: 188-92

1901 'Zur Steuer der Wahrheit' *Anglia* 24: 525-32

1903a 'Zu den altenglischen Denkmälern: Eine zweite Abwehr und Richtig-stellung' *Anglia* 26: 286-312

1903b 'Other Doubtful Words in Sweet's *Dictionary of Anglo Saxon*' *MLN* 18: 41-2

1903-5 'On the Old English Glosses Printed in Kluge's *Angelsächsisches Lesebuch*' *JEGP* 5: 139-52, 464-75

1906-10 'Anglo-Saxonica' *Anglia* 30 (1907): 123-34, 239-60, 394-400 / 31 (1908): 55-71, 135-40, 521-42 / 32 (1909): 503-14 / 33 (1910): 137-42, 239-51, 532; *MLN* 21 (1906): 236-8 / 22 (1907): 160 [correction of previous]

1907 'Zum Wortschatz des *Regius* und *Eadwine Psalters*' *EStn* 38: 1-27 / 39: 157-8 [correction]

1907-11 'Beiträge zur altenglischen Wortforschung' *EStn* 37 (1907): 177-87 / 42 (1910): 161-204 / 43 (1910-11): 305-39

1908a 'Gildas, *Libellus querulus de excidio Britannorum* as a Source of Glosses in the Cottoniensis (Cleopatra A III = W.W. 338-473) and in the Corpus Glossary' *AJP* 29: 432-48

1908b 'Review of Napier, *Contributions to Old English Lexicography*' *EStn* 38: 288-97

*1909 'Zum Wortschatz des *Eadwine*- und *Regius-Psalters*' *EStn* 40: 299-306. See Wildhagen's reply, *EStn* 40: 306-99

1910a 'Zu *Anglia Beiblatt* XXI, Nr. 5, S. 155-6' *Beibl* 21: 317-19

1910b 'Zum Wortschatz des *Eadwine Psalters*' *EStn* 41: 163-6

1910c 'Ae. *hyrþ* "pellis" = *bōcfell*' *EStn* 41: 323-8

1910d 'Ae. *lēwesa* "inopia"' *EStn* 41: 328-31

1910e 'Ae. *gamolian* "altern"' *EStn* 41: 454-5

1910f '*Werd* "rubeum"; *word* "consanguinitas"; *færbēna* "passenger"; **fennbēna* "worker of a fen-claim"' *EStn* 42: 146-53

1910g 'Ghost-Words' *MLN* 25: 80-81

1912a 'Zum Epinalglossar' *Anglia* 35: 137-41, 426-7

1912b 'Zur Frage des keltischen Ursprungs von ae. *gafol*' *Anglia* 36: 377-82

*1912c 'Zu den Trier Glossen' *Anglia* 36: 381

1912-13 'Zur altenglischen Wortkunde' *EStn* 44 (1912): 460-71 / 46 (1912-13): 156-63

1912-28 'Weitere Beiträge zur altenglischen Wortforschung' *Anglia* 36

(1912): 59-78 / 36 (1913): 41-53 / 38 (1914): 250, 512-16 / 40 (1916): 343-57, 505-7 / 42 (1918): 357-9, 451-6 / 43 (1919): 98-100, 195-6 / 44 (1920): 94-6, 291-6 / 45 (1921): 187-99 / 46 (1922): 143-71, 206-31, 286-8, 323-43 / 47 (1923): 34-52, 244-63, 287-8, 383-4 / 48 (1924): 101-4, 375-92 / 49 (1926): 92-6, 183-92, 376-83 / 51 (1927): 156-63 / 52 (1928): 83-7, 183-91; *EStn* 49 (1915-16): 156-7

1916 'Ae. *scinn* = ne. *shin* = nhd. *Schinne' Anglia* 40: 260-62

1919a 'Some Very Pertinent Remarks on Toller's *Supplement* to Bosworth-Toller's *Anglo-Saxon Dictionary' JEGP* 18: 137-43

1919b 'Old English Lexical Notes' *MLN* 34: 119-20

1920a 'Is There Sufficient Evidence to Warrant the Authenticity of OE *treppan* "to trap"?' *Neophil* 5: 351-2

1920b 'OE (Northumbrian *óht-ríp:* OHG *āhtsnit* "messis dominica"' *Neophil* 5: 352-4

1921a 'Additional Remarks on OE *scǽnan* = Modern English *sheen' Neophil* 6: 235-6

1921b 'OE *cléat* = Modern English *cleat;* OE *(ge)stéapan* = Modern English *to steep' Neophil* 6: 236-7

1921c 'OE *héolca* "pruina": ON *héla* "pruina"' *Neophil* 6: 237

1921d 'Traces of the Masculine Gender of OE *eorþe;* OE **bæsn, bysn* "fermentum"' *Neophil* 6: 237-40

1922a 'Zur Rechtfertigung meiner Stellung zu Holthausen' *Anglia* 46: 202-5

1922b 'OE *sárcréne* "so tender and sore to the touch as to make you cry with pain"' *Neophil* 7: 211-12

1922c 'Another Instance of OE *syla* "ploughman"' *Neophil* 7: 212-14

1922d 'OE *fótsetl* "a footstool"' *Neophil* 7: 214

1922e 'OE *stáncæstil* "acervus lapidum"' *Neophil* 7: 215

1922f 'OE *swínlic* "porcinus"' *Neophil* 7: 215

1922g 'OE *tíh* = MLG *tî* = OHG *zîch' Neophil* 7: 215-16

1923a 'OE *pillsápe* "soap for removing hair"' *Neophil* 8: 204-5

1923b 'Is There any Evidence for OE *weargincel* "butcher-bird"?' *Neophil* 8: 206-8

1923c 'Is There any Real Evidence for an Alleged OE *wyhtel* "quail"?' *Neophil* 8: 303-4

1924 'Some Further Remarks on Toller's *Supplement* to B-T' *Neophil* 9: 194-9

1927a 'Is There an OE Plant-Name *twínihte*?' *Neophil* 12: 117-18

1927b 'OE (Anglian) *gégan* "arsare" = ON *geya* "bellen, ausschelten"' *Neophil* 12: 118-19

1930a 'Is There any Evidence on Wich [sic] to Base the Assumption that OE *hólinga* is Equivalent in Meaning with *dearnunga* or *geresta* with *láf*?' *Neophil* 15: 262-3

1930b 'Further Remarks on Toller's *Supplement* to Bosworth-Toller' *Neophil* 15: 271-4

Schmidt, G.
1970 'Zum Problem der germanischen Dekadenbildungen' *ZvS* 84: 98-136

Schmoock, P.
1965 *Patientia: Die Terminologie des Duldens in der Leid-Synonymik der altenglischen und altsächsischen Epik: Semasiologische Studien zum Christianisierungsprozess des germanischen Wortschatzes* (Kiel diss.)
1976 '*Patientia*: Zum Christianisierungsprozess des Wortschatzes der altenglischen und altsächsischen Epik' in F. Debus and J. Hartig, eds., *Festschrift für Gerhard Cordes zum 65. Geburtstag* (Neumunster): II, 322-53

Schneider, C.
1978 'Cynewulf's Devaluation of Heroic Tradition in *Juliana*' *ASE* 7: 107-18

Schneider, K.
1959 'Zu den Inschriften und Bildern des Franks Casket und einer ae. Version des Mythos von Balders Tod' in H. Oppel, intro., *Festschrift für Walter Fischer* (Heidelberg): 4-20
1969a 'Runische Inschriftzeugnisse zum Stieropferkult der Angelsachsen' in *Mertner Festschrift:* 9-54
1969b 'Zu den ae. Zaubersprüchen *wið wennum* und *wið wæterælfadle*' *Anglia* 87: 282-302
1975 'Zu vier ae. Rätseln' in H. Beckers and H. Schwarz, eds., *Gedenkschrift für Jost Trier* (Cologne and Vienna): 330-54

Schneider, R.
1913 *Satzbau und Wortschatz der altenglischen Rätsel des Exeterbuches: Ein Beitrag zur Lösung der Verfasserfrage* (Breslau diss.)

Schnepper, H.
1908 *Die Namen der Schiffe und Schiffsteile im Altenglischen: Eine kulturgeschichtlich-etymologische Untersuchung* (Kiel diss.)

Schöffler, H.
1938 'Zur Kultursoziologie des englischen ablautenden Verbums' *Anglia* 62: 14-23

Schön, E.
* 1905 *Die Bildung des Adjektivs im Altenglischen,* Kieler Studien zur englischen Philologie, N.F. 2 (Kiel)

Schon, C.V. von
1977 *The Origin of Phrasal Verbs in English* (State University of New York, Stony Brook diss.; *DAI* 38: 1365A)

Schrader, A.
1880 *Das altenglische Relativpronomen mit besonderer Berücksichtigung der Sprache Chaucer's* (Kiel diss.)

Schrader, B.
1887 *Studien zur Ælfricschen Syntax: Ein Beitrag zur altenglischen Grammatik* (Göttingen diss.; Jena)

Schrader, W.
1914 For- *und* fore- *Verbalkomposita im Verlaufe der englischen Sprachgeschichte* (Greifswald diss.)

Schreuder, H.
1929 *Pejorative Sense Development in English* (Groningen diss.)

Schröder, E.
1891 'Belisars Ross' *ZfdA* 35: 237-44
1918 'Studien zu den deutschen Münznamen' *ZvS* 48: 141-50, 241-75
1922 'Die Nomina agentis auf -ster' *Niederdeutsches Jahrbuch* 48 (Norden and Leipzig): 1-8
1933 '*Wang* und -*wangen*' *Namn och Bygd* 21: 148-61

Schröder, F.R.
1951 'Erce und Fjǫrgyn?' in *Erbe der Vergangenheit: Germanistische Beiträge. Festgabe für Karl Helm zum 80. Geburtstage, 19. Mai 1951* (Tübingen): 25-36

Schröer, A.
1891 'Zur Texterklärung des *Beowulf*' *Anglia* 13: 333-48

Schubel, F.
1953 'Zur Bedeutungskunde altenglischer Wörter mit christlichem Sinngehalt' *Archiv* 189: 289-303
1961 'Die Bedeutungsnuancen von *bealu* in *Christ I-III*' in H. Viebrock and

W. Erzgräber, eds., *Festschrift zum 75. Geburtstag von Theodor Spira* (Heidelberg): 328-34

Schuchardt, R.
1910 *Die Negation im Beowulf* (Berlin diss.)

Schücking, L.L.
1906 'Das angelsächsische Gedicht von der *Klage der Frau' ZfdA* 48: 436-49
1912 'Altengl. *scepen* und die sogen. idg. Vokativreste im Altengl.' *EStn* 44: 155-7
1915 *Untersuchungen zur Bedeutungslehre der angelsächsischen Dichtersprache,* Germanische Bibliothek Abt. 2, Bd. 11 (Heidelberg)
1917 'Wann Entstand der *Beowulf?* Glossen, Zweifel, und Fragen' *BGdSL* 42: 347-410
1919-20 '*Wiðergyld* (*Beowulf* 2051)' *EStn* 53: 468-70
1922 'Ags. *scriðan' EStn* 56: 171-2
1923 'Die Beowulfdatierung: Eine Replik' *BGdSL* 47: 293-311
1929 '*Sōna* im *Beowulf'* in *Britannica: Max Förster zum sechzigsten Geburtstage* (Leipzig): 85-8
1933 *Heldenstolz und Würde im Angelsächsischen mit einem Anhang: Zur Charakterisierungstechnik im Beowulfepos,* Abhandlungen der phil.-hist. Klasse der sächsischen Akademie der Wissenschaften 42, Nr. 5 (Leipzig)

Schultze, A.
1941 *Das Eherecht in den älteren angelsächsischen Königsgesetzen* (Leipzig)

Schulze, F.W.
1969 'Die altenglische *Klage der Frau'* in *Mertner Festschrift:* 65-88

Schulze, W.
1918 'Ags. *húmeta' ZvS* 48: 136
1921 'Nordhumbrisch *speoft* und *beoftun' Archiv* 141: 176-80
1933 'Zur Blattfüllung: Ags. *nænigra* (*nánra*) *þinga' ZvS* 60: 144

Schwab, U.
1971 '**sibjō* nella più antica tradizione germanica' *Studi medievali,* ser. 3, 12 (Spoloto): 355-81
1972 '*Ær-æfter,* das *Memento mori* Bedas als christliche Kontrafaktur: Eine philologische Interpretation' in *Studi di letteratura religiosa tedesca in memoria di Sergio Lupi* (Florence): 5-134
1973-4 'Eva reicht den Todesbecher: Zur Trinkmetaphorik in altenglischen Darstellungen des Sündenfalles' *Atti dell'Accademia Peloritana* 51: 7-108

1978 'Huld und Huldverlust in der as.-ags. *Genesis*' in *Scritti in onore di Salvatore Pugliatti*, Scritti vari 5 (Messina): 961-1003

Schwabe, H.O.
1917-18 'Etymological Notes' *MLN* 32 (1917): 222-5 / 33 (1918): 85-9

Schwammberger, E.
1945 *Die Entwicklung der altenglischen Verben* beodan *und* biddan *zu neuenglisch* to bid: *Eine lautliche, syntaktische, und semantische Untersuchung* (Zurich diss.)

Schwentner, E.
1920 'Ags. *óleccan* "schmeicheln"' *BGdSL* 44: 500-1
1921 'Zur Wortsippe *dunkel* im Germanischen' *BGdSL* 45: 452-9
1923a 'Die Schallwurzel *hwĭs* im Germanischen und in den verwandten Sprachen' *BGdSL* 48: 73-9
1923b 'Germ. *hraþa, hurska, hrussa* und Verwandtes' *BGdSL* 48: 79-85
1934 'Ags. *stódla* = ahd. *stuodal*?' *BGdSL* 58: 290-93
1938a 'Vogelnamen' *BGdSL* 62: 30-33
1938b 'Ahd. *vitibeiten* "sulcare"' *BGdSL* 62: 419-20
1939 'Alts. *dref*, ags. *drep, dreb*' *ZvS* 66: 128-9
1940 'Ags. *wuduccoc*, altind. *vanakukkuta*' *IF* 57: 142
1943 'Ae. *hlōse*, ne. *looze* "Schweinestall"' *Archiv* 183: 122
1948 'Ags. *ent, entisc*, aksl. *ispolinz, spolinz*' *ZvS* 69: 128
1952a 'Aengl. *hrycigan* "resulcare" und Verwandtes' *ZvS* 70: 207-8
1952b 'Ags. *earsling*, ahd. *arselingûn*, mhd. *ersling(en)*, nhd. *ärschling(s)*, *ärschlich* und Verwandtes' *ZvS* 70: 228-37
1954 'Die Bezeichnungen für *venter, uterus, ventriculus, alvus, vulva, stomachus* im Altgermanischen' *IF* 61: 228-39
1955 'Lat. *petilus (petulus)*, ags. *fitel-*, alts. *fitil-*, ahd. *fizzil-*' *ZvS* 72: 235-41

Scragg, D.G.
1966 'Old English *bryt* in the Vercelli Book' *N&Q* 211: 168-9
1970 *The Language of the Vercelli Homilies* (Manchester diss.; ASLIB *Index* 20: 317
1977 'Old English *forhtleasness, unforhtleasness*' *N&Q* 222: 399-400

Sedgefield, W.J.
1921 'Suggested Emendations in Old English Poetical Texts' *MLR* 16: 59-61
1923-31 'Old English Notes' *MLR* 18 (1923): 471-2 / 26 (1931): 74-5
1933 'Further Emendations of the *Beowulf* Text' *MLR* 28: 226-30

Seebohm, F.
1890 *The English Village Community*, 4th ed. (London)
1902 *Tribal Custom in Anglo-Saxon Law* (London)

Seebold, E.
1966 'Die Geminata bei gm. *kann, ann* und anderen starken Verben' *ZvS* 80: 273-83
1968 'Ae. *twegen* und ahd. *zwēne* "zwei"' *Anglia* 86: 417-36
1971 'Das germanische Wort für den Heiden' *BGdSL* 93: 29-45
1973 'Die Stammbildungen der idg. Wurzel **u̯eid-* und deren Bedeutungen (2. Teil)' *Sprache* 19: 158-79
1974 'Die ae. Entsprechungen von lat. *sapiens* und *prudens:* Eine Untersuchung über die mundartliche Gliederung der ae. Literatur' *Anglia* 92: 291-333

Seelig, F.
1930 *Die Komparation der Adjektiva und Adverbien im Altenglischen*, AF 70 (Heidelberg diss.)

Segawa, S.
−1968 'Kodai eishi *Beowulf* no kōzō to sono ito' *Tōyō Daigaku Daigakuin Kiyō* 5, 3: 59-72 [The structure of *Beowulf* and its meaning]

Sehrt, E.H.
1950 'Altsächsisch *skîmo*' *MLN* 65: 89-92

Serjeantson, M.S.
1935 *A History of Foreign Words in English* (London)
1936 'The Vocabulary of Folklore in Old and Middle English' *Folk-lore* 47: 42-73

Severynse, M.
1980 *Three Old English Verbs of 'Turning': A Semantic Study of* wendan, cierran, *and* hweorfan (Harvard diss.)

Sheard, J.A.
1954 *The Words We Use* (London; repr. as *The Words of English* [New York 1966])

Shearin, H.G.
1903 *The Expression of Purpose in Old English Prose*, YSE 18 (Yale diss.; New York)

1909 'The Expression of Purpose in Old English Poetry' *Anglia* 32: 235-52

Shetelig, H. and Falk, H.
1937 *Scandinavian Archaeology*, tr. E.V. Gordon (Oxford)

Shimose, M.
1978 [A Variety of Expressions of 'Death' in *Beowulf* — Chiefly on Their Figurative Use] *Kumamoto Tandai Ronshū* 59, 9: 25-50

Shippey, T.A.
1972 *Old English Verse* (London)

Shook, L.K.
1939 *Ælfric's Latin Grammar: A Study in Old-English Grammatical Terminology* (Harvard diss.)
1940 'A Technical Construction in Old English: Translation Loans in -*lic*' *MS* 2: 253-7
1960-61 'The Burial Mound in *Guthlac A*' *MP* 58: 1-10
1965 'Old English *Riddle* No. 20: *heoruswealwe*' in *Magoun Festschrift:* 194-204

Shores, D.L.
1970 '*The Peterborough Chronicle:* Continuity and Change in the English Language' *South Atlantic Bulletin* 35, 4: 19-29
1974 'Old English *ge-*' *AS* 49: 281-3

Short, D.D.
1973-4 'The Old English *Gifts of Men*, line 13' *MP* 71: 388-9
1975 '*Leoðocraeftas* and the Pauline Analogy of the Body in the Old English *Gifts of Men*' *Neophil* 59: 463-5

Shteinberg, N.A.
— 1969a 'O drevneangliiskoi glagol'noi konstruktsii *waes* + prichastie I' *Voprosy struktury angliiskogo iazyka v sinkhronii i diakhronii* 2: 112-18 [On the OE verb construction *wæs* + participle I]
— 1969b 'O drevneangliiskoi glagol'noi konstrukstii *waes* + prichastie II' *Voprosy struktury angliiskogo iazyka v sinkhronii i diakhronii* 2: 119-24 [On the OE verb construction *wæs* + participle II]
1971 'K probleme glagol'noi prefiksatsii v drevneangliiskom iazyke' *Issledovaniia po angliiskoi filologii* 4: 59-65 [On the problem of verbal prefixation in OE]

Shuman, R. and Hutchings, N.
1959-60 'The *un*-Prefix: A Means of Germanic Irony in *Beowulf'* MP 57:
217-22

Sicardi, G. Petracco
1974 '*Sunberga:* Nota di etimologia germanica' *StG* (Roma) 12: 215-28

Siemerling, O.
1909 *Das Präfix* for(e)- *in der altenglischen Verbal- und Nominalkomposition*
(Kiel diss.)

Sievers, E.
1886 'Die Heimat des Beowulfdichters' *BGdSL* 11: 354-62
1887 'Altnordisches im *Beowulf?' BGdSL* 12: 168-200
1891 'Zu den angelsächsischen Glossen' *Anglia* 13: 309-32
1892 'Zur Texterklärung des *Beowulf' Anglia* 14: 133-46
1895 'Wie man Conjecturen macht' *BGdSL* 20: 553
1897 'Grammatische Miscellen' *BGdSL* 22: 255-6
1899 'Ags. *hnesce' BGdSL* 24: 383
1901 'Northumbrisch *blefla?' BGdSL* 26: 557
1903a 'Angelsächsisch *unna'* in *Album-Kern* (Leiden): 127-9
1903b 'Zu den angelsächsischen Diphthongen' *IF* 14: 32-9
1903-4 'Zum *Beowulf' BGdSL* 28 (1903): 271-2 / 29 (1904): 305-31, 560-
76
1909 'Angelsächsisch *wērig* "verflucht"' *IF* 26: 225-35
1909-26 'Ags. *hlæfdige' BGdSL* 34 (1909): 576-9 / 50 (1926): 16-17
1912a 'Ags. *scepen' EStn* 44: 295-6
1912b '*Beowulf* 1174' *EStn* 44: 296-7
1914-15 'Ags. *géagl' IF* 34: 337-8
1925 '*Theodoice snad' BGdSL* 49: 434-40

Sihler, A.L.
1981 'Early English Feminine Agent Nouns in -*ild:* A PIE Relic' *Sprache* 27:
35-42

Silber, P.
1977 'Gold and its Significance in *Beowulf' AM* 18: 5-19

Simpson, J.
1955-6 'A Note on the Word *friðstóll' SBVS* 14: 200-10

Singer, C.
1919-20 'Early English Magic and Medicine' *PBA* 9: 341-74

Singer, S.
1887 'Miscellen' *BGdSL* 12: 211-15

Singer, S.W.
1850a 'Ælfric's *Colloquy*' *N&Q* ser. 1, 1: 197-8, 248, 278
1850b 'What is the Meaning of *lærig*?' *N&Q* ser. 1, 1: 292-3, 387, 460, 463
1850c 'The Anglo-Saxon Word *unlæd*' *N&Q* ser. 1, 1: 430-32

Sisam, K.
1946 'Notes on Old English Poetry' *RES* o.s. 22: 257-68
1951 '*Genesis B*, lines 273-4' *RES* n.s. 2: 371-2
1953 *Studies in the History of Old English Literature* (Oxford)
1958 'Beowulf's Fight with the Dragon' *RES* n.s. 9: 129-40
1962 'OE *stefn, stefna* "stem"' *RES* n.s. 13: 282-3

Sizova, I.A.
1976 'Iz istorii glagol'noi prefiksatsii v angliiskom iazyke' in M.P. Alekseev, ed., *Teoriia iazyka, Anglistika, Kel'tologiia*, AN SSSR Institut iazykoznaniia (Moscow): 204-14 [One aspect of the history of verbal prefixes in English]

Skeat, W.W.
1872 'The Verb *to wit*' *Athenaeum* 2351: 634-5
1883 'Anglo-Saxon Numerals' *N&Q* ser. 6, 7: 365
1895 'English Words Borrowed from French before the Conquest' *Academy* 48: 252
1896 'Anglo-Saxon Plant-Names' *N&Q* ser. 8, 9: 163-4
1898 'Through-Stone' *N&Q* ser. 9, 1: 9-10

Skemp, A.R.
1911 'The Old English Charms' *MLR* 6: 289-301

Sklute, L.M.
1970 '*Freoðuwebbe* in Old English Poetry' *NM* 71:534-41

Slez, I.S.
— 1958 *Razvitie glagolov 'govoreniia' v angliiskom iazyke (VIII-XVII vv)* (Lvov, Universitet diss.) [The development of the 'speaking' verbs in English (VIII-XVII centuries)]

— 1965 'O smyslovykh i sintaksicheskikh sviaziakh odnoi gruppy glagolov (Na materiale drevneangliiskogo iazyka)' Tbilis, Ped. Institut inostrannykh iazykakh, *Trudy* 7: 103-51 [On the semantic and syntactic relationships of one group of verbs (based on OE)]

Small, G.W.
1924 *The Comparison of Inequality: The Semantics and Syntax of the Comparative Particle in English* (Johns Hopkins diss.; Greifswald)
1926 'The Syntax of *the* with the Comparative' *MLN* 41: 300-13
1929 *The Germanic Case of Comparison with a Special Study of English,* Language Monographs 4 (Philadelphia)
1930 'The Syntax of *the,* and OE *þon mā þe' PMLA* 45: 368-91

Smirke, E.
1848 'On Certain Obscure Words in Charters, Rentals, Accounts, etc., of Property in the West of England' *Archaeological Journal* 5: 20-24, 118-23, 164-9, 273-9

Smirnitskaia, O.A.
*1980 'Sinonimicheskie sistemy v *Beovul'fe' Vestnik Moskovskogo Universiteta* ser. 9, filologiia 5: 44-57 [Synonymic systems in *Beowulf*]

Smirnitskii, A.I.
*1955 *Drevneangliiskii iazyk* (Moscow) [The OE language]

Smith, A.H.
1959 'Two Notes on Some West Yorkshire Place-Names' in P. Clemoes, ed., *The Anglo-Saxons: Studies in Some Aspects of their History and Culture Presented to Bruce Dickins* (London): 311-15

Smith, G.G.
— 1931 *Recurring First Elements of Anglo-Saxon Nominal Compounds: A Study in Poetic Style* (Harvard diss.)

Smith, H.L.
1938 'Some Germanic Developments of IE **ǧeneu* and *ǧen-, **ǧenē' Language* 14: 95-103

Smithers, G.V.
1951-2 'Five Notes on Old English Texts' *EGS* 4: 65-85
1954 'Some English Ideophones' *ArL* o.s. 6: 73-111
1957-9 'The Meaning of the *Seafarer* and the *Wanderer' MÆ* 26 (1957):

137-53 / 28 (1959): 1-22, 99-104

1966 'Four Cruxes in *Beowulf*' in M. Brahmer, S. Helsztynski, and J. Krzyanowski, eds., *Studies in Language and Literature in Honour of M. Schlauch* (Warsaw): 413-30

1970 'Destiny and the Heroic Warrior in *Beowulf*'in *Meritt Festschrift:* 65-81

Snyder, W.H.
1971 'Zur Gemination in der dritten Ablautsreihe der starken Verben' *ZvS* 85: 70-84

Soeda, Y.
−1970 'Imagery of "Surging Water" in *Beowulf*' *Nagaski Daigaku Kyōikugakubu Jinbun Kagaku Kenkyū Hōkoku* 19, 3: 13-18

Sokolova, M.N.
1973 'Signification des termes *ham* et *tun* dans les documents anglo-saxons' *Cahiers de civilization médiévale* 16: 123-32

Soland, M.
1979 *Altenglische Ausdrücke für* Leib *und* Seele: *Eine semantische Analyse* (Zurich)

Solo, H.J.
1977 'The Meaning of **motan:* A Secondary Denotation of Necessity in Old English?' *NM* 78: 215-32

Sonnefeld, G.
*1892 *Stilistisches und Wortschatz im Béowulf: Ein Beitrag zur Kritik des Epos* (Strassburg diss.; Würzburg)

Spamer, J.B.
1978 'The Old English Bee Charm: An Explication' *Journal of Indo-European Studies* 6: 279-91

1979 'The Development of the Definite Article in English: A Case Study of Syntactic Change' *Glossa* 13: 241-50

Specht, F.
1935 'Ags. *scrúd*' *ZvS* 62: 242-3

Speyer, J.S.
1908 '*Blond*' *TNTL* 27: 1-9

Spinner, K.

1924 *Die Ausdrücke für Sinnesempfindungen in der angelsächsischen Poesie verglichen mit den Bezeichnungen für Sinnesempfindungen in der altnordischen, altsächsischen, und althochdeutschen Dichtung* (Halle diss.)

Splitter, H.W.

1948 'Note on a *Beowulf* Passage' *MLN* 63: 118-21

1952 'The Relation of Germanic Folk Custom and Ritual to *ealuscerwen* (*Beowulf* 769)' *MLN* 67: 255-8

Spolsky, E.

1974 'The Semantic Structure of the *Wanderer*' *Journal of Literary Semantics* 3: 101-19

1977 'Old English Kinship Terms and *Beowulf*' *NM* 78: 233-8

Sprengel, K.

1977 *A Study in Word-Formation: The English Verbal Prefixes* fore- *and* pre- *and their German Counterparts,* Tübingen Beiträge zur Linguistik 89 (Tübingen)

Sprockel, C.

1973 *The Language of the Parker Chronicle,* II: *Word-Formation and Syntax* (The Hague)

Standop, E.

1957 *Syntax und Semantik der modalen Hilfsverben im Altenglischen:* magan, motan, sculan, willan, Beiträge zur englischen Philologie 38 (Bochum-Langendreer; repr. London and New York 1968)

Stanley, E.G.

1956 'Old English Poetic Diction and the Interpretation of the *Wanderer,* the *Seafarer,* and the *Penitent's Prayer*' *Anglia* 73: 413-66

1957 'Some Notes on the *Owl and the Nightingale*' *EGS* 6: 30-63

1963a '*Hæthenra hyht* in *Beowulf*' in *Brodeur Festschrift:* 136-51

1963b '*Weal* in the Old English *Ruin:* A Parallel?' *N&Q* 208: 405

1964-5 'The Search for Anglo-Saxon Paganism' *N&Q* 209 (1964): 204-9, 242-50, 282-7, 324-31, 455-63 / 210 (1965): 9-17, 203-7, 285-93, 322-7; also publ. as monograph (Totowa, N.J. 1975)

1969a 'Old English -*calla, ceallian*' in D.A. Pearsall and R.A. Waldron, eds., *Medieval Literature and Civilization: Studies in Memory of G.N. Garmonsway* (London): 94-9

*1969b 'Spellings of the *waldend* Group' in Atwood and Hill *Studies:* 38-69

1971 'Studies in the Prosaic Vocabulary of Old English Verse' *NM* 72: 385-418

1974 'The Oldest English Poetry now Extant' *Poetica* 2: 1-24

1976 'Did Beowulf Commit *feaxfeng* against Grendel's Mother?' *N&Q* 221: 339-40

1977a *'Corona* in Old English' *N&Q* 222: 97-8

1977b '"Work" and "Exertion" in Old English' *N&Q* 222: 481

1978 *'Sum heard gewrinc (Genesis B* 317)' *N&Q* 223: 104-5

1979 'Two Old English Poetic Phrases Insufficiently Understood for Literary Criticism: *þing gehegan* and *seonoþ gehegan'* in D.G. Calder, ed., *Old English Poetry: Essays on Style* (Berkeley, Los Angeles, and London): 67-90

1981 'The Scholarly Recovery of the Significance of Anglo-Saxon Records in Prose and Verse: A New Bibliography' *ASE* 9: 223-62

Stanley, J.P. and McGowan, C.

1979 *'Woman* and *wife:* Social and Semantic Shifts in English' *Papers in Linguistics* 12: 491-502

Stapelkamp, C.

1947 'Oude Engelse Plantnamen' *ES* 28: 111-14

Štech, S.

1969 'A Few Remarks on the Etymology of OE *ædre* "vein"' *Brno Studies in English* 8: 179-81

Stenton, F.M.

1910 'Types of Manorial Structure in the Northern Danelaw' in P. Vino-gradoff, ed., *Oxford Studies in Social and Legal History,* vol. II (Oxford): 3-96

1927 'The Danes in England' *PBA* 13: 203-46; repr. in *Stenton Collected Papers:* 136-65

1932 *The First Century of English Feudalism 1066-1166* (Oxford; 2nd ed. 1961)

1936 'The Road System of Medieval England' *Economic Historical Review* 7: 1-21; repr. in *Stenton Collected Papers:* 234-52

1943a *Anglo-Saxon England* (Oxford)

1943b 'The Historical Bearing of Place-Name Studies: The Place of Women in Anglo-Saxon Society' *Transactions of the Royal Historical Society,* 4th ser., 25: 1-13; repr. in *Stenton Collected Papers:* 314-24

1970 'The Thriving of the Anglo-Saxon *ceorl'* in *Stenton Collected Papers:* 383-93

Stephan, K.
1937 *Das Aussterben und Fortleben der Nominalkomposita im altenglischen Beowulfepos und ihr Ersatz im Neuenglischen* (Graz diss.)

Stephens, G.
1878 'Thu(no)r in *Beowulf*' in *Thunor the Thunderer, carved on a Scandinavian Fort of about the Year 1000* (London): 54-6

Stephens, J.
1969 'Weland and a Little Restraint: A Note on *Deor* 5-6' *SN* 41: 371-4

Stephenson, J.
1930 'The Anglo-Saxon Borough,' *EHR* 45: 177-207

Stern G.
1921 Swift, Swiftly *and their Synonyms: A Contribution to Semantic Analysis and Theory*, Högskolas Årsskrift 17 (Göteborg)
1933-4 'Old English *fuslic* and *fus*' *EStn* 68: 161-73
1944-5 'On Methods of Interpretation' *SN* 17: 35-41

Steuernagel, K.
1921 *Der Wortschatz des Old English Martyrology unter besonderer Berücksichtigung des Gebrauchs der Präpositionen und Konjunktionen sowie einer ausführlichen Darstellung des syntaktischen Gebrauchs der Präpositionen* (Frankfurt)

Stevens, M.
1968 'The Narrator of the *Wife's Lament*' *NM* 69: 72-90
1978 'The Structure of *Beowulf*: From Gold-Hoard to Word-Hoard' *MLQ* 39: 219-38

Stevenson, W.H.
1885 'Errors in Anglo-Saxon Names' *Academy* 28: 29
1887 '*Molmen*' *EHR* 2: 332-6
1891 'Old English *efenehþ*' *Academy* 40: 14-15
1897 '*Burh-geat-setl*' *EHR* 12: 489-92
1898 'Some Old-English Words Omitted or Imperfectly Explained in Dictionaries' *TPS* (1895-8): 528-42
1902 'Dr. Guest and the English Conquest of South Britain' *EHR* 17: 625-42

Stevick, R.D.
1965 'Historical Selection of Relative *þat* in Early Middle English' *ES* 46: 29-36

Stewart, A.H.
*1979 'Kenning and Riddle in Old English' *PLL* 15: 115-36

Stibbe, H.
1935 Herr *und* Frau *und verwandte Begriffe in ihren altenglischen Äqui-valenten*, AF 80 (Heidelberg)

Stjerna, K.
1912 *Essays on Questions connected with the Old English Poem of Beowulf* (Coventry) [ed. and trans. J.R. Clark Hall]

Stokoe, W.C., Jr.
1957 'On Ohthere's *steorbord*' *Speculum* 32: 299-306

Stolzmann, P.
1953 *Die angelsächsischen Ausdrücke für* Tod *und* sterben: *Ihr Vorstellungs-gehalt und dessen Ursprung* (Erlangen diss.)

Storch, T.
*1886 *Angelsächsische Nominalcomposita* (Strassburg)

Storms, G.
1947 'An Anglo-Saxon Prescription from the *Lacnunga*' *ES* 28: 33-41
1957 *Compounded Names of Peoples in Beowulf: A Study in the Diction of a Great Poet* (Utrecht-Nijmegen)
1963 'The Subjectivity of the Style of *Beowulf*' in *Brodeur Festschrift*: 171-86
1972 'Grendel the Terrible' *NM* 73: 427-36
1977 'Notes on Old English Poetry' *Neophil* 61: 439-41

Strachan, L.R.M.
1931a 'Hernia among the Anglo-Saxons' *N&Q* 160: 192-3
1931b '*Rife, rive,* and *riveling*' *N&Q* 160: 291-2
1935 '*Rife = stream*' *N&Q* 169: 356
1936 'Old Vocabulary of Weaving' *N&Q* 171: 409-10

Stracke, J.R.
1970 *Studies in the Vocabulary of the Lambeth Psalter Glosses* (Pennsyl-

vania diss.; *DAI* 32: 987A)
1974 'Eight *Lambeth Psalter*-Glosses' *PQ* 53: 121-8
1976-7 '*Eþelboda: Guthlac B*, 1003' *MP* 74: 194-5

Strang, B.
1961 'Two Wulfstan Expressions' *N&Q* 206: 166-7

Stratmann, F.H.
1880 'Notizen zur angls. Grammatik' *EStn* 3: 472-3

Straub, F.
1923 'Lautlehre der altenglischen Übersetzung des Pseudo-Alcuin *Liber de virtutibus et vitiis* in der altenglischen Handschrift Vespasianus D.XIV. Fol. 104a-119a' *Anglia* 47: 66-96

Strauss, J.
1974 *Eine Komponentenanalyse im verbal- und situationskontextuellen Bereich: Die Bezeichnungen für* Herr *und* Gebieter *in der altenglischen Poesie*, AF 103 (Heidelberg)

Strite, V.L.
1970 *Old English Sea-Terms: A Word-List and a Study of Definitions* (Missouri diss.; *DAI* 31: 4147A)

Stroebe, K.
1911 *Altgermanische Grussformen* (Heidelberg diss.; Halle)

Stroebe, L.L.
1904 *Die altenglischen Kleidernamen: Eine kulturgeschichtlich-etymologische Untersuchung* (Heidelberg diss.; Borna-Leipzig)

Strunk, W.
1902 'Notes on Cynewulf' *MLN* 17: 186-7
1903 'Notes on the Shorter Old English Poems' *MLN* 18: 72-3

Stryker, W.G.
1953 'Old English Glossary Gleanings' *JEGP* 52: 372-7

Stuart, H.
1972 'The Meaning of OE **ælfsciene*' *Parergon* 2: 22-6
1975 'Some Old English Medical Terms' *Parergon* 13: 21-35
1976 'The Anglo-Saxon Elf' *SN* 48: 313-20

1977 '*Spider* in Old English' *Parergon* 18: 37-42

Stürzl, E.
1960 'Die christlichen Elemente in den altenglischen Zaubersegen' *Sprache* 6: 75-93

Sudo, J.
1965 'A Note on the Transitional Period from Old English to Middle English' *Kobe Gaidai Ronsō* 15, 5: 1-16

Süsskand, P.
1935 *Geschichte des unbestimmten Artikels im Alt- und Frühmittelenglischen,* SEP 85 (Halle)

Sugahara, S.
- 1975 'Kodai eigo ni okeru hitei – hiteiji *ne* o chushin ni' *Tamagawa Daigaku Bungakubu Kiyō* 15, 5: 31-63 [Negative in OE – centring on *ne*]
- 1977 'Considerations on Linguistic Phenomena in the OE Poem *The Seafarer*' *Tamagawa Daigaku Bungakubu Kiyō* 17, 3: 189-208
- 1978 'Considerations on the Linguistic Phenomena in the OE Conversation *Ælfric's Colloquy* (Part I)' *Tamagawa Daigaku Bungakubu Kiyō* 18, 3: 33-58

Sundby, B.
1958 'Old English *gumstōl* > Modern English *gumble-stool:* An Etymological-Semasiological Problem' *ES* 39: 110-16

Sundén, K.F.
1929 'The Etymology of ME *trayþ(e)ly* and *runisch, renisch*' *SN* 2: 41-55

Suolahti, H.
1909 *Die deutschen Vogelnamen: Eine wortgeschichtliche Untersuchung* (Strassburg)

Sutherland, C.H.V.
1973 *English Coinage 600-1900* (London)

Sutherland, R.C.
1955 'The Meaning of *eorlscipe* in *Beowulf*' *PMLA* 70: 1133-42

Swaen, A.E.H.
1895 'OE *seppan*' *EStn* 20: 148-9

1899-1943 'Contributions to Anglo-Saxon Lexicography' *EStn* 26 (1899):
125-33 / 32 (1903): 153-7 / 33 (1904): 176-8 / 35 (1905): 329-34 / 37
(1907): 188-97 / 38 (1908): 344-58 / 40 (1909): 321-31 / 43 (1910-11):
161-7 / 49 (1915-16): 337-59 / 53 (1919-20): 353-61 / 54 (1920): 337-
51 / 57 (1923): 1-7; *Neophil* 28 (1943): 42-9
1906 'An Old English Ghost Word' *Archiv* 117: 142
1907 'Some Old English Birdnames' *Archiv* 118: 387-9
1910 'Das angelsächsische Prosa-Leben des hl. Guthlac 14, 4' *Archiv* 124: 128
1915 'A Note on the *Blickling Homilies*' *MLN* 30: 126-7
1916a 'Old English *myl*' *Neophil* 1: 152-3
1916b 'Bestaat Oudengelsch *cocor* = "zwaard"?' *Neophil* 1: 209-12
1917 'As. *scǽnan* = ae. *sheen*' *Anglia* 41: 184
1917-18 'Three Mercian Words' *EStn* 51: 299-301
1918 'Two Old-English Ghostwords' *EStn* 52: 135-6
1920 'Note on the Anglo-Saxon *Indicia monasterialia*' *Archiv* 140: 106-7
1921 '*Unliss*' *Archiv* 142: 254
1930-31 '*Ærǽt*' *EStn* 65: 471-3
1931 'Anglo-Saxon Lexicography' *Anglia* 55: 8-9
1936-7 'Is *seo hiow* = "fortune" a Ghost-Word?' *EStn* 71: 153-4
1940 'Notes on the *Blickling Homilies*' *Neophil* 25: 264-72
1941a 'Riddle XIII (XVI)' *Neophil* 26: 228-31
1941b 'The Anglo-Saxon Horn Riddles' *Neophil* 26: 298-302
1942 '*Riddle* 63 (60, 62)' *Neophil* 27: 220
1946 'Riddle 9 (12)' *Neophil* 30: 126
1947 'Notes on Anglo-Saxon Riddles' *Neophil* 31: 145-8

Swanton, M.J.
1964 '*The Wife's Lament* and *The Husband's Message:* A Reconsideration'
Anglia 82: 269-90
1968 '*The Battle of Maldon:* A Literary Caveat' *JEGP* 67: 441-50
1969 'Ambiguity and Anticipation in the *Dream of the Rood*' *NM* 70:
407-25

Sweet, H.
1879 'Old English Etymologies' *EStn* 2: 312-16
1880a 'Disguised Compounds in Old English' *Anglia* 3: 151-4; repr. in
H.C. Wyld, ed., *Collected Papers of Henry Sweet* (Oxford 1913): 220-23
1880b 'English Etymologies' *Anglia* 3: 155-7
1881 'The Meaning of *æstel*' *Academy* 19: 395

Swiggett, G.L.
1905 'Notes on the *Finnsburg Fragment*' *MLN* 20: 169-71

Sytel', V.V.

−1957 *Suffiksal'nyi sposob obrazovaniia prilagatel'nych v drevneangliiskom iazyke* (Moscow, Universitet diss.) [The method of suffixation in the formation of adjectives in OE]

−1962 'K'istorii suffiksa lichnych imen sushchestvitel'nych -*er* v angliiskom iazyke,' Piatigorskii Pedagogicheskii institut. *Uchenye zapiski* 25: 209-14

Szemerényi, O.J.L.

1979 'Germanica I' *ZvS* 93: 103-25

Szogs, A.

1931 *Die Ausdrücke für* Arbeit *und* Beruf *im Altenglischen,* AF 73 (Heidelberg)

t

Talentino, A.V.
1970 *A Study of Compound* hapax legomena *in Old English Poetry* (State University of New York, Binghamton diss.; *DAI* 31: 6025A)
1973 '"Causing City Walls to Resound": *Elene* 151b' *PLL* 9: 189-93
1978 'Moral Irony in the *Ruin*' *PLL* 14: 3-10
1979 'Fitting *guðgewæde:* Use of compounds in *Beowulf*' *Neophil* 63: 592-6
1981 '*Riddle 30:* The Vehicle of the Cross' *Neophil* 65: 129-36

Taubert, E.M.
1894 *Der syntaktische Gebrauch der Präpositionen in dem angelsächsischen Gedichte vom heiligen Andreas (Ein Beitrag zur angelsächsische Grammatik)* (Leipzig diss.)

Taylor, I.
1898 'Ravensworth' *N&Q* ser. 9, 2: 96

Taylor, I., et al.
1898 'Leigh: lea' *N&Q* ser. 9, 2: 84-5, 215

Taylor, P.B.
1965 'OE *eoletes* Again' *Lingua* 13: 196-7

Teichert, F.
*1912 *Über das Aussterben alter Wörter im Verlaufe der englischen Sprachgeschichte* (Kiel diss.; Erlangen)

Temple, W.M.
1955 'OE *hlædfæt*-Welsh *lletwad*' *RES* n.s. 6: 63-5
1961 'The Song of the Angelic Hosts' *An Med* 2: 5-14

ten Brink, B.
1879 '*Eode*' *ZfdA* 23: 65-7
1882 'Das altenglische Suffix *ere*' *Anglia* 5: 1-4

Tengstrand, E.
1940 *A Contribution to the Study of Genitival Composition in Old English Place-Names* (Uppsala diss.)
1965 'A Special Use of Old English *ōþer* after *swilce*' *SN* 37: 382-92

Tetzlaff, G.
1954 *Bezeichnungen für die Sieben Todsünden in der altenglischen Prosa:*

Ein Beitrag zur Terminologie der altenglischen Kirchensprache (Berlin diss.)

Thiele, H.J.
1955 *Der Wortstamm* Wunsch *im Althochdeutschen, Altenglischen, und Altnordischen* (Berlin diss.)

Thiele, O.
1902 *Die konsonantischen Suffixe der Abstrakta des Altenglischen* (Strassburg diss.)

Thöne, F.
1912 *Die Namen der menschlichen Körperteile bei den Angelsachsen* (Kiel diss.)

Thomas, E.J.
1917 'King Alfred's *æstels* (*Pastoral Care*, pp. 7-9, ed. Sweet)' *Proceedings of the Cambridge Philological Society* 103-5 (1916): 12-13

Thomas, Elizabeth J.
1960 'Old Saxon *wurth* and its Germanic Cognates' *ArL* o.s. 12: 35-9

Thomas, P.G.
1917 'The OE *Exodus*' *MLR* 12: 343-5

Thompson, E.M.
*1885 'Ælfric's Vocabulary' *Journal of the British Archaeological Association* 41: 144-52

Thomson, E.
1853 'On a Passage in Orosius' *N&Q* ser. 1, 7: 399-400

Thomson, R.L.
1957 'Three Etymological Notes' *EGS* 6: 79-91
1961 'Aldrediana V: Celtica' *EGS* 7: 20-36

Thorpe, B.
1850 'Aelfric's *Colloquy*' *N&Q* ser. 1, 1: 232

Thun, N.
1968 'Germanic Words for Deer' *SN* 40: 94-113
1969 'The Malignant Elves: Notes on Anglo-Saxon Magic and Germanic

Myth' *SN* 41: 378-96

Thundyil, Z.P.
1969 *A Study of the Anglo-Saxon Concept of Covenant and its Sources with Special Reference to Anglo-Saxon Laws and the Old English Poems The Battle of Maldon and Guthlac* (Notre Dame diss.; *DAI* 30: 1997A)

Timmer, B.J.
1934 *Studies in Bishop Wærferth's Translation of the Dialogues of Gregory the Great* (Groningen diss.; Wageningen)
1941 '*Wyrd* in Anglo-Saxon Prose and Poetry' *Neophil* 26: 24-33, 213-28
1942 'The Elegiac Mood in Old English Poetry' *ES* 24: 33-44
1944 'Heathen and Christian Elements in Old English Poetry' *Neophil* 29: 180-85

Tinker, C.B.
1908 'Notes on *Beowulf*' *MLN* 23: 239-40

Tinkler, J.D.
*1964 *A Critical Commentary on the Vocabulary and Syntax of the Old English Version in the Paris Psalter* (Stanford diss.; *DA* 25: 1900)
1971 *Vocabulary and Syntax of the Old English Version in the Paris Psalter: A Critical Commentary*, Janua linguarum, series practica 67 (The Hague and Paris)

Tolkien, J.R.R.
1932-4 '*Sigelwara land*' *MÆ* 1 (1932): 183-96 / 3 (1934): 95-111
1936 '*Beowulf:* The Monsters and the Critics' *PBA* 22: 1-53
1953 'The Homecoming of Beorhtnoth Beorhthelm's Son' *E&S* n.s. 6: 1-18

Trahern, J.B., Jr.
1969 '*A defectione potus sui:* A Sapiential Basis for *ealuscerwen* and *meoduscerwen*' *NM* 70: 62-9

Trautmann, M.
1907 '*Werge (wyrge)* "verflucht"' *BBzA* 23: 155-6
1910 'Beiträge zu einem künftigen "Sprachschatz der altenglischen Dichter"' *Anglia* 33: 276-82

Trautmann, R.
1906 'Etymologien' *Beiträge zur Kunde der indogermanischen Sprachen* 29: 307-11, 328-30

Traver, H.
1935 *'Beowulf* 648-649 Once More' *Archiv* 167: 253-6

Tremaine, H.P.
1969 'Beowulf's *ecg brun* and Other Rusty Relics' *PQ* 48: 145-50

Trier, J.
1945 'Ags. *geormanleaf' BGdSL* 67: 64

Tripp, R.P.
1971-2 *'The Dream of the Rood:* 9b and its Context' *MP* 69: 136-7
1972a 'Language, Archaic Symbolism, and the Poetic Structure of *Beowulf' Hiroshima Studies in English Language and Literature* 19: 1-21
1972b 'The Narrator as Revenant: A Reconsideration of Three Old English Elegies' *PLL* 8: 339-61
1977-8 'The Restoration of *Beowulf* 2769b and 2771a, and Wiglaf's Entrance into the Barrow' *ELN* 15: 244-9
1979 'On "Post-Editorial" Editions of *Beowulf'* in L.C. Gruber and D. Loganbill, eds., *In Geardagum 3: Essays on Old English Language and Literature* (Denver): 18-25
1980-81a 'Hate and Heat in the Restoration of *Beowulf* 84: *þæt se secg hete āþum swerian' ELN* 18: 81-6
1980-81b 'The Restoration of *Beowulf* 2781a: *Hāt ne forhogode* ("did not despise heat")' *MP* 78: 153-8

Trnka, B.
1956 'K staroanglické deminutivní připoné *-incel' Časopis pro moderní filologii* 38: 1-5

Tsubaki, N.
−1977 *'Bēon* to *wesan* no tōgoronteki kenkyū' *Tottori Daigaku Kyōikuga- kubu Kenkyū Hōkoku (Kyōiku Kagaku)* 19, 2, 12: 75-89 [Syntactic research on *beon* and *wesan*]

Tucker, S.I.
1959 'Laughter in Old English Literature' *Neophil* 43: 222-6

Tuggle, T.T.
1977 'The Structure of *Deor' SP* 74: 229-42

Tupper, F.
1895 'Anglo-Saxon *dæg-mæl' PMLA* 10: 111-241

1912 'Notes on Old English Poems' *JEGP* 11: 82-103

Turville-Petre, G.
1962 'Thurstable' in N. Davis and C.L. Wrenn, eds., *English and Medieval Studies Presented to J.R.R. Tolkien on the Occasion of his Seventieth Birthday* (London) 241-9

Tuso, J.F.
*1966 *An Analysis and Glossary of Dialectal Variations in the Vocabularies of Three Late Tenth-Century Old English Texts, the Corpus, Lindisfarne, and Rushworth Gospels* (Arizona diss.; *DA* 27: 1357A)
1968 'An Analysis and Glossary of Dialectal Synonymy in the *Corpus, Lindisfarne,* and *Rushworth Gospels*' *Linguistics* 43: 89-118

Uemura, R.

−1959 '*Beowulf* ni okeru Substantive-Compound' *Ōsaka Kyōiku Daigaku Kiyō* 7, 3: 199-218 [On substantive compounds in *Beowulf*]
−1964 '*Beowulf* ni okeru shiteki koshō no ruikei' *Ōsaka Kyōiku Daigaku Kiyō* 12, 3: 227-44 [The varieties of poetic appellations in *Beowulf*]
−1969 'Kodai eigo ni okeru kyōishi *self*' *Ōsaka Kyōiku Daigaku Eibungaku-kaishi* 18, 3: 102-21 [The emphasis word *self* in OE]

Uhlenbeck, C.C.

1891 'Etymologica' *TNTL* 10: 283-4
1894-7 'Etymologisches' *BGdSL* 19 (1894): 327-33 / 20 (1895): 37-45, 563-4 / 21 (1896): 98-106 / 22 (1897): 536-42
1897-1901 'Etymologien' *BGdSL* 22 (1897): 199-200 / 26 (1901): 568-71
1901a 'Germanisches und Slavisches' *BGdSL* 26: 287-9
1901b 'Zur deutschen Etymologie' *BGdSL* 26: 290-312
1901c 'Zu *Beitr*. 26, 290ff.' *BGdSL* 26: 572-3
1907 'Etymologica' *BGdSL* 33: 182-6

Uhler, K.

1926 *Die Bedeutungsgleichheit der altenglischen Adjektiva und Adverbia mit und ohne* -lic (-lice), AF 62 (Heidelberg)

Umarova, B.S.

1976 'K semantike glagolov rechi v drevnegermanskikh iazykakh' Moscow, Universitet, Vestnik, Ser. 10, *Filologiia* [31] 5: 42-51 [Notes on the semantics of verbs of speech in Old Germanic languages]

ʋ

Vachek, J.
1976 'English Phonology, III: The Early Middle English Phoneme /J/ and the Personal Pronoun *she*' in J. Vachek, *Selected Writings in English and General Linguistics* (Prague): 194-203

Van Beek, P.
1940 *The be- Prefix in Verbs of King Alfred's Translation of Boethius' De consolatione philosophiae* (Iowa diss.; *Iowa Diss. Abstracts and References 1900-37* 1: 161-75)

Varah, W.E. and Anderton, H.I.
1933 'Minsters' *N&Q* 165: 148-9, 192

Varnhagen, H.
1892 'Zur Etymologie von *preost*' *EStn* 16: 154-5

Vasil'eva, S.A.
– 1958 'Otritsatel'naia chastitsa *ne* v drevneangliiskom povestvovatel'nom predlozhenii' Leningrad, Tekhnologicheskii Institut pishchevoi promish- lenosti, *Sbornik rabot:* 166-84 [The negative particle *ne* in OE narrative sentences]

Vat, J. [pseudonym]
1978 'On Footnote 2: Evidence for the Pronominal Status of *þær* in Old English Relatives' *Linguistic Inquiry* 9: 695-716

Vendryes, J.
1936 'Chronique XXV' *Etudes celtiques* 1: 390-91
1947 'Un mot irlandais dans l'évangéliaire de Lindisfarne' *Bulletin de la Société de linguistique de Paris* 43 (1946): 27-31

Verdonck, J.
1976 'Notes on Some Problematic Glosses in the *Liber scintillarum* Inter- lineation (MS. London, BM Royal 7 C. IV)' *ES* 57: 97-102

Vickrey, J.F.
1965 '*Selfsceaft* in Genesis B' *Anglia* 83: 154-71
1968 'An Emendation to *l(æ)nes* in *Genesis B* line 258' *Archiv* 204: 268-71
1970 'A Note on *Genesis* lines 242-244' *NM* 71: 191-2
1971 'The *micel wundor* of Genesis B' *SP* 68: 245-54
1972 '*Exodus* and the Battle in the Sea' *Traditio* 28: 119-40
1973 '*Exodus* and the Tenth Plague' *Archiv* 210: 41-52

1973-4 *'Egesan ne gymeð* and the Crime of Heremod' *MP* 71: 295-300
1975 *'Exodus* and the *herba humilis' Traditio* 31: 25-54
1977 'The Narrative Structure of Hengest's Revenge in *Beowulf' ASE* 6: 91-103
1979-80 'Concerning *Exodus* lines 144-145' *ELN* 17: 241-9

Viliuman, V.G.
− 1958 'O sviaszi zalogovoi differentsiatsii s leksicheskim znacheniem glagola (Na materiale drevneangliiskogo iazyka)' Leningrad, Ped. Institut im. Gertsena, *Uchenye zapiski* 154: 127-39 [On the connection of the distinction of voice with the lexical meaning of the verb (based on OE material)]

Vinogradoff, P.
1893 'Folkland' *EHR* 8: 1-17
1904a *The Growth of the Manor* (Oxford)
1904b *'Sulung* and *hide' EHR* 19: 282-6, 624
1908 *English Society in the Eleventh Century* (Oxford)

Viswanathan, S.
1979 'On the Melting of the Sword: *wæl-rāpas* and the Engraving on the Sword-Hilt in *Beowulf' PQ* 58: 360-63

Vleeskruyer, R.
1952 'Old English Vocabulary Research' in *Handelingen van het twee en twintigste Nederlands Philologen-Congres, Utrecht* (Groningen): 46-7

Vočadlo, O.
1933 'Anglo-Saxon Terminology' *Prague Studies in English* 4: 61-85

Vollrath-Reichelt, H.
1971 *Königsgedanke und Königtum bei den Angelsachsen bis zur Mitte des 9. Jahrhunderts,* Kölner historische Abhandlungen 19 (Cologne and Vienna)

Voyles, J.B.
1974 *West Germanic Inflection, Derivation, and Compounding,* Janua linguarum, series practica 145 (The Hague and Paris): 90-131

Vries, M. de
1879 'Woordverklaringen' *Taalkundige Bijdragen* 2: 1-61

ꟷꟷꟷ W

W., B.
1850 *'Lærig' N&Q* ser. 1, 1: 387

Wack, G.
1893 'Artikel und Demonstrativpronomen in *Andreas* und *Elene' Anglia* 15: 209-20

Wada, A.
ꟷ 1969 'Verb-Adverb Combination in the *Peterborough Chronicle* ꟷ An Inquiry into its Rudimental Stage' *Kanazawa Daigaku Kyōikugakubu Kiyō (Jinbun Kagaku hen)* 18, 12: 137-52

Wadstein, E.
1897 'Zur germanischen Wortkunde' *BGdSL* 22: 238-54
1925 'Le mot *viking:* Anglo-Saxon *wicing,* frison *wising,* etc.' in *Mélanges de Philologie offerts à M. Johan Vising par ses élèves et ses amis scandinaves à l'occasion du soixante-dixième anniversaire de la naissance le 20 avril 1925* (Paris and Göteborg): 381-6

Wärtli, H.
1935 *Stilistische Dämpfung als Mittel der Ausdruckssteigerung und der Ausdrucksmilderung im Altenglischen und im Neuenglischen, Litotes und Understatement* (Zurich diss.)

Wagner, N.
1980 'Der Name der Stellinga' *Beiträge zur Namenforschung* 15: 128-33

Wahlén, N.
1925 *The Old English Impersonalia,* Part I: *Impersonal Expressions Containing Verbs of Material Import in the Active Voice* (Göteborg)

Wahrig, G.
ꟷ 1953 *Die Ausdrücke des Lachens und des Spottes im Alt- und Mittelenglischen* (Leipzig diss.)
1955 'Das Lachen im Altenglischen und Mittelenglischen' *ZAA* 3: 274-304, 389-418

Wainewright, J.B.
1926 'Pound Sterling' *N&Q* 150: 427-8

Wakelin, M.F.
1969 '*Crew, cree,* and *crow:* Celtic Words in English Dialect' *Anglia* 87:

273-81

1970 'Names for the Cow-House in Devon and Cornwall' *SN* 42: 348-52

1971 'OE *brægen, bragen*' *Neophil* 55: 108

1974 'New Light on IE *r/n* Stems in Germanic?' *Studia Linguistica* 28: 109-11

Waldorf, N.O.

1953 *The* hapax legomena *in the Old English Vocabulary: A Study Based upon the Bosworth-Toller Dictionary* (Stanford diss.; *DA* 13: 558)

Walker, W.S.

1952 'The *brūnecg* Sword' *MLN* 67: 516-20

Wallace, F.E.

1927 'Color in *Beowulf*' in *Color in Homer and Ancient Art*, Smith College Classical Studies 9 (Northampton, Mass.): 69

Wallum, M.K.

1973 *The Syntax and Semantics of the English Modal Verbs from the Late Tenth to the Fifteenth Century* (University of Michigan diss.; *DAI* 35: 437A)

Ward, G.F.

1954 'The English *danegeld* and the Russian *dan*' *American Slavic and East European Review* 13: 299-318

Watanabe, K.

− 1971 'The Kennings in *Beowulf*' in *Collected Essays by Members of the Faculty* 14 (Women's Junior College, Tokyo): 1-18

Waterhouse, R.

1973 'Semantic Development of Two Terms within the *Anglo-Saxon Chronicle*' *SGG* 14: 95-106

Watts, T.

1850 'On the Anglo-Saxon Termination *ing*' *PPS* 4 (1848-50) 83-6

Weber, E.

− 1931 'Seelenmörder oder Unholdtöter?' *Neuphilologische Monatschrift* 2: 293-5

1941 'Zu dem Wort *Rune*' *Archiv* 178: 1-6

Weber, G.W.
1969 Wyrd: *Studien zum Schicksalsbegriff der altenglischen und altnordischen Literatur,* Frankfurter Beiträge zur Germanistik 8 (Bad Homburg, Berlin, and Zurich)

Wedgwood, H.
1884 *'Tar' N&Q* ser. 6, 9: 405

Wegner, R.
1899 *Die Angriffswaffen der Angelsachsen* (Königsberg diss.)

Wehrle, O.
1935 *Die hybriden Wortbildungen des Mittelenglischen (1050-1400): Ein Beitrag zur englischen Wortgeschichte* (Freiburg diss.)

Weick, F.
1911 *Das Aussterben des Präfixes* ge- *im Englischen* (Heidelberg diss.; Darmstadt)

Weijnen, A.A.
1965 'Oude Engels-Nederlandse Parallellen' *Verslagen en Mededelingen van de Koninklijke Vlamse Academie vor Taal- en Letterkunde* (Ghent) 385-401

Weimann, K.
1966 *Der Friede im Altenglischen: Eine bezeichnungsgeschichtliche Untersuchung* (Bonn diss.)
1976 'Battle of Maldon' in *Reallexikon der germanischen Altertumskunde* 2: 93-5

Weise, J.A.
1979 'Ambiguity in Old English Poetry' *Neophil* 63: 588-91

Weisweiler, J.
1923 'Beiträge zur Bedeutungsentwicklung germanischer Wörter für sittliche Begriffe' *IF* 41: 13-77, 304-68
1930 *Busse, Bedeutungsgeschichtliche Beiträge zur Kultur- und Geistesgeschichte* (Halle)

Weman, B.
1933 *Old English Semantic Analysis and Theory with Special Reference to Verbs Denoting Locomotion,* LSE 1 (Lund: repr. Nendeln 1967)

Wende, F.
1914 *Über die nachgestellten Präpositionen im Angelsächsischen* (Berlin diss.)

Wenisch, F.
1977 'Sächsische Dialektwörter in the *Battle of Maldon*' *IF* 81 (1976): 181-203
1978 'Kritische Bemerkungen zu Angaben über die Verbreitung einiger angeblich westsächsischer Dialektwörter' *Anglia* 96: 5-44
1979 *Spezifisch anglisches Wortgut in den nordhumbrischen Interlinearglossierungen des Lukasevangeliums*, AF 132 (Heidelberg)

Wentersdorf, K.P.
1970 'The Situation of the Narrator's Lord in the *Wife's Lament*' *NM* 71: 604-10
1971 'Beowulf's Withdrawal from Frisia: A Reconsideration' *SP* 68: 395-415
1972 'The Semantic Development of OE *dreorig* and *dreorigian*' *SN* 44: 278-88
1973a 'On the Meaning of OE *dreorig* in *Brunanburh* 54' *NM* 74: 232-7
1973b 'On the Meaning of OE *heorodreorig* in the *Phoenix* and Other Poems' *SN* 45: 32-46
1975a '*The Wanderer:* Notes on Some Semantic Problems' *Neophil* 59: 287-92
1975b 'Beowulf's Adventure with Breca' *SP* 72: 140-66
1977a 'Observations on the *Ruin*' *MÆ* 46: 171-80
1977b 'Shakespearian Shards' *SN* 49: 195-203
1978 '*Guthlac A:* The Battle for the *beorg*' *Neophil* 62: 135-42
1981a 'The Situation of the Narrator in the Old English *Wife's Lament*' *Speculum* 56: 492-516
1981b '*Beowulf:* The Paganism of Hrothgar's Danes' *SP* 78: 91-119

Werlich, E.
1964 *Der westgermanische Skop: Der Aufbau seiner Dichtung und sein Vortrag* (Münster diss.)
1967 'Der westgermanische Skop' *ZfdPh* 86: 352-75

Westphalen, T.
*1967 Beowulf 3150-55: *Textkritik und Editiongeschichte,* Bochumer Arbeiten zur Sprach- und Literaturwissenschaft 2 (Munich)

Weyhe, H.
1905-6 'Beiträge zur westgermanischen Grammatik' *BGdSL* 30 (1905):
55-141 / 31 (1906): 43-90
1911 *Zu den altenglischen Verbalabstrakten auf* -nes *und* -ing, -ung (Halle)
1924 'Ae. *ēawis* "offenbar"' in *Streitberg Festgabe* (Leipzig): 395-7

Whatley, E.G.
1975 'Bread and Stone: Cynewulf's *Elene* 611-618' *NM* 76: 550-60

Whitbread, L.
1938 'A Medieval English Metaphor' *PQ* 17: 365-70
1942a 'An Allusion in *Deor*' *JEGP* 41: 368-9
1942b 'Beowulfiana' *MLR* 37: 480-84
1943-4 *'Widsith* and *scilling*' *N&Q* 184 (1943): 152-4 / 186 (1944): 264-6
1945 'The Old-English Poem *Alms-giving*' *N&Q* 189: 2-4
1947 'Text-Notes on *Deor,* VIII-X' *MLN* 62: 15-20
1949a 'The Old English *Exhortation to Christian Living:* Some Textual
Problems' *MLR* 44: 178-83
1949b 'Some Etymologies' *N&Q* 194: 332-3
1957 'Notes on Two Minor Old English Poems' *SN* 29: 123-9
1963 'Old English and Old High German: A Note on *Judgment Day II*,
292-293' *SP* 60: 514-24
1965-6 'An Old English Gloss' *ELN* 2: 245-7
1966 'Old English *unbleoh*' *Neophil* 50: 447-8
1967 *'Beowulf* and Archaeology: Two Footnotes' *NM* 68: 28-35
1968 *'Beowulf* and Archaeology: Two Further Footnotes' *NM* 69: 63-72
1969 *'Beowulf* and Archaeology: An Additional Footnote' *NM* 70: 53-62
*1975 'Adam's Pound of Flesh: A Note on Old English Verse *Solomon and
Saturn (II)*, 336-339' *Neophil* 59: 622-6
1976 'The Old English Poem *Aldhelm*' *ES* 57: 193-7

Whitehall, H.
1941 'Interim Etymologies: *L**' *PQ* 20: 25-37

Whitehead, F.
1960 *'Ofermod* et *Desmesure*' *Cahiers de civilisations médiévales* 3: 115-17

Whitelock, D.
1941 'Wulfstan and the so-called Laws of Edward and Guthrum' *EHR* 56:
1-21
1949 'Anglo-Saxon Poetry and the Historian' *Transactions of the Royal
Historical Society* ser. 4, 31: 75-94

1951 *The Audience of Beowulf* (Oxford)
1968 'Wulfstan *Cantor* and Anglo-Saxon Law' in A.H. Orrick, ed., *Nordica et Anglica: Studies in Honor of Stefán Einarsson* (The Hague and Paris): 83-92

Whitesell, J.E.
1966 'Intentional Ambiguities in *Beowulf*' *TSL* 11: 145-9

Whitman, C.H.
1899 'The Birds of Old English Literature' *JGP* 2: 149-98
1906-7 'Old English Mammal Names' *JEGP* 6: 649-56
1907 'The Old English Animal Names: Mollusks; Toads, Frogs; Worms; Reptiles' *Anglia* 30: 380-93

Whitman, F.H.
1975 '*The Dream of the Rood*, 101a' *Expl* 33: item 70

Wiersma, S.M.
1961 *A Linguistic Analysis of Words Referring to Monsters in Beowulf* (Wisconsin diss.; *DA* 22: 570)

Wietelmann, I.
1952 *Die Epitheta in den 'Caedmonischen' Dichtungen* (Göttingen diss.)

Wijk, N. van
1906 'Ags. *cu,* an. *kyr*' *IF* 19: 393-8
1909 'Germanische Etymologien' *IF* 24: 30-37, 230-38
1915 'Zur Etymologie einiger Wörter für *leer*' *IF* 35: 265-8

Wilbur, T.H.
1963 'The Germanic Interrogatives of the *how* Type' *Word* 19: 328-34

Wild, F.
1962 *Drachen im Beowulf und andere Drachen, mit einem Anhang: Drachenfeldzeichen, Drachenwappen, und St. Georg,* Österreichische Akademie der Wissenschaften, phil-hist. Klasse, Sitzungsberichte 238, 5 (Vienna)

Wildhagen, K.
1909a 'Altenglische Miszellen' *EStn* 40: 152-3
1909b 'Entgegnung' *EStn* 40: 306-9
1913 'Studien zum *Psalterium Romanum* in England und zu seinen Glossierungen (in geschichtlicher Entwicklung)' in F. Holthausen and H. Spies,

eds., *Festschrift für Lorenz Morsbach*, SEP 50 (Halle): 417-72

Wilhelmsen, L.J.
1939 *On the Verbal Prefixes* for- *and* fore- *in English*, Avhandlinger utgitt av det Norske Videnskaps-Akademi i Oslo II, hist-fil. Klasse 1938, Nr. 2

Wilken, E.
1878 *'Nykrat' Germania* 23: 446-7

Willard, R.
1930 'Gleanings in Old English Lexicography' *Anglia* 54: 8-24
1936 'On Blickling Homily XIII: *The Assumption of the Virgin' RES* o.s. 12: 1-17
1951 'OE *oma* "rust"' *MLN* 66: 261-3
1961 *'Beowulf* 2672b: *līg ȳðum fōr' MLN* 76: 290-93

Willems, F.
1942 *Heldenwörter in germanischer und christlicher Literatur* (Cologne diss.)

Williams, E.R.
1958 'Ælfric's Grammatical Terminology' *PMLA* 73: 453-62

Williams, E.W.
1975 'The Relation between Pagan Survivals and Diction in Two Old English Riddles' *PQ* 54: 664-70

Williams, R.A.
1924 *The Finn Episode in Beowulf: An Essay in Interpretation* (Cambridge)

Willms, J.E.
1902 *Eine Untersuchung über den Gebrauch der Farbenbezeichnungen in der Poesie Altenglands* (Münster diss.)

Winter, W.
1955 Aeht, wela, gestreon, sped, *und* ead *im Alt- und Mittelenglischen: Eine bedeutungsgeschichtliche Untersuchung* (Berlin diss.)
1964 'Zur Methode einer bedeutungsgeschichtlichen Untersuchung' in D. Riesner and H. Gneuss, eds., *Festschrift für Walter Hübner* (Berlin): 26-39

Wissmann, W.
*1932 *Nomina postverbalia in den altgermanischen Sprachen nebst einer Voruntersuchung über deverbative ō-Verba, 1. Teil: Deverbative ō-Verba,*

Ergänzungshefte zur Zeitschrift für vergleichende Sprachforschung auf dem Gebiete der indogermanischen Sprachen 11 (Göttingen)
1975 *Die altnordischen und westgermanischen Nomina postverbalia* (Heidelberg)

Woesler, R.
– 1936 'Das Bild des Menschen in der englischen Sprache der älteren Zeit' *Neuphilologische Monatschrift* 7: 321-36, 383-97

Wolf, A.
1919 *Die Bezeichnungen für Schicksal in der angelsächsischen Dichtersprache* (Breslau diss.)

Wolf-Rottkay, W.-H.
1952-3 'Zur Etymologie von ae. *bāt' Anglia* 71: 140-47

Wolff, H.
– 1954 *Die Epitheta in den Cynewulfischen Dichtungen* (Göttingen diss.)

Wong, S.
– 1969 *A Linguistic Study of the Prefix* un- *in the Derivation of English Adjectives* (London diss.; ASLIB *Index* 19: 337)

Wood, C.
1960 '*Nis þæt seldguma: Beowulf* 249' *PMLA* 75: 481-4

Wood, F.A.
1898-1900 'Etymologies' *JGP* 2 (1898-9): 213-33; *MLN* 15 (1900): 48-51
1898-1917 'Etymological Notes' *MLN* 13 (1898): 144-6 / 15 (1900): 163-5 / 17 (1902): 3-6 / 18 (1903): 13-18 / 20 (1905): 41-4 / 21 (1906): 39-42 / 22 (1907): 234-6 / 23 (1908): 147-9 / 24 (1909): 47-9 / 26 (1911): 165-7 / 29 (1914): 69-72 / 32 (1917): 290-91
1898-1919 'Germanic Etymologies' *Americana Germanica* 3 (1899-1900): 309-25; *JEGP* 13 (1914): 499-507; *MLN* 13 (1898): 41-4 / 34 (1919): 203-8; *MP* 2 (1904-5): 471-6 / 11 (1913-14): 315-38
1899a 'Etymologisches' *BGdSL* 24: 529-33
1899b '*Understand, guess, think, mean,* Semasiologically Explained' *MLN* 14: 129-31
1899c 'The Semasiology of Words for "smell" and "see"' *PMLA* 14: 299-346
1900a 'Etymological Miscellany' *AJP* 21: 178-82
1900b 'The Semasiology of *understand, verstehen, ĕpístamai' MLN* 15: 14-16

1901-4 'Some Derived Meanings' *MLN* 16 (1901): 8-14 / 19 (1904): 1-5
1902a *Color-Names and their Congeners: A Semasiological Investigation* (Halle)
1902b 'Some Derived Bases' *AJP* 23: 195-203
1903 'The IE Root *selo-*' *AJP* 24: 40-61
1903-4 'The IE Base *ghero-* in Germanic' *MP* 1: 235-45
1905 '*Dürfen* and its Cognates' *MLN* 20: 102-4
1906-9 'Studies in Germanic Strong Verbs' *MP* 4 (1906-7): 489-500 / 5 (1907-8): 265-90 / 6 (1908-9): 441-52
1907 'Some Disputed Etymologies' *MLN* 22: 118-22
1910 'Gothic Etymology' *MLN* 25: 72-6
1913 *Some Parallel Formations in English*, Hesperia, Ergänzungsreihe: Schriften zur englischen Philologie 1 (Göttingen and Baltimore)
1920 'Names of Stinging, Gnawing, and Rending Animals' *AJP* 41: 223-39, 336-54
1920-21 'Germanic *w*-Gemination' *MP* 18: 79-92, 303-8
1926 *Post-Consonantal w in Indo-European*, Language Monographs 3 (Philadelphia)
1926-7 'Some Revised Etymologies' *MP* 24: 215-20
1927 'Some Words for *south*' *Language* 3: 184-6
1931a 'Prothetic Vowels in Sanskrit, Greek, Latin, and Germanic' *AJP* 52: 105-44
1931b 'Indo-European Bases Derivable from Skt. *áva* "down"' *SP* 28: 553-45

Woodward, B.B.
1859 'Anglo-Saxon Words in the *Liber Winton*' *N&Q* ser. 2, 7: 474-5, 507

Woodward, R.H.
1954 '*Swanrad* in *Beowulf*' *MLN* 69: 544-6

Woolf, R.E.
1953 'The Devil in Old English Poetry' *RES* n.s. 4: 1-12
1975 '*The Wanderer, The Seafarer*, and the Genre of Planctus' in *McGalliard Festschrift*: 192-207
1976 'The Ideal of Men Dying with their Lord in the *Germania* and in the *Battle of Maldon*' *ASE* 5: 63-81

Wrenn, C.L.
1944 'The Value of Spelling as Evidence' *TPS* (1943): 14-39
1959 'Sutton Hoo and *Beowulf*' *Mélanges de linguistique et de philologie: Fernand Mossé in Memoriam* (Paris): 495-507
1962a *Anglo-Saxon Poetry and the Amateur Archaeologist*, Chambers

Memorial Lecture, University College, London (London): 3-24
1962b 'Two Anglo-Saxon Harps' *CL* 14: 118-28; repr. in *Brodeur Festschrift* (1963): 118-28
1965 'Some Earliest Anglo-Saxon Cult Symbols' in *Magoun Festschrift*: 40-55
1967 *Word and Symbol: Studies in English Language* (London)
1969 'Some Aspects of Anglo-Saxon Theology' in Atwood and Hill *Studies*: 182-9

Wright, T.L.
1967-8 'Hrothgar's Tears' *MP* 65: 39-44

Wüest, J.
* 1969 *Die Leis Willelme: Untersuchungen zum ältesten Gesetzbuch in französischer Sprache,* Romanica Helvetica 79 (Bern)

Wülfing, J.E.
1891 'Ae. *wyrðe (weorð) = dignus* mit dem Dativ' *EStn* 15: 159-60
1892 'Ae. *sum* mit dem Genitiv einer Grundzahl' *EStn* 17: 285-91
* 1894-1901 *Die Syntax in den Werken Alfreds des Grossen* (Bonn)
1898 'Nochmals ae. *sum* mit dem Genitiv einer Grundzahl' *EStn* 24: 463
1899 'Einige Bemerkungen zu Swaen's "Contributions to Anglosaxon Lexicography"' *EStn* 26: 449-55
1901 'Kommt *and* in der Bedeutung von *if* schon im Altenglischen vor?' *Beibl* 12: 89
1902 'Einige Nachträge zu den altenglischen Wörterbüchern' *EStn* 30: 339-41

Wuest, P.
1906 'Zwei neue Handschriften von Caedmons Hymnus' *ZfdA* 48: 205-26

Wüst, W.
1955 'Zu Deutung und Herkunft des ae. *bāt* m.f. "Boot, Schiff"' *Anglia* 73: 262-75

Wullen, F.
1908 *Der syntaktische Gebrauch der Präpositionen* fram, under, ofer, þurh *in der angelsächsischen Poesie,* 1. Teil: fram, under (Kiel diss.)
1911 'Der syntaktische Gebrauch der Präpositionen *fram, under, ofer, þurh* in der angelsächsischen Poesie, Zweiter Teil: *ofer* und *þurh*' *Anglia* 34: 423-97

Wuth, A.
1915 *Aktionsarten der Verba bei Cynewulf* (Leipzig diss.; Weida i. Thüringen)

Wyatt, A.J.
1916 'A Passage in *Solomon and Saturn*' *MLR* 11: 215

Wyld, H.C.
1910 'Old English *gefyrhþe* and *friÞ* and the Latin Suffix *-ētum*' *MLR* 5: 347-8
1925 'Diction and Imagery in Anglo-Saxon Poetry' *E&S* o.s. 11: 49-91

Wyss, S.
*1977 *Le Système du genre en vieil anglais jusqu'à la Conquête* (Paris diss.)

ȝ

Yamaguchi, H.
1969 *Essays towards English Semantics,* 2nd ed. (Tokyo)

Yamakawa, K.
1971 'OE *þǣr* and *hwǣr:* A Study of *where* developing in the subordinating Function (1)' *Hitotsubashi Journal of Arts and Sciences* 12, 1, 9: 1-19

Yamanouchi, K.
— 1974-7 'Elegy ni arawareta *wyrd* no hyogen' *The Quiet Hill* 7 (1974): 88-97 / 8 (1977): 35-42 [The expression of *wyrd* in the elegy]

Yerkes, D.
1976-7 'Dugdale's *Dictionary* and Somner's *Dictionarium*' *ELN* 14: 110-12
*1979a *The Two Versions of Waerferth's Translation of Gregory's Dialogues: An Old English Thesaurus,* Toronto Old English Series 4 (Toronto)
1979b 'Twelve New Old English Words' *Sprache* 25: 171-3

Yoshino, T.
*1978 'Ko eigo no hitei ni tsuite — sanbun to shino hikaku (1)' *Ronsō* (Tamagawa) 18, 3: 75-106 [On negation in OE — a comparison between prose and poetry]

Yoshioka, G.-I.
1907 *A Semantic Study of the Verbs of Doing and Making in the Indo-European Languages* (Chicago diss.; Tokyo 1908)

Young, J.I.
1950 '*Glæd wæs ic gliwum:* Ungloomy Aspects of Anglo-Saxon Poetry' in *Chadwick Memorial Volume:* 275-87

Zabel, H.E.
1922 *The Semantic Development of Words for Mental Aberration in Germanic* (Chicago diss.)

Zachrisson, R.E.
1932-3 'OE *wise, usan, wassan, wær-, ur-:* Some Etymological Notes' *SN* 5: 70-76
1933 'OE *citel, cytel, cetel,* and O. Scand. *ketill* in English Place-Names' *NB* 21: 1-7

Zadorozhnyi, B.M.
1976 'Ob odnom mnimom arkhaizme v drevneangliiskoi epike' in M.P. Alekseev, ed., *Teoriia iazyka, Anglistika, Kel'tologiia,* AN SSSR Institut iazykoznaniia (Moscow): 173-6 [On a supposed archaism in an OE epic]

Zatochil, L.
—1959 '*Ge-* bei den sogenannten perfektiven und imperfektiven Simplizien' Sborník Filozofickej Fakulty Univerzity Komenského, *Philologica* 8, A 7: 50-64

Zeitlin, J.
1908 *The Accusative with Infinitive and some kindred Constructions in English* (Columbia diss.)

Zessin, H.
1937 *Der Begriff* Bauer *im Englischen im Spiegel seiner Bezeichnungsgeschichte und Bedeutungsgeschichte* (Halle-Wittenberg diss.)

Zettersten, A.
1969 'The Source of **mocritum* in OE' *SN* 41: 375-7

Zhigadlo, V.N.
—1961 'Puti vozniknoveniia predlozhnogo upravleniia v drevneangliiskom iazyke' *Issledovaniia po angliiskoi filologii* 2: 99-114 [Directions in the development of prepositional government in OE]

Ziatkovskaia, R.G.
1962 'Slovoobrazovatel'naia funktsiia iskonno-angliiskikh prefiksov v techenie X-XV st.' Kiev, Gos. ped. Institut inostrannykh iazykov, *Nauchnye zapiski* 5: 51-60 [The word-building function of native English prefixes during the X-XV centuries]

Zieglschmid, A.J.F.
1930 'The Disappearance of *werdan* in English' *PQ* 9: 111-15

Zimmer, H.
1895 'Keltische Studien 13: Ein altirischer Zauberspruch aus der Vikinger-
    zeit' *ZvS* 33: 141-56

Zupitza, J.
1881 '*Æstel*' *Academy* 19: 395
1885-6 '*Catchpoll* in Old English' *Academy* 28 (1885): 325 / 29 (1886): 95
1890 'Zu *Beowulf* 850' *Archiv* 84: 124-5